WIRED TO BECOME

The Brain Science of Finding Your Purpose,
Creating Meaningful Work, and
Achieving Your Potential

Britt Andreatta, PhD

7th Mind
Publishing

7th Mind
Publishing

This edition May 2023.
7th Mind Publishing
Santa Barbara, California

The following are all registered trademarks of 7th Mind, Inc.: Brain Aware®, Change Quest®, Four Gates to Peak Team Performance®, Three Phase Model of Learning™, Growth Culture®, Learn Remember Do™, and Survive Belong Become®.

For orders or bulk purchases of this book, please write Orders@7thMindPublishing.com.

For training materials affiliated with this book, visit BrittAndreatta.com/Training.

For speaking engagements, please contact Speaking@BrittAndreatta.com, or visit BrittAndreatta.com/Speaking.

ISBN: 978-0-9973547-9-9 (paper)
ISBN: 978-0-9973547-8-2 (ebook)

This book is printed on acid-free paper in the United States of America.

This book is dedicated to the scientists who
continually strive to expand our knowledge.
I appreciate your committment to discovery
and dedication to accuracy.

Content Warning
This book touches on the subject of trauma and suicide, which some readers might find difficult. We have placed a trigger warning at the beginning of those chapters.

CONTENTS

IV: Exploring Purpose + Meaningful Work

V: Continuing Your Journey to Find Purpose

VI: Building Purpose-Driven Organizations

INTRODUCTION

"The mystery of human existence lies not in just staying alive,
but in finding something to live for."

Fyodor Dostoyevsky, author

If you picked up this book, you are likely on your own journey of seeking more purpose in your life, or at least have noticed that a lot of other people are. It's hard to miss given that it's featured around the world in publications like *Forbes, Time, Entrepreneur,* and *Fast Company.* Consider these recent headlines:

Employees Want Purpose at Work: How to Deliver on This Top Priority

Finding Purpose at Work and the Growing Need for Corporate Values

Everyone Wants Meaningful Work.
But What Does That Really Look Like?

I started doing the research for this book at the beginning of 2018, after my community was torn apart by a natural disaster. On January 9th, in the span of 30 minutes, a 40-foot-high wall of mud and boulders the size of cabins slammed down, pulverizing cars and wiping away entire homes. The mudslide killed 23 people, including many children.

I saw firsthand that when all sense of happiness is gone, a sense of purpose is the only thing that gets you through. Purpose is also what motivates us to help others. We had this miraculous thing happen—people from hundreds of miles away started showing up to help. A loose volunteer organization formed, calling themselves the Bucket Brigade. They didn't live here but they showed up to remove the tons and tons of waist-high mud that buried streets and filled homes. They excavated people's living rooms, they dug out trees so they wouldn't suffocate, and they found and carefully organized possessions in hopes of returning them to their owners. It was an amazing act of generosity and kindness to witness and receive. It made those dark days a little more bearable.

At the same time, I began reading Aaron Hurst's book, *The Purpose Economy,* and realized that purpose was playing a far bigger role than what I could see in my own community. It was shifting the global economy.

Then the COVID-19 pandemic hit, scuttling my plans to write this book. My speaking income dried up overnight and I pivoted to supporting my 7th grader who was attending "Zoom school." As one of thousands of tech leaders charged with migrating a workforce to work-from-home employees in a matter of weeks, my husband's work intensified.

As we made our way through the lockdowns and worried about our loved ones, I started to notice a shift in my own sense of purpose. I felt a deep need to help in some way but wasn't sure how I could. At the time, I was recording the audiobook version of *Wired to Resist* and realized that I was uniquely positioned to help people live through this massive change we were experiencing. My team quickly built and offered a free online course on how to deal with change. I was stunned by the response. Nearly 1,500 people from around the world took the course and we were inundated with comments like: "Thank you for sharing it during this difficult and uncharted time. It's such a profound way of viewing change," and "What a blessing. This course was terrific, timely, and helpful!" and "It was an amazing gift to us during these difficult and challenging times. The concepts shared are all life changing!"

As time went on, I was asked to consult with several global organizations. I began to see the incredible toll burnout was taking on workers across every sector. I started doing research on the effects of burnout and realized we were headed toward high levels of disengagement and turnover, which ultimately became known as the Great Resignation.

We were living through a unique time as the whole world engaged in a simultaneous experience of reflecting on our values and clarifying our priorities. I was not surprised to see the many headlines about people's hunger for purpose and realized it was time to start up my research again. I quickly found that some amazing studies had been done during the pandemic, giving us new data and insights. If I had published this book earlier, it would already be out of date because things have shifted so significantly since 2019.

What is clear is the pandemic has changed us. Permanently. It accelerated what was already in motion, creating distinct pressures that magnified our need for purpose in significant ways. This societal shift impacts all age groups and all industries. There is no going back to "the before times" because we are different now. We are going through an amazing transformation, one that has shifted what we value, how we want to work, and ultimately the good that we wish to create in the world. While it has been challenging, it is also inspiring.

How to Use This Book

This book is designed to help you on your own journey to find your purpose and create meaningful work. I will share recent discoveries in neuroscience and other disciplines to give you new information and tools. You can apply this material to your own life immediately, starting today. If you have a role where you help or lead others, you will also gain new strategies for unlocking their potential and building more purpose-driven organizations. This book is organized into five sections:

I. We'll begin by diving into new findings about the science of becoming our best selves and why happiness, purpose, creativity, and innovation are all important elements.

II. Next, we'll explore the unique combination of forces and pressures driving this global quest for more purpose and how it's shifting human consciousness.

III. Then we'll dig into your individual journey toward finding purpose and creating a meaningful work. I'll share several tools and strategies you can use immediately to create more clarity.

IV. Next, I'll share new findings from research about meaningful work and what gives people a sense of purpose in their jobs and careers.

V. We'll continue your journey to find your own sense of purpose with additional tips and tools.

VI. We'll end with looking at purpose-driven organizations as the new future of work and practical strategies for employees, managers, and executives.

Throughout every section, you will find Purpose Stories, first-person narratives from 26 individuals from around the world including Ukraine, Brazil, The Netherlands, Australia, and the United States. They answered an open call for submissions and represent a wide range of industries from finance to manufacturing, from retail to education, and technology to healthcare. Each person tells their own story of finding purpose—sometimes at a young age, but more often discovered over the course of a career, learning what was *not* the right fit before finding what is.

Their journeys were shaped by a host of experiences from success and failure to burnout and tragedy. On multiple occasions, I found myself getting goosebumps as I read them and I hope you will find inspiration in learning how all of us are walking similar paths to finding our purpose. Each story is set off in a box with this compass icon. Consider this powerful story from Uvalde, Texas in the United States:

Purpose Story 1:
Purpose as a Way Through Tragedy
As a professional nonprofit fundraiser, I am driven by helping organizations secure the funding they need to serve communities. I consider myself a professional relationship builder. In this capacity, I matchmake—I match donors to causes that fulfill their deepest values.

Initially, I thought that academia would be the area where I could make the most impact. But after uncovering the deeply impactful work performed by nonprofits, I knew the sector offered a great fit for my aspiration and talents. Nonprofits are entrepreneurial spaces. Success is not dictated by the marketplace but rather by social change.

The work of a fundraiser is unique. You're positioned between the nonprofit and the funder. You're the curator of value-aligned relationships. It is hard work and often goes unrecognized. I have always found the work rewarding and it fulfilled my sense of purpose to help communities thrive.

But in 2022, a tragedy brought this work into sharp focus. My nonprofit organization was tasked with processing public donations after the mass school shooting in Uvalde, Texas. The kicker: I am from Uvalde and attended elementary school there.

This horrific situation made people across the country feel so helpless. I felt helpless. But being in a position where I could help facilitate the public outcry was quite fulfilling.

After the school shooting, everyday people and corporations wanted to help. Honestly, the only thing many felt that they could actually do was give a donation for the survivors and their families. In my role, I facilitated this along with my team. We created donation pages, responded to hundreds of emails, answered calls, and directed inquiries to the right people. We thanked everyone along the way for their light during this very dark time.

I relearned something that I already knew as a fundraiser—every donation matters. Every act of generosity deeply matters. People across the country gave what they could: $10, $15, and it added up. Everyone (and I do mean literally everyone) said, "I wish I could give more." We processed over $8 million in donations in the matter of a few months proving the collective power of caring.

Purpose comes at funny times, revealing itself when you're not desperately seeking it out. Follow what you love to do—it will reveal itself, in time. And most likely when you least expect it.

My Research Process

While I started researching purpose and meaningful work in 2018, when I resumed research I found many newly published studies had been conducted during the pandemic in every region of the world, showing a universal global experience. Countries included Afghanistan, Iran, Syria, Brazil, Mexico, Puerto Rico, Colombia, Ukraine, Yemen, Turkey, Romania, India, South Africa, Eretria, Korea, China, Japan, East Java, Indonesia, Spain, Italy, Netherlands, Canada, and the United States.

I first focused on neuroscience, reading journals like *Neuron, The Journal of Neuroscience,* and *Social Cognitive and Affective Neuroscience.* Inevitably, these studies led me to other disciplines and studies in biology, psychology, business, and education. I reviewed research from many branches of medicine and healthcare.

I also conducted a content analysis of the personal stories submitted to identify common themes and experiences.

Another important part of my research process is mapping what scientists find in their labs to issues that impact today's workplaces. I leverage research by data giants like Deloitte, Gallup, Gartner, and McKinsey, as well as professional organizations like the Association for Talent Development (ATD) and the Society for Human Resource Management (SHRM). Many of these global studies yielded fascinating insights about our hunger for purpose and meaning at work.

I also read over 30 books about purpose and meaningful work. I was especially struck by what they all had in common—when I looked at the totality of what the authors said, I saw clear patterns and themes that indicate a shared truth. I've attempted to synthesize them into a cohesive whole.

To be clear, I am not a neuroscientist; my PhD is in education, leadership, and organizations, and I have done my own research on the science of success. Because I am an active practitioner, designing and delivering learning experiences out in the field, I can see where lab studies do and do not translate to how people experience these concepts in the real world and especially at work.

I used this research to build science-based training programs that are proving to be exceptionally effective in all kinds of organizations and industries. If you want to learn more, visit www.BrainAwareTraining.com.

So, let's take a journey together. I'd like to introduce you to the fact that we are wired for purpose—it is part of our biological makeup as humans. We are neurologically designed to experience purpose and that it's different from happiness. The key to a meaningful life is to have them in balance.

It is also true that finding our sense of purpose is meant to be a journey that unfolds over time and shifts with life's experiences. Some people find many purposes over their lifetime, and others focus on one. There is no one right way but I have gathered some tools and information that can help you and others along the way. Let's get started!

Take a Learning Journey

I have learned that before I can write a book, I have to teach the concepts and content to live audiences. I always try to create a learning experience that shifts people's knowledge and behaviors. Before I wrote this book, I taught some of this content through workshops. In a live presentation, I model best practices in learning design based on the research of my previous book, *Wired to Grow: Harness the Power of Brain Science to Master Any Skill*. This includes having the audience pause and reflect on content every so often, applying it to their current situation.

Engaging with concepts in a personal way helps the brain learn and retain material and, more importantly, it's where any meaningful shift in actions starts. To help you gain the most from this book, you will find this light bulb icon marking an element called "Your Learning Journey" at the end of each section. Each includes instructions for applying the content to your experiences.

To make this easier, I have created a free downloadable PDF for you to fill out as you explore each concept (www.BrittAndreatta.com/Wired-to-Become). To maximize your experience, I also recommend you find a partner as social learning boosts long-term retention, and when you work in partnership, you gain the insights of each other's experiences. So, ask a friend or colleague who is seeking more purpose or meaning in their life and explore the content together.

THE SCIENCE OF BECOMING

"Being able to find one's purpose and meaning in life can—without a shadow of a doubt—make a person feel more alive, joyful, content, thankful, and even generous. Getting in touch with one's life mission and purpose has been proven to give huge psychological and emotional benefits that make life really worth living—and enjoying!"

Trevor Blattner, author,
Redefining the Top 1% and
7 Behaviors That Drive Shepard Leadership

1. Types of Well-being: Happiness and Purpose

Sometimes when people are on a search for purpose, they mistakenly focus on happiness. Both are important to our well-being, and we need them in balance but they are inherently different, even neurologically.

Two Types of Well-being

Hundreds of years ago, ancient Greek scholars identified two types of human well-being. Today's neuroscientists have discovered that they are important and also different.

- **Hedonic well-being focuses on attaining happiness and pleasure.** Happiness is more immediate—it's that fleeting sense of pleasure or joy. The pleasure I get from a good chocolate cake is real. It's a moment of a positive feeling that's entirely for me and my taste buds. I might not even share it! Hedonic well-being tends to be focused on the self and is self-enhancing. A good dessert is a form of desire but other values that drive happiness are money or fame/status/relevance. For example, many people get a brief feeling of happiness on social media when their story or post is "liked" by another person—that expresses our value for relevance.

- **Eudaimonic well-being results from striving toward meaning, purpose, potential, and self-realization.** Its hallmark is a longer-term, deep sense of fulfillment or satisfaction, though it is not always pleasurable. Striving for purpose or meaning often requires hard work as well as struggle. But the longer term and deeper satisfaction makes it worthwhile. This type of well-being often pushes us to ask ourselves these questions: *How can I be of service? How can I contribute to good in the world. How can I make a difference to other people?* As a result, eudaimonic well-being is self-transcending. It gets us out of the day-to-day in our own experience and moves us to thinking about the bigger community and the good that needs to be done for others. Oftentimes the values at play here are relationships, personal growth, and the community.

According to Brian and Gabrielle Bosché, authors of *The Purpose Factor: Extreme Clarity for Why You're Here and What to Do About It,* "Simply put, your purpose is what you have to help others. Fulfillment is the result of helping others with that you have." From the research, I have landed on this definition:

> *Purpose is an overarching sense of what matters in a person's life. It's driven by their core values and gives their life a sense of meaning. Purpose is self-transcendent where your actions result in service or benefit to others. Our sense of purpose acts as a North Star, even helping us know when we veered off the path and are no longer on purpose in our lives and work.*

So, I think of happiness as represented by a smiley face, and our sense of purpose and meaning as a North Star, guiding us forward for the good of others. Aristotle said, "There is a difference between the experience of pleasure and the notion of a 'virtuous activity of the soul.'"

Happiness/ Pleasure	Purpose/ Meaning
Hedonic well-being focuses on happiness and pleasure attainment.	Eudaimonic well-being results from striving toward meaning, purpose, potential, and self-realization.
Immediate	Long-term
Fleeting sense of pleasure or joy	Deep sense of fulfillment or satisfaction
"Having a good time"	"Living a good life"
Focused on self—self-enhancing	Focused on others—self-transcending
Values: money, fame/status, desire	Values: relationships, personal growth, community

Comparing hedonic and eudaimonic well-being

Dr. Zach Mercurio, from Colorado State University's Center for Meaning and Purpose writes, "When we serve others, we become better. More importantly, we transcend ourselves and become part of something bigger."

When you look at all the structures in our systems, it's clear that our species is wired for three key things:

- **To survive:** This is our most basic need to stay alive. Global conflicts and natural disasters highlight our primal need for food, water, and shelter. When we are not in crisis, this need expresses itself in our desire for job security because earning a paycheck is how we buy food and shelter. Anything that messes with our sense of job security, like a new boss, a performance review, or being assigned to a new team, can trigger these primal instincts. Needless to say, COVID-19 triggered survival fears, particularly before we had a vaccine.

- **To belong:** This is our need to be part of a community and form meaningful bonds. Belonging is tightly interwoven with our need to survive because our chances of survival are greater when we're part of a tribe. Entire structures of our anatomy are dedicated to helping us understand and connect with others, and our health suffers when we experience loneliness and isolation. This need was also strained when we had to practice physical distancing and avoid contact with family and friends.

- **To become:** Our deepest and greatest need is to become our best selves—to grow into our potential and make the contribution we are here to make. This is the "seeking" part of human nature and it distinguishes us from all the other living organisms on the planet. Our brains are wired to seek new levels of growth and we are called to identify and fulfill a sense of purpose. We'll explore this more in future chapters.

Some of you may recognize this as a simplified version of Abraham Maslow's hierarchy of human needs, and it is. While Maslow identified five levels, I find that collapsing them into these three categories better aligns with how issues play out in today's workplaces.

Leaders want their employees to show up and do their best work, but this cannot happen if the workplace isn't safe, both physically and psychologically. In addition, people have a need to belong at work, which may be difficult if a culture of inclusion is not intentionally cultivated.

A disservice of Abraham Maslow's model was framing self-actualization as the *peak* of human experience. Maslow initially conceived of a hierarchy in the shape of a pyramid, with self-actualization—becoming everything that one is capable of becoming—at the top or the pinnacle of the journey through human needs. It launched a movement of personal growth that focused on the self, which people sometimes misinterpreted as a focusing on their happiness.

Most people don't know that Maslow originally sourced his famous model from the Siksika Tribe of the Blackfoot Nation, but he made some changes that don't align with their original concepts. Over the course of his career, he realized his error and was seeking to rectify it when he passed.

Let's look at the differences: the Siksika and other First Peoples do not hold the concept of self-actualization as something we must do. They believe we are born *already* self-actualized and, as such, that each child should be treated with dignity and respect. That every person has inherent wisdom within them.

In the Siksika tradition, wealth or success is not measured by money or property but rather generosity. The wealthiest person would have almost nothing, as a sign of how much they gave to others. In fact, they have "giveaway ceremonies" where people give their possessions to those most in need.

For the Siksika Nation, the concept of community actualization was the most important—that each person was responsible for contributing to the health and safety of the entire tribe, and also ensuring its cultural perpetuity by adding to and passing on the ancestors' wisdom. According to one scholar, "First Nations often consider their actions in terms of the impacts of the 'seven generations.' This means that one's actions are informed by the experiences of the past seven generations and by considering the consequences for the seven generations to follow."

Maslow eventually acknowledged and updated his view, as described by Dr. Scott Barry Kaufman,

> *Toward the very end of his life, Maslow was working on an unfinished theory, which included "self-transcendence" at the top of his hierarchy of needs. In his description, self-transcendence involves furthering a cause beyond the self and*

experiencing a radical shift in perspective, including a communion beyond the boundaries of the self through "peak experiences."

Happiness vs. Purpose

Modern science proves the ancient Greeks and First Peoples right. Dr. Barbara Fredrickson, a researcher in positive psychology who studies happiness, found that 75 percent of the participants who score high on happiness scored low on purpose/meaning.

If you have ever chased happiness, you have probably experienced this yourself. Those fleeting moments of pleasure, while enjoyable, don't provide a sense of deeper fulfillment. We quickly feel empty again so can end up in a cycle of craving that next hit of pleasure when really what we need is to focus on how we can serve others.

Happiness is important and you may want to explore more on your own. I highly recommend these scholars and their researched-based books:

- Dr. Barbara Fredrickson, *Positivity: Groundbreaking Research to Release Your Inner Optimist and Thrive*
- Shawn Achor, *The Happiness Advantage: How a Positive Brain Fuels Success in Work and Life*
- Dr. Russ Harris, *The Happiness Trap: How to Stop Struggling and Start Living*
- Dr. Sonja Lybomirsky, *The How of Happiness: A New Approach to Getting the Life You Want*
- Catherine Price, *The Power of Fun: How to Feel Alive Again*
- Dr. Arthur Brooks, *From Strength to Strength: Finding Success, Happiness, and Deep Purpose in the Second Half of Life.*
- Dr. Robert Waldinger and Dr. Marc Schulz, *The Good Life: Lessons from the World's Longest Scientific Study of Happiness*
- Dr. Martin Seligman, *Authentic Happiness: Using the New Positive Psychology to Realize Your Potential for Lasting Fulfillment* and *Flourish: A Visionary New Understanding of Happiness and Well-being*

If you want to boost your happiness today, Dr. Martin Seligman offers this piece of advice: "Doing a kindness produces the single most reliable momentary increase in well-being of any exercise we have tested. Here is the exercise: find one wholly unexpected kind thing to do tomorrow and just do it. Notice what happens to your mood."

Dr. Seligman created the PERMA model, which includes these science-based strategies to increase happiness in your life:

1. Positive emotion

Intentionally boost how often you experience positive emotions like hope, joy, amusement, and gratitude. You can do this by spending time with people or on activities that elicit these emotions. Other options include listening to uplifting music and writing or speaking about things you are grateful for.

2. Engagement

If you've ever lost track of time while doing something you enjoy, you've experienced engagement. This state of "flow" tends to happen when we are using our skills in a way that challenges us and people who do so every day are happier. Activities include sports, puzzles or games, creative activities like painting or knitting, or being present through a practice of mindfulness.

3. Relationships

Positive relationships, where you feel supported, valued, and even loved by others are a key ingredient of happiness. In fact, Dr. Robert Waldinger and Dr. Marc Schulz, authors of *The Good Life: Lessons from the World's Longest Scientific Study of Happiness,* found that positive relationships not only contribute to happiness but also better health and longer lives.

They recommend that you decrease time spent in "depleting" relationships that induce tension, frustration, or anxiety and make you feel worried, or even demoralized. Instead, increase your time in "energizing" relationships that enliven and invigorate you, giving you a sense of connection and belonging that remains after you part.

4. Meaning

This is about our human need to have a sense of value or purpose. Seligman claims that this is about serving something greater than ourselves. Activities include spiritual activities, donating to or volunteering for a cause, teaching or mentoring others, honoring a loved one's memory, or doing an act of kindness.

5. Accomplishments

This aspect of happiness comes from working hard to achieve a goal or master a skill, which gives us a sense of pride. Activities that boost happiness include learning something new, starting and finishing a challenging project, or setting a goal and taking the steps to complete it.

Happiness scholar Dr. Christopher Boyce, recently traveled to Bhutan, a small Himalayan country that measures its "gross national happiness" or GNH and uses it to make important policy decisions. Bhutan now finds itself as the pioneer of the "well-being economy" and continues to break ground on critical issues that other countries are following.

Boyce said he learned more about happiness on that trip than in his many years as a scholar. He states, "The kind of happiness I value is deeper—grounded in connection, purpose, and hope, yet has room for sadness and anxiety too. Indeed, it's this kind of happiness that a country like Bhutan aspires to, and I think more countries (and people) should, too."

The Science of Purpose

It's clear that both happiness and purpose are necessary for well-being. Neuroscientists have studied both and found them neurologically different, lighting up different regions of the brain when studied on fMRI machines. Hedonic well-being or happiness activates a circuit between the medial shell, ventral pallidum, opioid neurotransmitters, and orbito-frontal cortex. It lights up a brain region near the top and right of center, as identified in a study titled, "The Structural Neural Substrate of Subjective Happiness."

Whereas eudaimonic well-being activates network connectivity between the insular cortex, precuneus, and ventral medial prefrontal cortex. In an article titled, "Neural Correlates of the 'Good Life': Eudaimonic Well-being Is Associated with Insular Cortex Volume," fMRI images show activity on both sides of the brain, lower down, near the ears. Several subsequent studies have confirmed these findings.

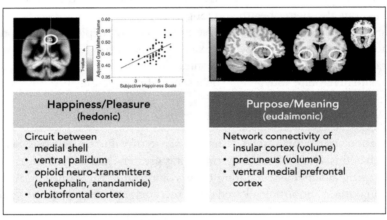

Neurological differences between happiness and purpose

While we might know that happiness and purpose feel different, we now have scientific proof that they are neurologically different—that we experience them differently in our biology.

It's no wonder, then, that we hunger for purpose and meaning. We are wired for purpose—to become our best selves. This is why, when you set a goal for yourself and you achieve it, you'll celebrate for a few days, and then what's the next thing you do? You set a new goal.

We are biologically designed to continually grow and reach for our potential, like the ever-turning upward spiral that is our very DNA.

Capital P or Small p

While we are wired for purpose, it doesn't always mean that we have a clear sense of what our purpose is. When we hear quotes like Aristotle's "virtuous activity of the soul," it can be a bit intimidating and put purpose up on a pedestal—like you're only living your purpose if you're doing something serious or it feels highly spiritual (cue the angels singing).

But we can think of two kinds of purpose: Purpose and purpose. Purpose with a capital P happens anytime we are of service or benefit to others. This can certainly include creating a nonprofit organization that helps a population in need and it also includes making another person feel like they matter and belong. It might include finding a cure for a disease as well as creating amazing food that brings people a sense of comfort. Or it might include donating to or volunteering at organizations that help animals or making a piece of art that touches people.

Stephanie Hsu, the actress nominated for her role in the Oscar-winning movie *Everything Everywhere All at Once,* spoke about this. The movie wrapped before the pandemic lockdowns began and so,

> *There was no way to predict how much the world would need our little offering… My biggest conflict with being an actor or being a part of this industry is that I fear that what we do is not enough. How is it possible that when there is a war, when there is climate disaster, when everything feels like it's crumbling, how is art going to help it?…I'm proud of this movie for so many reasons but the biggest gift has been that I very palpably feel that it is offering people healing. And that is all I could ever wish for—for any piece of art that I put out into the world. It's helpful to remember that art is capable of doing that, for moving us into action.*

Media and the news give us examples of what purpose can look like, but it's vital to remember that scale does not matter, nor does visibility. Purpose with a capital P is made through intention and commitment to be of service or benefit to others, whether one person or a million.

Many people are still on a journey of discovering their Purpose (capital P) is, and that's okay. There is also the day-to-day sense of purpose and meaning that gives us a sense of satisfaction in life. We can consider purpose (small p) as having an intention, an objective, or a goal. You can wake up and have a sense of purpose for getting your kids off to school or for working on a project with a colleague. Small p purpose also matters.

Purpose Story 2:
Purpose in Parenting
I was a newly single parent and my children were 10 and 12 years old at the time. I had been the family breadwinner throughout the marriage, while my partner had been the stay-at-home parent. I was transitioning to the routine of making all the breakfasts and dinners, taking out the garbage, fixing minor house issues, understanding the school routines, etc. And I was helping my kids navigate the hard emotions of this time. Many days I felt overwhelmed and exhausted.

One of the ways I coped was to use my drive home to mentally plan the dinner. On this particular evening, I decided on a quick and easy dinner: jarred spaghetti sauce, browned beef, and boxed pasta. I got home, caught up with my kids, and walked into the kitchen. I opened the pantry door and…no pasta. It just wasn't there. It wasn't anywhere. I stood, with my hand on the pantry door feeling such despair, such disappointment. And then I started crying silently—broken and exhausted.

I wanted to provide everything for my children. Ease their broken hearts. Be consistent and trustworthy. My sense of purpose was to ensure that my children were cared for in a similar fashion prior to me becoming a single mother. Providing a home-cooked meal made with love meant a lot to me, and the non-existent box of pasta almost did me in.

That moment will stay frozen in my mind for the rest of my life. I really had a sobering moment knowing that I was crying over pasta. But, with tears streaming down my cheeks, I told myself, "This cannot beat you." Thinking beyond what was in front of me, I asked myself, "How else can I get this done?"

I happen to own a hand-cranked pasta maker that only comes out at Christmas to make pierogi. I wiped my tears, pulled out the pasta machine, grabbed eggs, flour, salt, and I made my own pasta that night. I used my actions to turn a disappointing reality into achieving my goal of having a home-cooked meal for my kids.

I learned that a sense of purpose contributes to a resilient mind and family. There are other ways to approach challenges and I learned I could be flexible and creative. I also learned that it was okay to cry in the pantry! Life will bring disappointment, frustration, and sadness. But digging into your sense of purpose is how you find the way forward.

The other phrase that purpose researchers use is "purpose in life" or PIL. Purpose in life is the desire and effort people put forth to accomplish their goals, make significant contributions to society, and maintain a meaningful existence. In the next chapter, we will explore more about this research and the amazing benefits that having a sense of purpose in life brings us.

The term "meaningful" is often mentioned when people talk about purpose. It includes things that have value, significance, or importance. This is very personal to each individual but also arises from our core values.

Researchers also explore the concept of "meaningful work" or the way we express the meaning or purpose of our lives through the activities of work that take up most of our waking hours. We'll dig into this more in section IV.

We can now see that purpose and meaning are slightly different but very intertwined. As we continue in this book, we'll explore each of them so that you gain more information and tools to find and live your own sense of purpose.

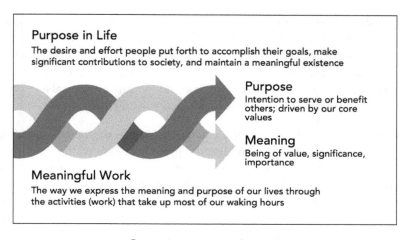

Purpose in Life
The desire and effort people put forth to accomplish their goals, make significant contributions to society, and maintain a meaningful existence

Purpose
Intention to serve or benefit others; driven by our core values

Meaning
Being of value, significance, importance

Meaningful Work
The way we express the meaning and purpose of our lives through the activities (work) that take up most of our waking hours

Comparing purpose and meaning

Drivers of Purpose

One tool I want to introduce you to now is the work of Aaron Hurst. In 2016, he wrote *The Purpose Economy: How Your Desire for Impact, Personal Growth and Community Is Changing the World.* I've since had the pleasure to meet and work with him. His research identified that people have three drivers of purpose: impact, values, and craft.

Impact
The first purpose driver is the impact we want to create. It answers the question, "Who do you want to impact?" Hurst found that people are drawn to work at one of the three levels:

- **Individuals:** At this level, people want to bring about change in individual lives by addressing their needs or challenges. An example here might be helping homeless people in your community or teens with mental health challenges. This might include working directly with homeless people living on the street or volunteering at a shelter. Or a person might become a therapist or school counselor working directly with teens. This level is about relationships and being able to look into people's eyes and see the impact you're having.

- **Organizations:** This level is about expanding the impact to touch many lives by enabling an organization or team to succeed. Here, the focus is on the larger work the organization is doing. This might mean working for or donating to organizations that focus on the mental health of youth or taking a job at a company that produces electric cars or organic food. You may not be able to look into the eyes of the people you are helping but you can track the organization's impact on the community you want to serve.

- **Society:** People drawn to this level care about impacting people by changing society. Even small changes at the society level can have a huge impact to organizations and individuals. This level often includes working with laws, government agencies, and media campaigns. For example, we can work to change laws at the state or national level or film a documentary designed to educate people and change behavior.

Sometimes, we start at one level and journey to another. For example, veterinarian Dr. Kwane Stewart started providing free veterinary care to homeless people with pets. He found a profound sense of purpose in helping each animal and their owner. Over time, he saw a greater need, so he started a nonprofit organization, Project Street Vet, to fund raise so he could offer more services to more communities—thus working at the organization level. His organization has worked with Congress and endorsed bill HR8074, known as the PUPP Act, to help homeless people with pets. Dr. Steward was named a 2023 CNN Hero by the news network.

Hurst argues that we usually find one level to be particularly fulfilling and that level is our personal purpose driver for impact. Which one speaks to you or is evident when you look over your life so far? This reflection can be a source of insight too because sometimes we shift levels without realizing that it might dilute or enhance our sense of purpose. Consider if that is something you should explore in your own life.

Values

The next purpose driver is the "why" and is sourced in our values or moral view of the world. Hurst believes that we hunger to drive progress toward where our values are universally achieved. Hurst identifies two categories here:

- **Karma:** This value focuses on the idea that when people are supported in realizing their potential, they will be able to accomplish great things. It is about supporting individuals in becoming better and knowing that if we invest in people, they will solve the other problems. Progress is achieved through hard work and resourcefulness. They tend to work best in challenging environments that reward bold ideas and action.

- **Harmony:** This focuses on society and expresses the value that our society will become truly great once we achieve equality for all people. They believe that we cannot get there until we fix the structures that keep people from achieving their potential, so society must come first. Progress is achieved through equality, justice, and balance. They tend to work best in inclusive environments that encourage everyone's participation.

Craft

The final category is "the how" and answers the question, "How do you want to achieve success?" Hurst found four ways that people approach their work, solve problems, and engage in the creative process:

- **Community:** People with this driver generate purpose most when empowering others to work together by leveraging collective capabilities to tackle obstacles. Their problem-solving approach is collaborative. They enjoy facilitating connections and building motivation among team members, leadership, support staff, and clients.

- **Human:** People with this driver generate purpose most when engaging with people and exploring contexts to determine needs and propose authentic solutions. Their problem-solving approach is intuitive. They enjoy creating a practical solution based on the needs and desires expressed by the individuals they serve.

- **Structure:** People with this driver generate purpose most when designing and implementing the tools and systems necessary to take on a challenge. Their problem-solving approach is process based. They enjoy outlining all the steps needed to address a problem or scale a solution, and to define the process that will move things forward.

- **Knowledge:** People with this driver generate purpose most when investigating new theories by exploring possible solutions through rigorous research and analysis. Their problem-solving approach is research based. They enjoy mastering the technical issues of the problem and sharing their insights and knowledge with others.

As you can see, these four approaches can be found in different types of roles or jobs. When we align with the right one, we find work much more fulfilling and can feel that we are "on purpose" in our lives.

Based on these descriptions, what do you think are your purpose drivers? Which ones resonated for you the most? Are there any you need to adjust to bring you closer to your sense of purpose and meaning? I will share other models for exploring your sense of purpose in sections III and V. Hurst's model is one way to reflect on purpose in your life. He also built a company that helps organizations create a purpose-driven workplace (check it out at Imperative.com). I have partnered with Aaron Hurst to offer you a free North Star Reflection Exercise to explore your purpose drivers—you will find it at Imperative.com/britteq.

2. Benefits of Purpose: Individual Health

In doing the research for this book, I was astounded to learn of the many biological benefits of purpose. It turns out that we are so wired for purpose that it provides all kinds of protections to us, both as individuals and communities. In this chapter, I'm going to share the robust and growing evidence that shows the positive impact that having a sense of "purpose in life," or PIL, has on people across their lifespan. This section is data heavy as I "bring the receipts."

What really made me take notice is how the researchers studying different aspects of purpose were all arriving at the same conclusion. Purpose is a biological imperative—we thrive when we have it and we struggle when we don't.

Neural Protection

We know that nutrition and regular exercise contribute to our overall health but it turns out that having a sense of purpose in your life does too. In fact, as Dr. Trevor Blattner explains, "One particular area of health where PIL is proving to be very useful is known as a cognitive reserve or cognitive resilience, which is the human brain's ability to recover from trauma and protect against diseases."

A sense of PIL boosts brain cell resilience to injury and degradation. As a result, they enjoy a reduced risk for stroke. Researchers use the Purpose-in-Life Scale which gives respondents a score ranging from 20 to 140. One study found that as PIL scores go up, the risk of stroke goes down by up to 22 percent. Another study found that a strong sense of purpose reduced the risk of death via stroke as much as 72 percent for men.

Neuropsychologist, Dr. Patricia Boyle, found that older people who had a sense of purpose in their lives reduced their risk of Alzheimer's by 50 percent. Another study found that a sense of purpose also slows age-related decline and reduces the risk of dementia.

Other researchers have found this same effect and also that PIL significantly moderated the relationship between race/ethnicity and cognitive decline, especially among Black participants. These studies are not just among small populations but have sample sizes in the tens of thousands.

Purpose in life also proves to be helpful in enhancing healthy cognitive aging among older adults. Higher PIL scores are associated with better health status, higher use of preventative care, lower healthcare costs, and most importantly, higher quality of life.

Older adults who have recently lost their spouse or life partner are particularly prone to rapid cognitive decline. In a 2022 study of over 12,000 widows, cognition was shown to decrease in the years following their partner's death, but those with a purpose in life showed an increase cognitive health that counterbalanced the effect of their loss.

Another study assessed the health of 13,000 adults five times over an eight-year period. Having a purpose in life was associated with key health behaviors:

- 24 percent decrease in the likelihood of becoming inactive
- 33 percent lower likelihood of developing sleep problems
- 22 percent decrease in developing unhealthy body mass index (BMI)
- A slight decrease in a smoking relapse

There is no question that a sense of purpose in life is a powerful neural protectant, especially as we age. But it positively impacts all age groups.

Mental Health Protection

People with a sense of purpose experience some powerful protection for their mental health. One important study found that teenagers with a sense of purpose experienced significantly lower bouts of depression.

That is especially important since the pandemic created such a rise in mental health challenges for teens. In 2021, the US Surgeon General, Dr. Vivek Murthy, issued an advisory titled *Protecting Youth Mental Health*. This 53-page report details biological and environmental factors that shape the lives of children and can create the conditions for challenges to become mental health issues and grow into maladaptive disorders.

He points to a robust body of research on adverse childhood experiences (ACEs), which can impair the children's healthy development, physically and psychologically. Adverse experiences include various forms of abuse, neglect, and household dysfunction.

If you have not yet explored the ACE research, I highly encourage you to watch the TED talk by Dr. Nadine Burke Harris titled, "How Childhood Trauma Affects Health Across a Lifetime." Dr. Burke Harris is the current Surgeon General for the state of California and authored the book *The Deepest Well: Healing the Long-Term Effects of Childhood Trauma and Adversity.*

One study by Dr. Kristin Homan and Dr. Jooyoung Kong found that adverse childhood experiences tend to give sufferers a restricted or lower sense of purpose in life. So, trauma at a young age lowered PIL then impacted them over the course of their lifetime, causing poorer mental and physical health.

Fortunately, increasing a person's sense of purpose can mediate this impact at any stage in life. An increased PIL has been shown to decrease isolation as well as symptoms of anxiety and depression in adulthood, even well into late life. PIL also motivates people to increase self-care behaviors like seeing a therapist or consistently taking medications.

Even during the pandemic, PIL offered significant mental health protection to frontline healthcare workers. One study found that it modulated the appearance of mental health distress even during the height of the crisis. It also reduced anxiety when people learned that they or a family member had been exposed to COVID-19.

Before the vaccines were available, that waiting period tended to cause great anxiety as the death rates were still high and people who became ill had to hospitalized without visits from family members. PIL reduced that anxiety.

Finally, having a sense of purpose modulates life's daily stressors. Studies show that people with higher PIL scores have more positive emotions on a day-to-day basis. And they weather daily stresses better, seeing less decline in positive emotions (or rise in negative ones). Finally, they report fewer physical symptoms of stress. The researchers go on to suggest that PIL serves a homeostatic function by reducing a negative reaction to stress, creating more emotional stability.

It's clear that a sense of purpose protects against developing mental health challenges and reduces the effect of symptoms once they begin.

Purpose Story 3:
A Career of Helping Others

This is a past, current, and ongoing success story. I've had the honor of doing this work, if you want to call it that, for the last 18 years. Always incredibly fulfilling and purposeful, the "work" is becoming even more so lately with the emergence of a new organization I've had the privilege of helping to launch. My horizons have broadened. And I'm making even more of a positive impact in people's lives. What more can there be?

I have the pleasure of facilitating a circle practice, council—attentive listening coupled with authentic expression—in addition to team building. I do this work with a wide variety of organizations, schools, and prisons. I think of Tony (all names changed), who's been incarcerated his entire adult life, looking around our circle with excitement. "I've seen these guys a lot, but now I feel closer to them. I'm actually getting to know them," he says. In moments like these, my spirit is full.

When 17-year-old Bella shares with tear-filled eyes, "I always thought I was the only one who felt this way, and now I don't feel so alone," I wonder what the world would be like if we all felt more connected to others I've learned through these experiences to be more empathic, more open to differing perspectives, and kinder to myself and others.

Additionally, I'm blessed to facilitate Rites of Passage programs for high school seniors. Over five days on 36 beautiful acres of land, students gather to explore the transition they're about to make. Able to slow down, they're offered opportunities to reflect on their lives, who they've been, and what "boxes" they've been put into—and then decide who they would like to be as they step into adulthood. With all of my work, I know I'm in the right place, doing the right thing, at the right time.

And now, as the newly appointed director of outreach, I will be able to connect with more organizations and reach an even wider audience. As Whitney, a council trainee, says, "I've learned this practice is portable and available to me in any situation at any time." It's true. The world needs more of us listening and speaking from the heart. To glimpse the wider ripple effect of the work I do is a blessing I do not take for granted.

Physical Health

The benefits of having purpose in life also positively impact physical health. One study found that people with purpose in life reduced their risk of death from cardiovascular disease by 44 percent and heart attack by 48 percent.

In research published in the journal *Proceedings of the National Academy of Sciences*, Dr. Kim and colleagues found that people with greater senses of purpose in life were more likely to embrace preventive healthcare: things like mammograms, prostate exams, colonoscopies, and flu shots. They were more committed to acts of self-care like eating more healthfully and exercising regularly.

Several studies show that a purpose in life even lowers the body's inflammatory response, thus reducing risks of autoimmune diseases like multiple sclerosis and Crohn's disease. When we are under stress, the adrenal glands produce cortisol, which naturally and temporarily suppresses the immune system. This is fine for short periods but, when this happens over a longer time, our body can become desensitized to cortisol. When the immune system is out of balance, it can turn on itself, attacking the tissues instead of foreign bodies like viruses.

In fact, some researchers go so far as to call purpose "a buffer against mortality." Dr. Victor Strecher is a medical professional who authored the book *Life on Purpose: How Living for What Matters Most Changes Everything*. He outlines the many health benefits of purpose including better sex, better sleep, being more relaxed, better levels of the "good" cholesterol, and an increase in cells that attack viruses and cancer. Even a one-point increase on the PIL scale reduces the risk of dying by 12 percent. "We find that people with the strong sense of purpose literally have their DNA repaired more effectively," he says. "They have more antibodies and fewer pro-inflammatory cells. We find that people with the strong purpose live longer."

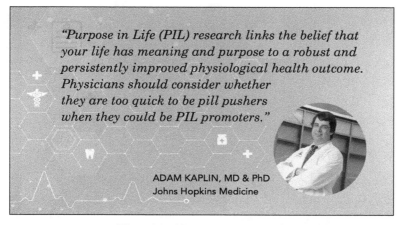

"Purpose in Life (PIL) research links the belief that your life has meaning and purpose to a robust and persistently improved physiological health outcome. Physicians should consider whether they are too quick to be pill pushers when they could be PIL promoters."

ADAM KAPLIN, MD & PhD
Johns Hopkins Medicine

The value of having a purpose in life

Adam Kaplan, MD and PhD, from Johns Hopkins Medical Center said, "Purpose in life research links the belief that your life has meaning and purpose to a robust and persistently improved physiological health outcome. Physicians should consider whether they are too quick to be pill pushers when they could be PIL promoters."

And he's not alone in this view. Another study published in the 2021 *American Journal of Preventive Medicine* looked at the mortality rates of over 13,000 adults older than age 50. They found that the "people with the highest level of purpose consistently tended to have lower mortality risk."All this evidence clearly indicates that a sense of purpose in life creates significant benefits for our physical and mental health. In the next chapter, we'll learn about how these benefits also impact our organizations and communities.

3. Benefits: Community and Organizational Health

Purpose also plays an important role in the health of our communities. Several studies point to benefits that impact all of us as we coexist as neighbors, friends, and coworkers.

Community Health

Let's first explore the many benefits purpose provides our communities.

Increased comfort with diversity
Three different studies found that people with a sense of purpose are more comfortable with diversity. We know that people who have a sense of purpose for themselves don't feel as threatened by those who are different. They're much less likely to engage in negative behaviors, such as judging or suppressing others' experiences, perhaps because they have their own sense of fulfillment.

Decreased perception of difficulty
When you give people with a sense of purpose a task, they perceive it as less hard compared to others who don't have a sense of purpose. Having a sense of purpose helps people walk through life and not feel overwhelmed. They may perceive obstacles as easier to overcome because they are motivated from an internal source.

Better rehabilitation
Many studies point to the powerful effect purpose has on rehabilitation. According to Dr. Victor Strecher, "People who enter drug and alcohol rehab programs with purpose are half as likely to relapse within six months of completing treatment."

I have had the privilege of doing leadership development with prison wardens through the Warden Exchange Program. When people are given a sense of purpose, for example, training service dogs, their rehabilitation goes way up, and their recidivism (returning to prison after release) goes way down.

This is important for our communities because 95 percent of prisoners, approximately 600,000 per year in the US, are released. Helping them develop a sense of purpose helps incarcerated people become better citizens and more successful in life.

One documentary, titled *Prison Dogs,* details the power of using inmates to train service dogs. They immediately find a strong sense of purpose, both in caring for the animal and preparing them to successfully serve their future owner. Data shows that prisoners create more successful dogs with 70 to 87 percent placed in service versus the 40 to 50 percent rate of nonincarcerated trainers. In addition, the prisoners experience significant benefits like these:
- More patience and kindness
- Less depression and anxiety
- Better physical health

- Better behavior and fewer infractions
- Fewer return after release (recidivism)

Helping incarcerated people find and experience a sense of purpose creates long-lasting and important effects for us all.

Purpose Story 4:
From Addiction to Transforming Lives
One of my greatest passions is nurturing and developing potential. I believe that potential is something that's already within each one of us, and in everything around us. Sometimes potential may not be visible yet and is just waiting to be noticed and brought to the surface. Or, maybe it's already visible but hasn't received the right kind of support and encouragement needed to reach its fullest capacity.

Looking back, I can see that my life has really been a search for my own potential. Although I was always bright and outwardly successful, inwardly I was often plagued by self-doubt, fear, and uncertainty about the future. Depression was common and I developed an addiction to alcohol that lasted for 16 years. This addiction, more than once, threatened to take everything away from me that mattered most. Fortunately, I was able to find recovery and my life was transformed from the inside out.

One of my clearest memories from this transitional time in my life was during my role as Urban Forester for a community government agency. This position involved incredible opportunities to make a difference in something I cared deeply about. I worked closely with local citizens, governmental departments, schools, businesses, and other organizations. I was regularly featured in the local newspaper for positive initiatives and participated with community organizations that helped support a variety of causes related to education, health, wellness, and of course, environmental care.

At the same time, something was wrong, and I knew it. I was struggling with alcohol use, and it wasn't getting any better. In fact, it was destroying my life. It was all I could do to maintain some semblance of sanity during the day, trying desperately to manage hangovers and daily withdrawal symptoms, just so that I could get home and drink again. It was no way to live, but I didn't know what else to do. I had tried so many ways to stop and had very little success.

I felt so caught between having a sense of purpose and also watching it disappear right in front of my eyes. Ultimately, my alcohol use disorder progressed, and I got the help I needed. I began a journey that took five years of trying and relapsing, but it fortunately has led to the life I'm blessed to live today.

I've been sober and in active recovery since February of 2006. In recovery, I began to experience life in ways I had never known before. I started to understand how I was causing my own suffering and misery without even realizing it. This understanding helped me to find a deep sense of freedom, empowerment, and true happiness for the first time. My whole attitude and outlook on life were dramatically changed for the better. Each day became a quest for purpose and the fulfillment of my potential. That quest is what led me to become a coach.

These years have been the best of my life. I really didn't expect to live to see 30, and probably shouldn't have made it past 20. But today I have an amazing, loving family that I feel was handpicked for me. We belong to each other. And now as a Purpose Coach and Addiction Recovery Coach, I have a career that fulfills my life purpose and helps others to do the same.

Protection for marginalized communities

Research shows that the very possibility of getting stereotyped may harm the work/school performances of people who are part of groups likely to be stereotyped. Known as the "stereotype threat," it's something that impacts people of color, women, 2SLGBTQI people, as well as people with disabilities. [Note: 2S stands for Two Spirit, the term used in Native or Indigenous communities and, since they are the first peoples, 2S is added to the front of LGBTQI acronym that stands for lesbian, gay, bisexual, trans, queer, and intersex.]

Being judged or viewed negatively (via stereotypes) is a form of threat that activates the brain's survival center. For all of us, being in a threatened state takes the executive center of the brain offline as energy is diverted away from higher-order thinking (analysis, logic) to funnel toward the fight-flight-freeze reaction that increases our chance of survival. This process temporarily reduces our intelligence and can negatively impact our performance.

Stereotypes inevitably impact the beliefs, values, and actions of others, and that prejudice can cause them to deny people access to opportunities. For example, not interviewing female applicants for engineering jobs or not renting a home to a family of color. Findings from several different studies show how this effect impacts all kinds of groups.

One study found that Black students asked to identify their race when taking a standardized test consistently performed lower than other Black students who were not asked to do so. In another study, women were asked to take a notoriously difficult math ability test. Participants were randomly assigned to one of three groups labeled as women, residents of the Northeast, or students at an elite private college. The third group (elite college) consistently performed the best on the exam, even though all the labels were true of all the women.

Stereotypes matter. Currently and historically, Black people are extremely overrepresented in the US prison systems, a result of racial profiling and biased laws and sentencing. While Blacks are 13 percent of the US population, they comprise 38 percent of the state prison system, meaning they are incarcerated an average of 5.1 times the rate of Whites (in some states it's as high as 10:1). Chicano/Latino people are also overrepresented in the prison at 18 percent of the population but 21 percent of those incarcerated. Native Americans are 2 percent of the prison population while only 0.9 percent of the US population.

While a small percentage of the population knowingly believes stereotypes and intentionally uses them to guide actions (supremacy and extremist groups, for example), the majority happens through unconscious bias.

This is why unconscious bias and inclusion programs are so important in our schools and workplaces. They can help us become aware of these invisible forces and make different choices.

Additionally, we can use the power of purpose to give some protection against the stereotype threat. I find Dr. Geoffrey Cohen's research on this topic particularly compelling. He's a Stanford professor who studies self-concept and belonging. In one study, subjects were asked to spend 15 minutes writing about their values or something important to them. This brief exercise boosted their confidence, acting like a "mental vaccine" against the stereotype threat.

In fact, one study found that Black students who did this purpose exercise closed a 40 percent performance gap that existed between them and their White peers (not true for the students who had not focused on purpose). Another study by Dr. Jonathan Sepulveda and his colleagues found that adolescents who attended a program specifically designed to increase their sense of purpose enjoyed many benefits, including general self-efficacy, increased GPAs, a decrease in comparing themselves to others, and avoiding situations where they risked failure or social consequences. Similar results have been found in studies with the 2SLGBTQI community and people with disabilities.

New studies show that a sense of purpose counterbalances or can partially shield against the harm of the stereotype threat, allowing people in *all* marginalized groups to perform better.

Often, people don't understand the real scale of how many people feel targeted. One Harvard study found that 61 percent of employees feel pressure to cover some facet of their identity at work. The numbers are higher for members of marginalized or targeted communities:

- 83 percent for 2SLGBTQI
- 79 percent for Black
- 66 percent of women
- 63 percent for Chicano/Latino/Hispanic
- 61 percent of Asian/Pacific Islander

Even 45 percent of heterosexual, white men feel this way because they are covering up something like a mental health issue or a physical disability.

We know that having a sense of purpose can help *all* of these communities not only do better themselves but also create a better environment for others. We need to actively work to dismantle systems of oppression, ending bias and microaggressions. But until that happens, we can also help targeted communities by giving them a shield of purpose to provide a small sense of relief against the daily onslaught of threat.

Percent of employees who feel pressure to cover their identify at work

Healing through tragedy and loss

A final benefit for our communities is that purpose helps us heal from painful experiences. In the face of tragedy and loss, sometimes healing begins with the initial purpose of making arrangements for the service or taking care of the daily demands of kids and pets. Sometimes it occurs during the subsequent court proceedings and the purpose of finding justice or in turning tragedy into efforts that will prevent others from suffering a similar loss.

In addition to the mudslides of 2018, my community suffered two other big tragedies. In 2019, a deadly boat fire killed 29 people, making it the worst maritime disaster in California since 1865. Several families have been actively involved in creating legislation to improve safety on small passenger vessels.

And in 2014, our community was ripped apart by a mass shooting in the neighborhood where college students live. One of those students went on a stabbing and shooting rampage killing 6 students and injuring 14 others. Several of the victims' parents have been involved in ongoing efforts to change gun laws and provide better support for people with mental illnesses.

A sense of purpose may also come from people's spiritual traditions, as most have beliefs and traditions around eternal life and lost loved ones being with the divine. Finding meaning is a natural part of the grieving process—we'll explore this more in chapter 7.

Organizational Health

Interestingly, data shows that organizations also greatly benefit from purpose. This occurs on two levels: When employees have a sense of purpose, it enhances the success of the organization. And the work culture of a purpose-driven organization enhances the experiences of its employees, customers, and stake-holders. Let's look at some key data points.

Recruitment, engagement, and retention

If you hold a leadership role, you may want to further explore the reports and studies I mention in this chapter.

In McKinsey's 2021 report *The Search for Purpose at Work*, they found that those employees who say that they live their purpose at work are

- 6.5 times more likely to report higher resilience,
- 4 times more likely to report better health,
- 6 times more likely to want to stay at the company, and
- 1.5 times more likely to go above and beyond to make their company successful.

Living your purpose at work can mean that the employee's personal sense of purpose is fulfilled by the job they do and/or their organization's mission and vision.

Deloitte's *2020 Global Marketing Trends Report* found that purpose-driven companies report 40 percent higher employee retention than their competitors. And when employees are deeply connected with their company's giving and volunteering efforts, turnover drops by an average of 57 percent. This yields real cost savings, given that replacing an employee costs 50 to 250 percent of their salary plus benefits, according to the Society for Human Resource Management (SHRM).

Millennials and Gen Z particularly care about working for socially responsible companies, another form of purpose. One study found that 64 percent of Millennials won't take a job if the company doesn't demonstrate a sense of social responsibility through its policies. An astounding 83 percent said they would be more loyal to a company who helped them make contributions to social and environmental issues.

Gen Z is even more focused on purpose—75 percent believe that work should have greater meaning than their paycheck. They want their employer to actively take a stand for equality and the environment. A report by WeSpire states that Gen Z is also "Obsessed with authenticity and will actively publicize ugly corporate cultures."

Customer loyalty

Gen Z's focus on purpose translates to their behavior as consumers as well. If a brand is socially responsible, studies find that Gen Z is

- 85 percent more likely to trust that brand,
- 84 percent more likely to buy their products, and
- 82 percent more likely to recommend that brand to others.

But they are not alone. According to the *Wall Street Journal*, consumers in general are more focused on purpose than ever before. Nearly 60 percent of Americans said their purchasing behavior was based on the brand's stand on societal issues, up 13 percent from 2017.

Accenture, in their report titled *From Me to We: The Rise of the Purpose-Led Brand*, found that brand loyalty is largely impacted by the brand's stand on societal issues. More than half of consumers would complain if they were disappointed by a brand's words or actions on a social issue, and nearly just as many would walk away in frustration, with nearly 20 percent leaving for good.

This can create an opportunity for brands as well—two-thirds of consumers (and 91 percent of Millennial consumers) would switch to buying from a purpose-driven company. Nearly two-thirds of adults believe that "making the world better" should be a primary purpose of companies—furthermore, they are willing to pay more for products from brands that want to do good. For those companies that align with this belief, they have an opportunity to gain great market share over their competitors that don't.

Productivity and financial performance
Studies by Google, Bain & Company, and PricewaterhouseCoopers found that employees with a sense of purpose have 50 percent stronger leadership potential, 125 percent higher productivity, and 400 percent higher performance.

Deloitte's *2020 Global Marketing Trends Report* also found that purpose-driven companies report 30 percent higher levels of innovation than their competitors.

The *2020 Kantar Purpose Study* studied brand growth over a 12-year period, comparing how companies were perceived by consumers in terms of positive impact in the world. The brand value growth was highest for companies perceived as having a high positive impact (175 percent) versus 86 percent for medium perceived impact and 70 percent for low perceived impact.

The most compelling research is the Torrey Project on financial performance on the NASDAQ and NYSE. They compared four sets of companies over the past 20 years: (1) S&P 500, (2) companies from Jim Collins' book *Good to Great*, (3) purpose-driven companies featured in *Firms of Endearment*, and (4) Ethisphere's 2019 "most ethical companies." The top performers? The purpose-driven companies with stock price 100 percent higher than the S&P 500.

Each one of these findings drives real gains for the organization and combined can create a significant competitive advantage. In section VI, we will look at how to build purpose-driven organizations.

4. Creativity and Innovation

This section on the Science of Becoming would not be complete without a chapter on creativity and innovation. Both people and organizations express their path to purpose through these processes. A series a of "aha!" moments often is what lead us to our purpose.

Creativity vs. Innovation

Bob Iger, CEO of Disney, says, "The heart and soul of the company is creativity and innovation." Just like happiness and purpose, creativity and innovation are different but connected. You need a balance of both in order to create success. But it is also a question of which came first—the chicken or the egg? In this case, we know. It's creativity.

Creativity is unleashing the potential of the mind to conceive of new concepts. These can manifest themselves in any number of ways, but most often they become something we can see, hear, smell, taste, or touch—some tangible thing we experience.

However, creative ideas can also be thought experiments within the mind, so to speak.

Contrast that with innovation—the work required to make an idea viable. Innovation is also about introducing change into relatively stable systems. By identifying an unmet need, an organization can apply its creative resources through innovation, to design an appropriate solution and reap a return on investment.

Creativity is that "aha!" moment—a flash of insight, whereas innovation is a process, like design thinking. Creativity is coming up with an idea, where innovation is capitalizing on that idea. Creativity is spending money to generate ideas and innovation is spending ideas to generate money.

Creativity	Innovation
Creativity is unleashing the potential of the mind to conceive new ideas.	Innovation is the work required to make an idea viable.
Those concepts could manifest themselves in any number of ways, but most often, they become something we can see, hear, smell, touch, or taste. However, creative ideas can also be thought experiments within the mind.	By identifying an unmet need, an organization can use innovation to apply its creative resources to design a solution and reap a return on its investment. It's also about introducing change into relatively stable systems.
The "aha!" moment; flashes of insight	A process, like design thinking
Coming up with an idea	Capitalizing on an idea
Spending money to generate ideas	Spending ideas to generate money

The differences between creativity and innovation

The pandemic pushed us through an intense period of creativity and innovation, where entire industries found new approaches in a matter of weeks, if not days, to successfully navigate our changing world. Workers in healthcare, teaching, and technology had to be especially resourceful while problem-solving massive challenges in real time. And each one of us had to dig into creativity and innovation to make our way through those difficult lockdowns, whether we were still at home or essential workers out in the field.

If your organization leaned hard into innovation, there is a cost to innovation at speed. People can't do it at a sustained pace without also getting breaks and opportunities to fill their tanks. This has contributed to rising burnout, which we'll explore more in chapter 9.

It's clear that we need both creativity and innovation to drive success, that these are separate but related processes, and that creativity comes first. Let's explore creativity in more depth.

The Science of Creativity

Creativity is birthed in the human mind—that flash of insight that brings something entirely new into reality. Humans are naturally creative beings, and our brain is designed to have these "aha!" moments.

Dr. John Kounios studies the neuroscience of "aha!" moments and discovered, through fMRI imaging, that the brain is very active in the seconds before a person is conscious of having that flash of insight. One-third of a second before that moment, there is burst of gamma waves above the right ear, in the anterior temporal gyrus. Blood rushes into that part of brain, making the activity quite easy to detect with modern diagnostic tools.

One full second before that, a burst of alpha waves in the right occipital cortex suppresses vision for a millisecond. Scientists call this the "brain blink"— we essentially darken our sight to the outer world to give birth to our in(ner) sight. You can read more about this research in the book *The Eureka Factor: Aha Moments, Creative Insight, and the Brain.*

When I speak to audiences around the world, I ask the questions, "Where do you get your best ideas?" and "What are you doing when those 'aha!' moments hit you?" Never once has anyone said, "Sitting at my desk thinking." Isn't that funny? We can try and try to focus and have flashes of insight, but we can't just squeeze them out of our brain.

The most common answers to my question? The shower, going for a walk/run, right after waking up, and gardening. It turns out, we are all living examples of what the brain is built to do—take information in, stir it around, and let new connections form.

Our brain is incredibly complex. Sitting on your shoulders is the most complicated object in the known universe with 86 billion neurons and 10,000 different types of neurons. The brain has 300 times more connections than there are stars in the Milky Way Galaxy. If that's not motivation to wear a helmet, I don't know what is.

Cognitive scientist. Dr. Scott Barry Kaufman studies human creativity. He details his findings in the book, *Wired to Create: Unraveling the Mysteries of the Creative Mind*, that he co-authored with *HuffPost* writer Carolyn Gregoire. He identifies three neural networks that play a role in creativity:

- **Executive center:** Comprising the prefrontal cortex and positive parietal, this allows us to have focused attention on something and take in new information through learning.

- **Imagination:** The medial temporal and posterior cingulate allow us to engage in musing or daydreaming, picturing fanciful, unexpected, or seemingly impossible things.

- **Salience:** The anterior insula and anterior cingulate work together to toggle between concentration and monitoring your environment. For example, part of you is reading this paragraph but can switch over to noticing the temperature in your room or any ambient noises.

The magic happens when we step away from concentrating, giving our neo-cortex a rest. We take a break and go for a walk or hop in the shower, and that unfocused state primes the brain for new connections to be made—and BAM! Or rather, "AHA!"

The shower seems to be a great incubator for insight because it brings together three elements that facilitate flashes of insight. First, between the steam and fairly neutral materials, there is not much visual stimulation, mimicking the brain blink. White noise and warm temperature create a comfortable zone of low stimulation, also known as sensory gating. And finally, there is water, which is particularly powerful for shifting us to a state of musing or daydreaming.

Dr. Wallace Nichols states,

> *Being by water meditates you. It puts you in that relaxed state. You don't need to study or practice meditation, you just need to pay attention to the water around you. You can do it in the bathtub, the hot tub, the swimming pool, the creek, the lake, the river, the ocean. When you unplug and let go, disconnect from a clock altogether, you do what neuroscientists call mind wandering. Rather than data crunching, you're letting things come and connect. You're letting innovation happen.*

Discover more of water's powerful benefits in Wallace's book *Blue Mind: The Surprising Science That Shows How Being Near, In, On, or Under Water Can Make You Happier, Healthier, More Connected, and Better at What You Do.*

Water is powerful because it's part of nature. Nature in general boosts our creativity because many things in nature are made up of fractals, the magical proportion known as the "Golden Mean." The fractals we unconsciously see align with the fractals in the optical nerves and other aspects of our biology, creating a calming effect that gives us access to the musing state that boosts creativity.

When we go for a walk or run, or when gardening, we usually do so outside. Even densely populated cities still have nature in the form of trees, grass growing in the sidewalk cracks, and birds. Besides creativity, time in nature is proven to lower blood pressure and stress, improve mood, reduce anxiety and depression, and also help us heal from burnout.

Dr. Jonas Salk often credits his time in nature, particularly near the water, for helping him find the cure for polio. He had been working tirelessly for months, working 16-hour days when he was finally persuaded to take a vacation. He went to Italy and there he had his own "aha!" moment that changed everything.

He went on to build the Salk Institute in San Diego, California, with nature at its core. Situated on the bluffs overlooking the Pacific Ocean, every room has a view of the ocean and high ceilings to promote expansive thinking.

| Preparing Brain | Resting Neocortex | Sensory Gating |

The brain science of inducing insight

To boost creativity in your life or organization, leverage neuroscience to set yourself up for those flashes of insight. First, prepare your brain by taking in a lot of information. Read everything and push yourself to learn from sources outside your norm. Next, take a break and rest the neocortex. Go for a walk, get out in nature, or take a nap. Sleep is important too, which is why many people wake up with new ideas.

Finally, engage in sensory gating by reducing stimulation from images, sounds, etc. This naturally happens in the shower, but you can do it with meditation or sitting quietly in nature. Looking at water is also helpful.

One last word about creativity: People often don't believe they are creative. They often mistakenly equate being artistic with being creative and deny themselves the credit they are due. Gordon MacKenzie, the Chief Creative Officer at Hallmark, would often go to elementary schools to talk with children. He said that in the early grades, children saw themselves as creative but by the time they got to just third or fourth grade, many had lost that belief. I highly recommend his book, *Orbiting the Giant Hairball: A Corporate Fool's Guide to Surviving with Grace.*

School tends to impact our perception of our potential because it doesn't teach or measure all the ways in which we can be smart. Traditional schooling,

IQ tests, and college entrance exams only measure the first two of the nine types of intelligence identified by Harvard's Dr. Howard Gardner. Many of us attended school environments that did not support nor measure other forms of intelligence—we felt out of place or, even worse, stupid.

And because K–12 education leads to college and college degrees are often required for jobs, we have a whole world that is overly skewed to just two types of intelligence and is missing out on the creative brilliance many have to offer. Perhaps Albert Einstein said it best: "Everybody is a genius, but if you judge a fish by its ability to climb a tree, it will live its whole life believing that it is stupid."

There are multiple ways to be creative and neuroscientists have proven Gardner's model because each type of intelligence has its own neural signature; that is they each activate different areas of the brain. Dr. Branton Shearer and Dr. Jessica Karanian published a study titled "The Neuroscience of Intelligence: Empirical Support for the Theory of Multiple Intelligences?" They reviewed the research, mapping the brain regions to each of the intelligences along three levels of neural analysis: primary brain regions, subregions, and particular brain structures within the subregions. The results were quite astounding, showing a clear alignment for each intelligence. The authors concluded that there was robust evidence that each of the intelligences "possesses its own unique neural architecture."

Here is the list of intelligences that Dr. Gardner identified. Which ones are your strengths?

- **Linguistic:** The ability to learn languages, analyze information, or create products involving oral and written language. Writers, poets, lawyers, and speakers often have high linguistic intelligence.

- **Logical-mathematical:** The ability to develop equations and proofs, make calculations, and solve abstract problems, as well as detect patterns, reason deductively, and think logically. This intelligence is most often associated with scientific and mathematical thinking.

- **Musical:** The ability to produce, remember, and make meaning of different patterns of sound and the capacity to recognize and compose musical pitches, tones, and rhythms. People with this intelligence often have skills in performance and composition.

- **Bodily-kinesthetic:** The ability to use one's own body to create products or solve problems, and to use mental abilities to coordinate bodily movements. Athletes and dancers exhibit this intelligence.

- **Spatial:** The ability to recognize and manipulate large-scale and fine-grained spatial images. This can be with open space, like that used by navigators and pilots, as well as the patterns of more confined areas such as those used by sculptors, surgeons, chess players, artists, or architects.

- **Intrapersonal:** The ability to recognize and understand one's own moods, desires, motivations, and intentions. In Howard Gardner's view it involves having an effective working model of ourselves, and to be able to use such information to regulate our lives.

- **Interpersonal:** The ability to recognize and understand other people's moods, desires, motivations, and intentions. It allows people to work effectively with others. Educators, salespeople, religious and political leaders, and counselors all need a well-developed interpersonal intelligence.

- **Naturalist:** The ability to identify and distinguish among different types of plants, animals, and weather formations found in the natural world.

- **Existential/spiritual:** The capacity to tackle deep questions about human existence, such as the meaning of life and death.

Purpose Story 5:
Epiphany on a Plane

After attending a sales conference a few years back, I found myself in Los Angeles International Airport (LAX), waiting for my plane home to Sydney, Australia. I decided to buy a book that I thought was all about sales, called *Go-Givers Sell More* by Bob Burg and John David Mann.

I should mention that I wasn't really looking to learn anything from said book. As far as I was concerned, I was already the Yoda of selling. I had been in sales a long time, and I was successful. But hey, I had many hours to fill, so why not. If anything, it would reinforce how awesome I thought I already was. Boy, was I in for a surprise!

When I settled into my seat and started reading, I soon realized the book wasn't about the sales process and skills as I expected. It was about purpose and values in sales and I soon realized that I did not have any!

Turning the pages, I remember starting to feel heavy. It was like someone had placed a couple of those cartoon anvils on my shoulders. In reality, what was weighing me down was the realization that everything I thought I knew was wrong. I wasn't the Master Jedi salesperson I thought I was. I'd been so consumed with what I wanted all these years, I had totally failed to understand or embrace what my role as a true sales professional should really have been all about. The truth I had to accept was that I had no purpose. Other than to close deals. To crush my quota. And to be lauded and applauded by my colleagues and superiors. That all felt so hollow and meaningless now.

How had I become so shallow? This wasn't at all how I saw myself. It was a very strange experience. The more I read and reread the words on these pages, the more my mood sank. This was like a self-inflicted intervention I didn't know I needed. I was an emotional wreck.

During the flight, I read and reread that book. After a while there was a shift. I realized I could change. I could become the person they wrote about—someone who lives with generosity. Someone who creates exceptional value for others. Someone who creates a swelling tide that raises all ships.

I went through just about every emotion but after 14-hours of contemplation and reflection, I landed at home a man reborn. I often refer to it as my Amazing Grace moment—"I once was blind, but now I see." I was resolved to rebuild and commit to finding my purpose, being a better man and sales professional.

That experience powerfully influenced who I am and the future direction of my life. I made it my personal mission to understand what this whole purpose thing was all about. Because no matter how many sales I would have made, or commission I would have earned, or recognition I would have received, it would never have been enough to fill this hole I had in my soul for so long.

Looking back, I had never contemplated something was missing. So, I had never even thought to look. If I hadn't by some stroke of serendipity or happenstance found that book when I did—or maybe it found me!— I wouldn't be who I am today.

I can now say that everything I do is driven by my deeply held purpose. As a result I live a life with far greater meaning and fulfillment. Although I started my own journey by accident. I am resolved to help my fellow sales professionals find and activate their own purpose, on purpose. The journey continues.

Cultivating Creativity

The truth is that we are wired to be creative—we just need the right conditions and our brains will do the rest. And we can use strategies to further boost our natural creativity.

First, we can leverage our many strengths. Honor our intelligences and trust in our natural ability to be creative. This includes looking for jobs and organizations that align with our strengths and give us opportunities to learn and grow.

Second, we can work with the brain to induce insight. By preparing the brain, resting the neocortex with breaks, and sensory gating by taking a shower or being in nature, we can facilitate flashes of insight.

Third, we can play brain games designed to boost our natural creativity. For example, word pair games (like the game show $10,000 Pyramid) and visual puzzles with hidden images can activate the brain in new ways.

Neuroscientist Dr. Trisha Stratford from Sydney's University of Technology conducted a study where she had participants focus on a problem, then used calming techniques and hands-on tactile materials like clay and blocks to allow participants to "feel their way through the problem and activate the parietal cortex." The results were impressive:

- 80 percent showed improved performance in creative thinking
- 63 percent generated more viable solutions to problems
- Their brain's cognitive function improved by 33 percent, with a 26 percent increase in problem-solving accuracy and reduced failed problem-solving attempts by 25 percent
- 100 percent of participants showed increased gamma waves, the brain signature of insight

Consider how you can use this information to boost creativity in your own life and the teams you work with.

5. Obstacles to Innovation

While creativity comes first and is the birthplace for great ideas, innovation is the process by which those great ideas change the world. Often making an impact and serving others requires innovation.

Two Pathways

There are two main paths to innovation:

- **Breakthrough** is what you think it is—transformative, because it fundamentally changes things. Executives and investors speak of trying to find that "unicorn"—that one unique idea that will make millions. It can be the thing that disrupts an industry or even launches an entirely new one.

  The breakthrough path involves some level of risk and is a journey of many trials and failures. I think of breaking glass because you need to make some messes before achieving success. Some organizations have entire teams or departments dedicated to breakthrough innovation and while it can cost a lot in resources (time, energy, money), the payoffs can be big.

- **Incremental** is about taking small steps to systematically improve or enhance something you already have. For example, improving the efficiency or cost of a product by just 10 percent can yield millions of dollars. As can growing your market share or productivity—small improvements can yield big results over time.

  It's a slow process, requiring lots of little tweaks along the way, so I think of a sloth—small and steady steps will get you up that tree.

Though the breakthrough path gets more press, incremental is equally as valuable. When you think about your own life, which path do you prefer? Do you take big risks, try new things, and endure some failures to get there? Or are you more focused on taking something that is working and using a slow process of making small changes to make it better?

Innovation is very important to organizations. According to the *Global Innovation Survey* by McKinsey, 85 percent of executives consider their organization's future success very or extremely dependent on innovation.

But many have a hidden bias for the incremental pathway. CB Insight's *State of Innovation Report* found that 78 percent of innovation portfolios are allocated to continuous improvement rather than disruptive risks. The top five innovation goals demonstrated this bias with only one being breakthrough:

- Generate revenue by enhancing existing products and services
- Generate revenue by launching new products and services
- Improve customer satisfaction
- Improve operational effectiveness/productivity
- Reduce costs for existing products and services

Common Obstacles

Clearly, lacking a set process or structure is going to thwart innovation from happening. But there are other factors that tend to cause problems. Planbox's study found that the top five obstacles were being a risk-adverse industry (42 percent), problems with execution (39 percent), unsupportive culture (36 percent), lack of clear objectives (32 percent), and lack of resources for innovation (29 percent). This can become a checklist for issues you need to solve to boost innovation in your life or organization.

In my work as a consultant, I have seen both execution and culture be major derailers, so I want to dive a little deeper here.

Execution

Innovating the great ideas is part of the process, but so many organizations have failed because they had great ideas, and no one got them to market. Some classic examples include Xerox who didn't stumble because they hadn't noticed that Canon had introduced personal copiers—no, they had their own plans but didn't execute them fast enough.

Kodak failed for a similar reason—they were not blind to the rise of digital photography; they just didn't execute on their innovations in that area. Retail giant Sears didn't suffer a decline because they had no awareness of Walmart's new everyday discount format. They just didn't follow through on their own plan fast enough.

According to the authors of *The Other Side of Innovation: Solving the Execution Challenge,* failed execution can nullify outstanding performance in creativity and innovation, "We like to think of an organization's capacity for innovation as creativity multiplied by execution. We use 'multiplication' rather than 'sum' because, if either creativity or execution has a score of zero, then the capacity for innovation is zero."

There are lots of ways to drive execution. If you don't yet have a great process in place, I highly recommend the four disciplines of execution as outlined in the book of the same name by Chris McChesney, Sean Covey, and Jim Huling.

Culture and climate

The next large obstacle to innovation is not having the right culture to support it, mentioned as the number 3 obstacle in the *State of Corporate Innovation* report.

Culture matters—71 percent of top performers said their organization's culture was highly supportive of innovation. In addition, high performing organizations are five times more likely to build a culture of innovation across business functions.

Climate matters too, and is the steppingstone to a great culture. Let's compare them. Climate is the actions, channels, and tools to support new idea development within an organization. When these resources and resulting actions become a *daily* part of the organization, a "culture" of innovation is in place.

Purpose Story 6:

Mentors Can Give You a Needed Nudge

As most success stories do, mine began as a struggle. I was stuck between a rock (a company that treated employees as disposable) and a hard place (a lack of education or experience that would lead to future career opportunities). I was enrolled in a Human Resources Management degree program and learning about our rights and protections as workers. The more I learned, the more aware I became of the laws that my then-employer was breaking. I also realized how little most employees truly understood about the laws put in place to protect them.

My employer at the time had no mission, vision, or even human resources (HR) department, and my sense of purpose had nothing to align with. As I fine-tuned more skills and continued through my degree, I also began completing LinkedIn Learning courses and eventually came across one created by Britt Andreatta, "Leading with Emotional Intelligence." It led me to more of her courses and connecting with her on LinkedIn. I reached out and asked for guidance about my work environment at the time. Britt was kind enough to send me a well-crafted response and tips, stating, "You deserve to work in a place that feels fair, ethical, and even fun and positive!" It truly changed my perspective and reminded me I could find another job worthy of my time.

I was empowered in my job search and took control of my application process by proving my knowledge and willingness to align my purpose with a new organization. My mentor at the university recommended I investigate positions at my alma mater. Once I began researching, it was very clear that they stood by what they taught in their HR management degree. I was hired at the end of my second interview and started shortly thereafter.

The support and training I received enabled me to succeed quickly and eased any leftover nerves I had about my fit for the position. My attitude, mental health, and outlook on life improved within months of starting the position. I now am happy to begin work and know that I make a difference in the lives of my students as I help them bridge pathways to opportunity. My employer is a safe space where I can learn from my mistakes, trust my development path is in good hands, and grow within an organization that cares about me and my future endeavors, whether with them or elsewhere.

My current leader puts mental health above all else—I was able to attend multiple resiliency and well-being trainings and learn about thinking traps, emotional awareness, and self-management. I am an entirely different person now.

Having an organization that respects its employees and empowers them in their position and beyond is life changing. I can accomplish things I never thought I could before, thanks to my new power over my mindset, and am ready to turn any struggle into a success story or at least a lesson learned.

For creativity and innovation, there are two cornerstones.

- **Collaboration:** One of the three types of teamwork on a continuum along with cooperation and coordination. What distinguishes collaboration is that the outcome or result is created by the unique contributions and input of all the contributors. As people tussle with ideas, creative tension drives innovation. Collaboration requires trust and respect, as well as a mindful process for conflict resolution.

  Contrast that with cooperation, where a group of people perform their distinct portion of an agreed upon task. A smooth process drives efficiency and requires planning, alignment, communication, and a clear process for execution. Collaboration often occurs at the creativity or brainstorming part of the innovation process, along with design thinking. Then, as the idea becomes viable, the process morphs into cooperation with a focus on execution.

- **Psychological safety:** This is crucial for both creativity and innovation. It's especially critical for work in the breakthrough pathway and risk-adverse industries. Many studies show that psychological safety is the key differentiator between high-performing teams and the rest, so building or increasing psychological safety is going to yield payoffs across your organization.

Harvard's Dr. Amy Edmondson was the first to identify and define psychological safety. She states, "It is a sense of confidence that the team will not embarrass, reject, or punish someone for speaking up with ideas, questions, concerns, or mistakes." Let's pause and appreciate what a low bar that is, to not be embarrassed, rejected, or punished. And yet, many people at work don't have that.

Signs of psychological safety among a team

One study by VitalSmarts found that half of employees (50 percent) don't regularly speak their minds at work, whether to colleagues or managers. And only 1 percent o employees feel "extremely confident" when it comes to voicing their concerns in the workplace at critical moments. These moments not only cost the organization thousands of dollars but may also endanger employee or customer safety, in certain circumstances.

I cannot think of a single industry that does not benefit from a workforce feeling like they can bring forward their ideas, questions, concerns, mistakes, and even critiques. Employee input is the built-in feedback loop that every organization should be elevating, not suppressing. And the top-performing organizations do exactly that.

In a global study of all its teams, Google found that psychological safety was so crucial that it is now the focus of all of their manager and leadership development programs. Read more in the *New York Times* article, "What Google Learned from Its Quest to Build the Perfect Team."

Psychological safety means that it is okay to take risks and make mistakes, both of which are core to creativity and innovation. Failing is how we learn and improve. If failing leads to being judged or sidelined, especially by a manager, innovation will come to a screeching halt.

The other critical benefit of psychological safety is that it naturally supports inclusion and belonging. Dr. Edmondson goes on to say that psychological safety, "describes a team climate characterized by interpersonal trust and mutual respect in which people are comfortable being themselves."

Studies have proven that exclusion is incredibly damaging to both people and teams. It drives isolation, poor performance, reduced productivity, anxiety, and depression, as well as poorer physical health. Neuroscientists discovered that even mild experiences of exclusion activate the same region of the brain as physical pain. Think about that. When you're excluded, your body registers it as if you were hit. You can read more about this fascinating research in my book, *Wired to Connect: The Brain Science of Teams and a New Model for Creating Collaboration and Inclusion.*

Humans are a tribal species and we're designed to live and work in community. Inclusion and belonging are elemental needs and, when met, people thrive and teams excel. Fortunately, creating psychological safety is a skill that anyone can learn. And it's vital that managers and leaders do learn it. It should be a key part of training for any teams engaged in creativity, innovation, or execution.

We need both creativity and innovation to fulfill our sense of purpose so that we can serve or benefit others. I love this quote by Sarah Ban Breathnach, who says, "The world needs dreamers and the world needs doers. But above all, the world needs dreamers who do."

Your Learning Journey

Take a few minutes to reflect on your own experiences with the concepts from this section.

- Share some examples of your own experience with the two types of well-being: happiness and purpose. Do you have the right balance?
- After you complete the free North Star Reflection Exercise found at Imperative.com/britteq, share what you learned about yourself.
- Which of the many benefits of purpose do you most need in your life?
- Share some of your experiences with creativity and innovation. What are some ways you can boost them in your life and work?
- Do you experience psychological safety in your workplace? If not, how might you change that environment or find a better fit?

OUR RISING HUNGER
FOR PURPOSE

"The greatest challenge in life is to be our own person and accept that being different is a blessing and not a curse. A person who knows who they are lives a simple life by eliminating from their orbit anything that does not align with his or her overriding purpose and values. A person must be selective with their time and energy because both elements of life are limited."

Kilroy J. Oldster, author,
Dead Toad Scrolls

6. Primed for More Purpose

The research is clear. People are hungering for purpose and meaningful work in record numbers. It's happening in every sector and every region of the world.

While there has been a recent, sharp increase, this trend is not new. In 2017, *Forbes* ran a story entitled "The New Workplace: Where Meaning and Purpose Are More Important Than Ever." The author, Renelle Darr, stated, "People are wanting more out of work than money. They want more meaning and more purpose. They want to be able to see how their contribution to the workplace makes a difference." In 2018, *Harvard Business Review* published "9 Out of 10 People Are Willing to Earn Less Money to Do More Meaningful Work" and *Forbes* ran another article headlined "The Why of Work: Purpose and Meaning Really Do Matter."

Initially, it seemed that this was driven by the younger generations in the workforce. *The Guardian* claimed, "Millennials are bringing purpose to the forefront of today's business culture." Daniel Goleman, the father of emotional intelligence, calls Millennials (born 1981 to 1996) "The Purpose Generation." Nearly two-thirds believe that "improving society" should be the primary focus of organizations.

A study by the Society for Human Resource Management (SHRM) found that 94 percent of Millennials want to use their skills to benefit a cause and 57 percent wish that there were more company-wide service days. Millennials, who will comprise 75 percent of the global workforce by 2025, are likely to see their work as their "life calling."

But the pandemic made purpose a top priority for nearly all working adults. More and more people are searching for purpose and meaning. This growing trend caught the attention of researchers and global organizations, like Gartner and McKinsey, published in-depth reports.

In 2022, McKinsey released a report titled *The Search for Purpose at Work*. They found that 70 percent of people (all generations) say they define their purpose *through* work. In other words, people want their jobs to bring a "significant sense of purpose to their lives."

Certainly, the pandemic is part of this. McKinsey's report stated, "One of the really interesting pieces that we found in the research is that nearly 7 out of 10 employees are reflecting on their purpose because of the coronavirus disease, or COVID-19. In fact, we found that, as a result of COVID-19, half of American employees are reconsidering the work that they want to do."

Gartner found a similar trend with the majority of respondents agreeing or strongly agreeing with the statements: "The pandemic has made me...

- ...question the purpose of my day-to-day job." (52 percent)
- ...want to contribute more to society." (56 percent)
- ...rethink the place that work should have in my life." (65 percent)

Members of Gen Z (born 1997–2012) also care about deeply about purpose. Gen Z currently represents 13 percent of the workforce but will reach one-third of the workforce by the end of this decade, according to the US Bureau of Labor Statistics.

A report by WeSpire found that Gen Z is the first generation to prioritize purpose over salary. When applying for jobs, they read corporate mission statements and expect work cultures where the stated values are consistently modeled. They have a higher desire for service-oriented work than previous generations, wanting to work at places with a focus on social good, public service, or not-for-profits.

Purpose Story 7:
All Experiences Contribute Valuable Information
It is interesting to look back on my journey and connect the dots. A series of professional crises led me to find my passion. I had to abandon a successful executive career path to start a new one at 40.

This shift in my professional identity was a bumpy road, with lots of ups and downs. Slowly, I created a new sense of identity, and my indicator that it was going well was that I started to feel proud, competent, and relevant.

My first career was in electrical engineering, working at television manufacturer. But I realized early on that there was no bright future for me as an electrical circuit designer in Brazil, my home country. I transitioned to a business administration role in various companies then had the opportunity to earn an MBA where I decided to migrate to human resources when I returned to work.

Six years later, I was working in managerial positions and suffering to spend most of my time on company politics and very little learning new things. When I lost my job due to company downsizing, I decided not to come back to the same type of work.

This second professional crisis led me to pursue some dreams: studying psychology and working as a consultant where I had freedom to choose how to spend my time and create opportunities to learn. At the same time, I was invited to work as a professor for a local business administration school. Voilà! I finally found what I was looking for!

I believe that my purpose was present inside of me, somewhere, but latent for a long time. I remember that while at engineering school, I wanted to learn how a TV works (crazy me, I know). When I realized the engineering course didn't include that topic, I managed to get external funding and hire a specialist that created and taught a TV engineering course to me and my colleagues. To learn what I really wanted was one of the greatest moments of my life, both because of the knowledge and because of pursuing and sharing this knowledge with others.

I never imagined at that time that working with knowledge and learning would be my professional future. So, 16 years later, I realized that my real purpose is to transform lives and leaders through education. I can say I am privileged to work on what I love and in what I find deep meaning. There is no paycheck that matches the feeling I get when someone tells me that I was part of their evolution or transformation.

However, it does not mean that I was not happy while working at different jobs and various companies before my current career. It was all part of my soul-searching process and gave me real-world experiences that were crucial for learning what activities resonated with me. They also helped to discover which types of organizational cultures and manager styles helped me to thrive.

The Convergence of Three Global Forces

We'll dive into the impact of the pandemic in a future chapter but while it accelerated certain trends, three related global forces were already in play:

- Increased focus on employee engagement
- The rise in human consciousness
- Shift from the information economy to the purpose economy

Employee engagement

In 2013, Gallup released its first report on employee engagement, driving a global conversation about what engagement is and why it matters. The data on employee engagement is robust: engaged employees are unquestionably more satisfied, more productive, stay longer, and even act as brand ambassadors. Further, disengaged employees do a lot of damage because their cynicism and poor performance can impact coworkers and customers. Gallup found that disengaged employees can cost organizations as much as one-third of their salary plus benefits per year.

Leaders everywhere started examining employee engagement, instituting annual surveys and focusing on how to raise their scores. The competition for top talent in every sector only fueled these efforts. But engagement is really an outcome or effect, not the cause. None of us as children sat around dreaming that one day we would be engaged, at least not in the work sense. We dreamed of being happy and fulfilled. It turns out that having a sense of purpose or meaning at work is the real driver, fostering engagement, which then drives the outcomes (productivity, retention, etc.) that leaders crave.

We have spent the last decade shining a light on engagement and asking people annual questions about how they feel at work, what makes them feel fulfilled, and what leads them to give more than is expected for their role. Employees everywhere have spent the past ten years reflecting on what matters to them and how they feel about work.

When the pandemic hit and we all went into lockdown, people had even more time to reflect on what matters as they faced their own mortality. No wonder it added fuel to the already burning fire.

Consciousness

Another global trend for the past couple decades is the accelerated rise of human consciousness. Human consciousness evolves in sudden transformations, and we are currently in a unique time when consciousness is evolving very rapidly.

Scholars study human consciousness from many disciplines including neuroscience, biology, psychology, sociology, and even anthropology. They have discovered that human consciousness develops through stages, and scientists have chosen colors to denote each stage, starting with infrared, which occurred approximately 100,000 years ago and magenta, which was about 50,000 years ago. In contrast, within the past 100 years, we have now shifted through five levels of consciousness—assigned the colors red, amber, orange, green, and teal—which are actively shaping today's organizations.

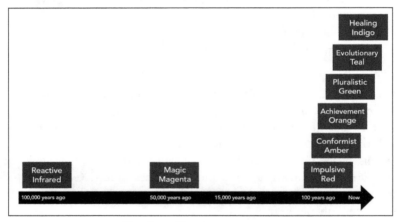

Timeline of human consciousness

The most recent levels of consciousness, green and the newly emerging teal, are focused on purpose and meaning, so it's no surprise that these influence what people are seeking. As we look ahead, scientists predict that human consciousness will eventually shift to indigo and violet levels over the decades to come.

Frederic Laloux reveals some very interesting developments in his book *Reinventing Organizations: A Guide to Creating Organizations Inspired by the Next Stage of Human Consciousness.* Laloux discovered that organizational development maps to these stages of human consciousness and, as humans evolve, so do the organizations they build. He states, "Every transition to a new stage of consciousness has ushered in a whole new era in human history. At every juncture, everything changed: society, the economy, the power structures…and organizational models."

Laloux is one of many people talking about the intersection of consciousness and business. Former Whole Foods CEO John Mackey partnered with

Raj Sisodia to write *Conscious Capitalism*. Dr. Fred Kofman wrote *Conscious Business* and now consults with companies and governments around the world to bring conscious practices to the forefront. And it's not just a feelgood exercise. Companies operating in the green and teal levels of consciousness significantly outperform the others. According to *Firms of Endearment: How World Class Companies Profit from Passion and Purpose* (by Raj Sisodia, David Wolfe, and Jagdish Sheth), it can be as much as 1,400 percent!

In every organization I work with, I see clear evidence of this conscious evolution, so I consider it an essential tool when assessing organizations in every sector. I write more about this model in chapter 21. I strongly recommend you read Laloux's book and view some of the videos and resources he posts on his website ReinventingOrganizations.com.

The economy

As consciousness rises, it impacts every aspect of society, including work and business. Josh Bersin is an international thought leader who analyzes global industries. In 2015, he published a timeline of management models as part of his work at Deloitte. He characterized the 1960s through the 1980s as focused on hierarchical leadership, the 1990s as collaborative management, and the 2000s as networks of teams. At the time, he was predicting that in the 2020s we'd move to organizations that were driven by purpose and meaning. His prediction is coming true.

Aaron Hurst's 2016 book, *The Purpose Economy*, went even further, making the case that purpose would be the fourth great American economy, the first three being agrarian, industrial, and information. In 2016, 40 percent of the US and 37 percent of the global workforce stated that purpose was their primary reason for working, while the rest prioritized status or money. In just eight short years, McKinsey's research indicates we have climbed to 70 percent of people wanting more purpose. Hurst predicted this, saying "I now believe we are in the early days of the emergence of a 'purpose economy.' It is likely that in fewer than 20 years, the pursuit of purpose will eclipse the third American economy—the Information Economy."

Hurst's book details some critical moments in history that have led us here. First is the Industrial Economy that began in 1750 and lasted until 1950. In that 200 years, a major shift drastically changed society: In 1860, nearly half of all workers were self-employed, working small businesses in their hometowns as farmers, bakers, cobblers, etc. But by 1900, two-thirds became wage earners, working for an organization and most likely a factory.

Think about that—in just 40 years, a significant portion of the workforce changed. Critically, that shift took people away from seeing the direct impact of their work. Prior, farmers and bakers could see the families they were feeding and likely knew them by name. The cobblers and tailors knew the people they were clothing and probably lived close by or sat next to them in church. People could see the fruits of their work and how it impacted their community.

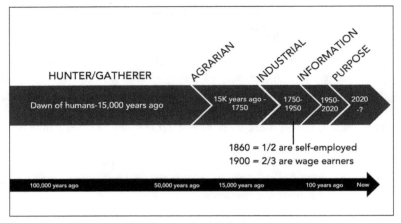

The four recent global economies

When people went to factories, they became one piece of a larger process with little, if any, contact to the ultimate customer. Hurst argues that this moment disconnected us from a sense of purpose in our work and why we're hungering to come back to it. It's more challenging today for people to find a sense of purpose at work because working for an organization can make it harder to see the impact of your work and the good it's doing in the world.

As the industrial economy was ending, Abraham Maslow noted this transition. In 1943, he stated, "Individuals who do not perceive the workplace as meaningful and purposeful will not work up to their professional capacity"—in other words, our potential.

Others also saw this rising need for purpose. Dr. Viktor Frankl, a physician trained in psychiatry and neurology and a Holocaust survivor, wrote the seminal book *Man's Search for Meaning.* In 1950, he wrote, "There is nothing in the world that would so effectively help one to survive even the worst conditions as the knowledge that there is a meaning in one's life."

Purpose and meaning continue to be a central focus. Currently, one of the bestselling nonfiction books in history—with more than 35 million copies sold and translated into over 50 languages—is *The Purpose-Driven Life: What on Earth Am I Here For?* As Written by Reverend Rick Warren, he says that people are hungering for answers to three very important questions:

- Why am I alive? A question about our existence
- Does my life matter? A question about significance
- What am I here for? A question about purpose

Warren brings a Christian perspective to this exploration, as do other authors like Parker Palmer and Thomas Moore. Christianity and many other faiths include the belief that a Divine Being has a plan for your life, and your have a unique service to bring to the world. On the one hand, this clearly frames the idea that everyone has a purpose and it's your job to discover what it is and then do your best to live a life that fulfills it. But on the other hand, this also creates a lot of pressure, especially when the answer is not yet clear.

Many people are not Christian nor any other religious faith. Over the past few decades, the role that religion plays in society has shifted significantly. Studies show that religiosity—a person being affiliated with a particular faith or church—has decreased over time. This is a global trend with many countries becoming less religious between 2007 to 2019.

Within the US, the decline is particularly sharp. The Pew Research Center found that in 1972, 90 percent of Americans defined themselves as Christian but by 2020, the number had fallen to 64 percent and trends show that it could be as low as 35 percent by the year 2070.

Approximately 6 percent of those Christians now define themselves as agnostic or "spiritual but not religious" while atheism increased from 2 to 3 percent. Not surprisingly, the same study found that church attendance also declined. The researchers state, "Over the last decade, the share of Americans who say they attend religious services at least once or twice a month dropped by seven percentage points, while the share who say they attend religious services less often (if at all) has risen by the same degree."

This shift is most notable when looking at the generations. In a 2021 study, researchers found that 29 percent of Millennials identify as *not* affiliated with a religion, compared to Gen X at 25 percent, Baby Boomers at 18 percent, and the Silent Generation at 9 percent. Gen Z is the least religious of all the generations with 34 percent unaffiliated.

The scholars add, "It's not only a lack of religious affiliation that distinguishes Gen Z. They are also far more likely to identify as atheist or agnostic (18 percent). In contrast, fewer than 1 in 10 (9 percent) Baby Boomers and 4 percent of the Silent Generation identifies as atheist or agnostic."

Taken together, this data signals that populations who maybe once found a sense of purpose or meaning through their religious practice are now seeking a new source. For a vast majority, it is now the workplace.

In 2016, Aaron Hurst predicted that purpose and meaning will become the driving force of the economy. Consumers will seek to purchase from companies contributing to the greater good and employees will seek to work for them as well. Employees will also want a sense of purpose or meaning in their day-to-day job. Hurst's prediction is appearing to come true, with a strong nudge from the impact of the COVID-19 pandemic.

7. The 4 Pressures of the Pandemic

While our hunger for purpose increased as we moved to working in factories, it's always been a part of our DNA as a species. As we learned in chapter 1, we are wired to survive, belong, and become. These key needs and how people feel about their workplaces were already in play before the first person was infected with COVID-19. We are now living through a time when our hunger for purpose and meaning is greater than ever, as a result of four pressures:

- Facing loss and grief
- Reflecting on our values and priorities
- Overworking to burnout
- Entering post-traumatic growth

Facing Loss and Grief

The first pressure is facing our mortality as the pandemic raged around the world. None of us could escape the horrifying reality that the virus was deadly. During those early months, we watched daily images of overcrowded hospitals, people dying without being able to see their loved ones, and morgues unable to keep up with the death toll.

Our neurological system is especially attuned to danger, and we were seeing images from not just our own community but from every region of the globe, which magnified our sense of danger and fear.

We were also dealing with grief. We've gone through a very traumatic experience collectively and it's still playing out in our lives today.

Grief expert David Kessler was quoted in a *Harvard Business Review* article during the lockdowns titled "That Discomfort You're Feeling Is Grief." "We're feeling a number of different griefs," he says. "We feel the world has changed, and it has…. The loss of normalcy; the fear of economic toll; the loss of connection. This is hitting us and we're grieving. Collectively. We are not used to this kind of collective grief in the air."

And the numbers agree with him. In the US, 40 percent of American adults know at least one person who died of COVID-19 and 7 percent know three or more people—15 percent lost a family member. These numbers are even higher for people of color because the disease hit those communities disproportionately hard.

Globally, over 7 million people have died from COVID-19 since the onset of the pandemic and the numbers continued to rise daily. Each loss is a person loved by somebody. They are our grandparents, parents, siblings, children, coworkers, neighbors, and friends.

An additional tragedy unfolded during the first year of the pandemic that undoubtedly took a toll on mental health: people were denied the opportunity to actively grieve. They couldn't be with loved ones in the hospital nor gather with family and friends for a service.

But how is grief related to our sense of purpose? According to the research of Dr. Elizabeth Kubler-Ross and David Kessler, people move through six stages of grief, which are not linear; people can move back and forth across them or go at a different pace than others in the same situation. But the last stage is "finding meaning."

It's important to note that these stages may be experienced *before* a death, when people learn of a terminal diagnosis and are processing their fear, or *after* a death, as people make sense of the loss.

1. Denial
The first stage is denial, when we cannot believe or accept what is happening. This is a form of shock, and while it helps us deal with tragedy by numbing us, it might also make us feel that the world is meaningless and overwhelming.

2. Anger
In this second phase, people begin to process the feelings of the loss, with anger being a natural emotion and the first step towards healing. In this phase, people often feel that the situation is unfair and look for someone to blame. Feeling and expressing anger is part of the healing process but sometimes this phase is extended, when people try to suppress or shove down their feelings.

3. Bargaining
In the third phase, we try to bargain with a higher power or the universe in an attempt to change the outcome. For a diagnosis, it might be something like, "Please, if you let them survive this, I promise to be kinder to everyone." And after the loss, the bargaining phase focuses on attempting to relieve the pain: "Please, if you help me not hurt so much, I will dedicate my life to helping others in this situation."

The six stages of grief

4. *Depression*

Feeling depression is the hallmark of the fourth stage when we fully feel the enormity of the loss. The pain can feel even stronger in this stage than the previous ones and sometimes it feels like it will last forever. This is a stage of deep sadness and healing can be shortchanged if people feel that they need to "snap out of it" or are scared to feel the full depth of their loss (for example, not crying for fear of not being able to stop).

5. *Acceptance*

The fifth stage is about accepting the reality of the loss and finding a way to live with it. It's not about being "over it" but rather accepting that we must live our lives without that person in it, or that we're going to say goodbye ourselves. Over time, people eventually begin to find moments of happiness, make new connections, and have meaningful relationships.

6. *Finding meaning*

David Kessler's research added a new stage to the journey, finding meaning. While grief is a process of healing, the sixth stage can transform people into a "more peaceful and hopeful" state by helping them honor their loved ones.

This last stage is collectively driving an increased search for purpose and meaning in life around the world. Millions of people have spent recent years moving through their grieving process and are now turning their focus on finding meaning.

Purpose Story 8:
From Tragedy to Connection
I experienced a terrible loss when I had a miscarriage at five months. The pandemic was about to hit in Mexico, so I never returned to the office after my medical leave. The lockdown was extremely tough for me and it took me a while to bounce back. It was not easy, nor fast, but I had a lot of help from many fabulous people surrounding me, so I couldn't remain in that super dark place for long.

A sense of purpose is what got me through. First, I had to come back for my five-year-old son. I worked with a psychologist and took several wellness courses, all of which taught me how to overcome hardships. I had the amazing support of my direct reports, my boss, and the entire company, which made this super difficult situation bearable.

Second, I wanted to help people within my organization thrive through the pandemic. My team and I run the development programs, so I got to help people navigate the hardship of lockdowns while helping myself. I moved away from asking "why?" and invested in asking "what for?"

I learned that I am extremely strong, and that it is okay to reach out to people for help. I also learned that although my problem might seem hard, there are other people experiencing hardships and losses too. We just need to spread kindness and help other people as much as we can.

I couldn't come back from that without the support of my family, which I think is important to acknowledge as not everyone has a strong support system. We, as managers, need to be mindful about that, and offer to help our people as much as we can.

8. Reflecting on Our Values and Priorities

In addition to grief, the pandemic drove three other pressures that accelerated and intensified our search for more purpose and meaning in our lives. The second is that the lockdowns created an extended period of intense reflection.

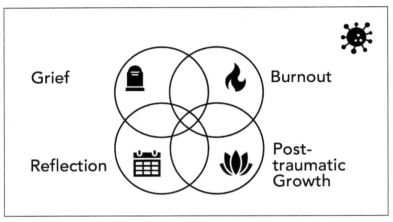

The four pressures of the pandemic

People were no longer going out to dinner, running errands, or taking trips. In fact, we were not leaving our homes except for the most basic of needs and even then we were wearing protective gear and wiping everything down with disinfectant. Even essential workers, who carried an immense burden during those early days, spent what little down time they had in lockdown at home.

This period of a global pause gave us an unprecedented amount of time to reflect. People contemplated their lives, not just for a day or two, but months on end. Simultaneously, we were confronted with mortality and the fragility of life.

As any cancer survivor will tell you, facing your mortality brings your values and priorities into sharp focus. But this time of reflection was significant because we participated in a shared, simultaneous, and global contemplation of what mattered. It's like we gave the whole world this quote by poet Mary Oliver and asked them to journal on it for months.

"Tell me, what is it you plan to do with your one wild and precious life?"

It was bound to impact society in measurable ways, and it has. People became clear about what mattered to them and started making moves to change their lives in three key areas: their homes, their relationships, and their jobs.

Where We Live

Shifting where we live was made possible by the massive pivot to working from home. Gallup found that, due to the pandemic, nearly 62 percent of working adults worked from home. Add this to the number of people who were already working remotely and by May of 2020, nearly 7 out of every 10 employees were no longer going to a workplace.

This created an opening for many to leave urban areas to work remotely from smaller, more affordable communities. According to a study by Zillow and the US Census, nearly two million renters who could not afford homes in the cities were able to in other areas.

A housing frenzy ensued where people bought homes, sight unseen, sometimes with all-cash offers and well over the asking price. As *Forbes* claims, the pandemic "changed the housing market forever," as the intensive demand for housing in smaller communities drove up prices for single-family homes. Being in lockdown and realizing that COVID-19 may not be the last pandemic of our lifetime, many reflected on what they wanted in a home. Highly sought-after features included home offices and outdoor spaces for gathering.

Besides affordability, many moved to be closer to family. The inability to travel and see loved ones, especially older parents, shifted the priorities around location. Many people in lower-income households, who experienced the highest job losses, moved back in with family or co-rented with other families to reduce costs.

Who We Love

Ending or redefining relationships was the second major shift people made as restrictions eased. Being in lockdown strained many relationships as people were not prepared for spending so much time together. According to Dr. Pamela Lannutti of the Center for Human Sexuality Studies, how couples handle worry and stress factored in, as did the growing divide over opinions of masking and vaccines. Many people discovered some differences with their partner not previously visible and it led to a spike in divorces after lockdown.

The *Journal of Social and Personal Relationships* published a special issue on research conducted on relationships during the pandemic. Their findings indicated that gender roles intensified in heterosexual relationships as women took on more responsibilities around the house. While both partners saw the imbalance in the workload, men were not bothered by it while women experienced an increase in dissatisfaction with their relationship.

Another study found that, despite being lonely, single people didn't lower their standards. Researchers expected that single people might settle, given the unusual situation the pandemic created, especially the difficulty with dating. But people continued to search for the same criteria as before.

Another study focused on 2SLGBTQI couples. The researchers found that the couples who discussed their complaints were happier than the ones who did not. Those who stayed silent experienced more anxiety and depression as well. Interestingly, 20 percent of the couples in the study had decided to move in together because of the pandemic.

A final study, by Dr. Helen Lillie at the University of Utah, found that couples who focused on these five specific behaviors weathered difficult times better than those who did not:

- "Crafting normalcy" by keeping to their routines as much as possible
- Talking about their worries or concerns with their partner and other supportive people
- Affirming their identity by focusing on their values
- Constructing a positive framework or view of what was happening
- Focusing on potential positive outcomes

These are strategies worth using in your own relationships as they help couples cope with all kinds of challenges, not just the pandemic.

How We Work

The third major shift people made was in their work life.

Many were forced to seek employment elsewhere as they were laid off or furloughed. Georgetown University's Center on Education and the Workforce tracks ongoing data about job loss. By April 2020, over 23 million people had lost their jobs due to the pandemic. This group was naturally forced to explore what work they wanted to do and given that entire industries, like hospitality, were shut down for the foreseeable future, they contemplated other options, and many began new careers.

Another group, often called "non-essential," pivoted to working from home since going to the office was no longer an option. This group stayed employed and experienced a break from many of the frustrating elements of work, like commuting long distances or dressing in more formal clothes. This group found many benefits working from home and has strongly resisted returning to the office. The *2022 Pulse of the American Worker Survey* found that 87 percent of people want to work from home at least one day per week—68 percent say that a combination of working remotely and onsite ("hybrid") is the perfect work model.

A third group were pushed into an intensive time of high productivity. Workers deemed "essential" were asked to work longer shifts in dangerous conditions. Breaks and downtime were difficult, if not impossible, to come by. While many essential workers felt that their work had purpose and meaning, the overwhelming and unsustainable pressures of the pandemic caused significant exhaustion and burnout as well as the resulting mental health challenges. Healthcare workers in particular bore the brunt of the devastating death toll and their inability to save so many people.

It's not surprising that essential workers across many sectors—but especially in healthcare, education, and technology—were the first to start quitting in record numbers during the "Great Resignation," a term coined by organizational psychologist Dr. Anthony Klotz to describe the period between 2021 and 2022 where quitting hit the highest level in two decades. Each month brought a new resignation record, with four million people quitting on average, or nearly 3 percent of the workforce.

A Harvard study found that "Resignation rates were higher among employees who worked in fields that had experienced extreme increases in demand due to the pandemic, likely leading to increased workloads and burnout."

The quit rate in the hotel/restaurant industry was nearly 7 percent, over double the average across all sectors. During 2021, these workers were more likely to take the brunt of abusive behavior as they dealt with angry guests who argued with mask and vaccine mandates.

It comes as no surprise that healthcare workers also left in droves. Healthcare lost 20 percent of its workforce in the past year, including 30 percent of its nurses. In the US, approximately 3 percent of the workforce, or 500,000 employees, quit per month. Nearly one-third cite burnout as the cause (more on burnout in the next chapter).

Former trauma nurse, Will Patterson, states, "When you're taking on responsibility for more lives than you can reasonably handle—for days at a time—you burn out quickly. Now, after over two years of fighting the pandemic, that burnout is at an all-time high. And as the nurse shortage worsens, that burnout is only going to continue to accelerate."

And the exodus is not over. In a study by Elsevier Health, nearly half (47 percent) of healthcare workers in the US plan to leave their positions by 2025 and a shocking 90 percent of nurses said they are considering leaving within in the next year!

From the start of the pandemic, healthcare workers were physically and emotionally exhausted after working long shifts for months, and even sleeping away from their families to avoid exposing them to the virus. In addition, the high death tolls became unbearable, taking a physical and mental toll. A study in the *Journal of General Internal Medicine* found that "the trauma experienced by healthcare workers during COVID is comparable to that of military veterans in post-9/11 combat zones."

Of further concern, they went from being applauded by their communities every night to the target of verbal and physical harassment by people who believed the pandemic was a hoax. President of the American Medical Association (AMA) Dr. Gerald Harmon, commented, "The AMA is deeply concerned about this threatening behavior and how it has contributed to an increasingly hostile working environment across medicine, particularly for those on the front lines of our nation's response to COVID-19."

I have recently worked with senior executives at several hospital systems in the US who told me horrible stories of verbal and physical harassment, to the point that many healthcare workers no longer wear their scrubs out in public for fear of being targeted.

Tech is another industry that was hit hard by the Great Resignation. According to a recent article in *Business Insider*, "Those in tech and healthcare jobs, specifically, are quitting at the highest rates. And it's not just because of pay, but because they don't feel valued at work."

Tech workers bore the burden of enabling work to continue through the lockdowns by moving their entire workforce to online communication and collaboration tools. Futurist Amy Webb states, "2020 saw a decade of digital transformation in the span of a few months." At the same time, tech workers lost many of the benefits their offices provided, like onsite meals, gyms, and childcare.

Education is also losing a record number of teachers. A *USA Today* article from March 2023 claims "More teachers than usual exited the classroom after last school year, confirming longstanding fears that pandemic-era stresses would prompt an outflow of educators." The author cites the main stressors as being burnout, student behavior challenges, and the politicization of teaching and the curriculum.

A global study by Gallup found that women across all industries also resigned in record numbers, many during the early stages of the pandemic to handle childcare and school closures. While this population saw a reprieve when schools reopened, they were exhausted and continued to outpace men in quitting rates each month, labeled as the "shecession." Only recently have women returned to the workforce near pre-pandemic numbers. Hybrid and remote work options have contributed greatly to this increase.

A February 2023 article in *Business Insider* claims that the Great Resignation created a new normal for Gen Z. "For a certain subset of younger workers who entered the workforce as the Great Resignation picked up steam, quitting has become a way of life…. Gen Z has adapted to a new normal: When in doubt, find a new job. Welcome to Generation Quit."

The Great Resignation affected board rooms too. A study of nearly 1,100 companies across 24 countries found 103 newly appointed new chief executives in the first half of 2021, more than double the previous six months.

While many people who quit during the Great Resignation found work in another organization or industry, many chose to leave traditional work altogether to start their own business. According to the Census Bureau, a record number of new businesses were created in the US, a 53 percent increase over 2019. Pre-pandemic, the number used to hover around 3 to 3.5 million but the past two years have both topped 5 million.

Many people took the leap to pursue a long-held dream. Social media channels are bursting with side giggers who transitioned to verified influencers with six-figure salaries. Many found their audience during the lockdowns as people flocked to social media applications like Instagram and TikTok to stave off lockdown boredom.

Researchers found that there was a sharp increase in what they term "parasocial relationships," which occur when a person feels a form of attachment to a celebrity or online influencer even though that person doesn't know them. As celebrities and influencers filmed from their homes, it created a sense of camaraderie and intimacy that accelerated this attachment. Dr. Jennifer

Bevan, coeditor of the *Journal of Social and Personal Relationships*, states that while people stayed connected with friends during the lockdowns, they felt much closer emotionally to the people they followed online.

This time of reflection impacted us and motivated many people to make big changes in their lives. A break from our routines gives us time to take stock of what we're doing and why. Much of our identity is wrapped up in the activities we do—our work, hobbies, and relationships. So, naturally, people began to question things that had previously felt solid. Besides our homes, relationships, and careers, we also started looking more deeply at our sense of purpose.

Purpose Story 9:
Shifting Skills into a New Future

I was unsatisfied, unhappy, and unsure of myself. For the last 12 years I'd been doing something professionally that I did not enjoy. As a financial advisor, my job, as I saw it, was to help my clients grow their wealth over time and align their portfolio risk with their personal tolerance. The large firm I worked for paid me based on how much my clients paid it in fees. The two concepts were in conflict, as was I.

Growing wealth is a task that no person can accomplish 100 percent of the time in all market conditions, regardless of their education, skill, or expertise. All it takes is one global pandemic, one financial crisis, or one CEO's public PR debacle to send all your clients' portfolios down by more than they had made in the past several years. All that well-intentioned planning out the window.

My unhappiness was of course bleeding into everything I did. I was not present; I was in my head. I would fret all weekend over some careless statement by an elected official that sent the overseas markets tumbling because I knew our US markets would likely do the same Monday morning. I worried about running into clients because, even if I understood they did not blame me for their portfolio being down, I took it personally that I could not prevent what happened. My wife told me I was distant, and I was missing out on my kids' lives.

But, what can I do? I'm in my later 40s, stuck on the track, no way to reset, restart or reinvent. Right?

Of course not, but it was going to be a collective, herculean effort by me and my family to do something new. I would not have a job with predictable hours and benefits anymore. My wife would have to return to work, which meant I would need to be available for school drop-offs and pick-ups as well as after school sports and cooking (eek!).

Beginning a new business was going to take time, money, and learning lots of new things, things outside of my comfort zone. But as it turns out, outside of one's comfort zone is where all the growth happens. I needed to find a career that aligned with my values. I like helping people. I believe in service and fairness. I appreciate that people make mistakes and should have a second chance to do the right thing. My skillset is in analysis, finance, and emotional awareness.

Through reflection and research, a new business idea came together and I now help people work through the finances of divorce. The mission of my business is "Helping couples amicably identify, evaluate, and equitably divide assets in a fair and respectful manner during divorce to achieve a peaceful financial separation." I get to use my skills, talents, and values every day.

I had to do everything, from the education it would take to get the certification, to learning how to design my website, name my company, register my business, determine pricing, and become an expert in a new field. This was in no way a passive change.

Starting a business has been hard, and it has pushed me to work harder than I did. But I love what I do now, and it colors every part of my life. I am satisfied, happy, and confident in my ability to help others. I am present. I look forward to meeting with clients. My relationships with my wife and kids have improved, and I feel I am better at every facet of my life. Except maybe cooking. But there is still time to improve on that.

I had known for years that I was unhappy and needed to find a way to align my career with my values. It took introspection and emotional rock-bottom to give me the determination to make the change. I regained my sense of purpose and it inspired me to grow.

I am a lot more capable than I gave myself credit for, and I have reinvigorated myself for any new challenges ahead.

9. Burnout: The Erosion of the Soul

During the Great Resignation, burnout was the number one reason employees cited for leaving their current jobs, and burnout rates continue to be exceptionally high.

Burnout was a serious problem even before the pandemic, costing nearly $200 billion in related healthcare costs in the United States alone. In 2019, the World Health Organization declared burnout an occupational disease due to workplace stress not being successfully managed. At that time, about 53 percent of the workforce was burned out but it has since risen to extraordinary levels. In the spring of 2021, up to 70 percent of people were experiencing burnout. Recent studies show that it rose to a high of 89 percent in the fall of 2021 and then dropped a bit in 2022 after things opened up and people were able to take some vacation.

Burnout is a diagnosable state of emotional, physical, and mental exhaustion brought on by long-term stress. Leadership coach Dr. Kim Hires posted a video in 2021 saying, "People are not alright. And it's been a long time coming, but I think everything with COVID and the last 18 months has just sent everyone over the edge; entire industries are about to implode." More telling are the comments left by the thousands of viewers, including:

"I am not alright, and I don't know if I can be the same employee I used to be. I'm a different person now. I just don't GAF about anything."

"I cry daily at work. I'm not even saving lives. I just work in Corporate America."

"I have no motivation to work anymore. I don't even care if I get fired… #overit."

"We were just discussing this in my HR Management class. It was coming but COVID escalated it. People won't settle anymore!"

This unprecedented state of burnout grew from the intensity of the pandemic and lockdowns. During natural disasters, Dr. Ann Masten says that humans can tap into what scientists call our "surge capacity," mental and physical systems designed to help us survive acutely stressful situations, like a hurricane or earthquake.

But we deplete that capacity after about six months—the time most communities need to begin processing the physical and emotional wreckage. This is when we expect to see signs of recovery (funerals are held, debris is cleared, and construction begins) but the pandemic was far more intense. It lasted longer, did more damage, and impacted everyone everywhere. This meant that, unlike regional disasters, there was no safe place to go to or people who could be leaned on for support.

Three Components of Burnout

In their book *Burnout: The Secret to Unlocking the Stress Cycle*, Dr. Emily Nagoski and Amelia Nagoski, DMA, identify three components of burnout:

- **Emotional exhaustion:** This is the fatigue that comes from caring too much for too long. Symptoms include chronic fatigue and, ironically, insomnia, putting sufferers in a cycle of accelerating exhaustion. This leads to impaired concentration or forgetfulness, anger, increases in anxiety and depression, increased illness, and physical symptoms like heart palpitations, chest pain, shortness of breath, GI pain, dizziness, headaches, and fainting.

- **Lack of accomplishment:** The second component is an unconquerable sense of futility, a feeling that nothing you do makes any difference. People experience feelings of apathy and hopelessness along with increased irritability. The projects that used to give them satisfaction or the teams they used to enjoy working with now make them feel, "meh" at best. This leads to a lack of productivity and, ultimately, poor performance.

- **Depletion of empathy:** The hallmark of this component is detachment and depersonalization because the person has depleted their ability to give empathy, care, or compassion. Not just for others, but for themselves too. This leads to loss of enjoyment, pessimism, increased isolation, and disconnection. Joy and compassion seep away and even if the person realizes they need help they don't care enough to seek it for themselves.

This has contributed greatly to the sharp increase in mental health issues that began during the lockdowns and continue to this day.

The three components of burnout

Purpose Story 10:
From Depression to Purpose

I graduated from college in the 2009 recession and the work I could find took me down the path of law enforcement. I started as a public safety officer on a college campus where I felt like an armed babysitter, and then progressed into the corrections world where I described myself as a social worker with a gun.

I was able to get to know my clients, help them successfully navigate the justice system, and work with them to understand the reasons behind the sanctions they received for violating the terms of their probation. The respect and rapport I built with the people there was such that one notorious offender called me while "on the run" and asked me to arrange for him to turn himself in—which he did, and even thanked me for my assistance.

When I moved to another state and joined their version of probation (Community Corrections), the culture shock of becoming a disciplinarian with no real ability to help the people on my caseload spiraled me into a deep depression.

To escape the stress, I began seeking out opportunities to do other things, like learning about the hearings process, coordinating social events, and volunteering to be a traveling instructor for topics like first aid and emergency management. As I stepped into the front of the classroom, I began to feel empowered to make a difference in people's lives again.

The complexities of the criminal justice system and the frustration at our inability to do more than hand out demerits and jail time was felt across many field offices and programs. When I was able, I used the classroom time to encourage discussions about what we could do for our clients, how our decisions impacted the community, and what options for change and reform might exist. At the time, my background in adult education was informal—a side hobby at best. Yet I began finding my sense of purpose in the classroom more than I was out on the streets.

When an internal job opportunity appeared for a curriculum development role, I did not think I was qualified. I had a thousand reasons not to apply, but my supervisor saw that I was burning out in the field and encouraged me to try. In what I still see as the most fortuitous decision of my career, I applied, and the training team decided to take a chance on me. While it was not common for curriculum developers to step in front of the classroom, a shortage of instructors and an increase in new staff resulted in opportunities for me to teach.

As my confidence in the classroom grew, word of my passion for the work and exceptional abilities in handling disruptive behaviors spread (with several years of experiences walking into rooms of convicted felons, the students did not faze me). It became a cycle of improvement—the more I witnessed the new staff understand and apply the knowledge and skills they were learning, the more encouraged I was to become a better facilitator.

By the end of my first year in the training role, I was assigned to help rebuild our instructor development program, deliver train-the-trainer workshops, and oversee new instructor certifications.

I found my purpose—my calling to help others recognize and develop their abilities to serve themselves, their families, and their communities. Being an officer was a job. Writing curriculum was a project. Helping others achieve success and influence others inside the classroom and beyond—that was my purpose.

Do not ignore your mental health and wellness. If you are being stressed out to the point of depression and burnout in your job, something is wrong.

The Costs of Burnout

Burnout is insidious, creeping up slowly and making us too tired to care or take positive action. By the time we realize we are in trouble, we don't have the motivation or self-compassion to take action. Psychologist Dr. Christine Hohlbaum describes it this way, "Sadly, most people don't even notice its gradual grip over their lives until it's too late. By then, external intervention is necessary to move burnout patients toward positive change."

Scientists call burnout "the erosion of the soul." Reading that struck me hard in the solar plexus—it's not just exhaustion; it slowly drains away the core of who you are.

Lack of accomplishment and depletion of empathy are particularly responsible for the rise in resignations. No matter how hard people work, many feel like they are spinning their wheels. And as their negative feelings grow, some inevitably project those feelings onto their job, which makes them think they need to find another one.

The truth is that the only cure for burnout is to rest, not start another job. This is why hiring managers saw an increase in ghosting behavior, both by applicants and 25 percent of new hires who failed to show up for their first day. New employees who did show up were still in danger of quitting within a short period. Hiring managers also saw boomeranging—employees who quit their jobs due to burnout returning to their organizations after taking time off to recover and heal.

As psychologist Dr. Sherrie Bourg Carter puts it, "When you are in the throes of full-fledged burnout, you are no longer able to function effectively on a personal or professional level." It is likely that burnout is contributing to the recent rise in conflict and incivility occurring in workplaces around the world. Employee surveys now feature comments like these:

*"I'm seeing a lack of professionalism and
passive aggressiveness up to overt aggression."*

"I was on a call that was the most unprofessional interaction I've ever had."

"I've seen more people cry in the last four months than I have in my entire career."

People appear to be literally losing control of their emotions, or lacking empathy or compassion for damage their outbursts might do to others. This ultimately takes a toll that can lead to more resignations. Dr. Christine Pearson and Dr. Christine Porath studied how the bad behavior of one employee negatively impacted their coworkers. They found:

- 80 percent lost work time worrying about the incident
- 78 percent said their commitment to the organization declined
- 66 percent felt their performance declined
- 48 percent intentionally decreased their work effort and time at work
- 12 percent left the job

Burnout drives people to seek healthier workplaces

The Causes of Burnout

While studies have long shown that remote employees work just as hard as their in-person counterparts, the lockdowns created a recipe for burnout—overworking and under resting. According to a 2020 survey by the Society for Human Resource Management (SHRM), 70 percent of workers who transitioned to remote work because of the pandemic say they now work on the weekends, and 45 percent say they regularly work more hours per week than they did before the lockdowns.

In fact, during the pandemic, the workday increased from 9 to 12 hours. Work even crept into our sleep time. One of the symptoms of burnout is insomnia, and email providers saw spikes in logons from midnight to 3:00 a.m.

During the height of the lockdowns, when people lost access to how they normally rest and recharge—going to dinner, traveling, getting pedicures, going to the gym, etc.—they often leaned into doing *more* work. Gone were the clear boundaries that commuting to a workplace provides, and many found that working seemed to soothe the uncertainty and anxiety the pandemic caused.

Many companies not only held profits steady during 2020 but actually had one of their best years ever. I get worried when I hear executives tout that success because that short-term gain was not sustainable. We're paying the price now with record-setting burnout and resignations across every sector. In addition, it's driving a drop in employee engagement and a sharp increase in labor movements as workers fight for better conditions and pay.

In Gallup's *State of the Global Workplace 2022 Report*, they found engagement had dropped to the lowest levels in a decade. In addition, people are not thriving. In fact, only 33 percent of employees are thriving with their overall well-being. When broken out by region, many parts of the world are struggling more. They identify people on this continuum:

- **Thriving:** People with positive views of their present life and of the next five years
- **Struggling:** People who struggle in their present life and have uncertain or negative views of the future
- **Suffering:** People who report their lives are miserable and have negative views of the future

SUFFERING ⬅———————➡ THRIVING

Gallup tracks additional measures, asking questions about how much people experienced the following the previous workday: worry (40 percent for worry), stress (44 percent), anger (21 percent), and sadness (23 percent). Only 11 percent of people felt they were treated with respect at work, ranging from a low of 6 percent (Commonwealth of Independent States) to a high of 19 percent (South Asia).

People are reporting the highest levels of workplace stress since Gallup started tracking it in 2009. Stress is responsible for 75 percent of doctor's visits with work pressures and financial worry the biggest sources. Stanford's Dr. Jeffrey Pfeffer estimates that stressful workplace environments are responsible for 120,000 employee deaths per year, just in the US.

When people are struggling or suffering, they are 61 percent more likely to experience burnout. Thriving employees have 53 percent fewer missed workdays due to health issues. It's clear that today's employees are not in good shape and shifting this is now a top focus for researchers from many disciplines.

Safety Moves to the Forefront

Working from home created its own zeitgeist. People saw how much time had been dedicated to commuting and dressing professionally. Instead, they spent their days surrounded by decor they enjoyed, foods they preferred, and pets they loved. A sharp contrast to sterile workplaces.

Over recent decades, we have slowly stripped people's humanity out of the workplace. We went from offices where people could create a sense of space for themselves to cubicles where those personal touches had to become much smaller, to open floor plans where you can't have anything personal at all since you just grab whatever table is free. While this shift may save organizations money, a Harvard study found that it does not boost collaboration in any significant way; on the contrary, it makes people less emotionally attached to their workplaces. Many people discovered how much happier and productive they are when surrounded by things they love.

Many tech organizations had wooed employees with what I call "free food and fun furniture" to convey a positive workplace culture. But when lockdowns cut off access to those perks, employees were left with their laptops and their workloads. The real culture was stripped bare for all to see, and many realized that they did not have supportive managers, visionary leaders, or purpose-driven organizations. Is it really a wonder that tech organizations saw turnover as high as healthcare?

For many groups of employees, losing access to the office was not really a loss as they gained a sense of safety. With all communication planned (via meetings) and miniaturized (via screens), people also got a break from all the negative interactions that can impact us at work. In particular, many groups realized they were now protected from the insensitive comments of their peers, or the inappropriate touch of a colleague, or the microaggressions from their boss.

For example, in a *New York Times* article, Emma Goldberg writes how one Black woman quit her job because she faced persistent micro-aggressions at work. It is not surprising that women and people of color are leaving their jobs in record numbers. Over 200,000 Black and Latina women have left since the beginning of the pandemic, according to *Fast Company*.

Are you aware that 75 percent of workers experience workplace bullying? It's four times more common than either sexual harassment or racial discrimination on the job. But employees got a break from those too.

While burnout is the number one reason that people are leaving their jobs (at 40 percent), instances of discrimination came in third (at 20 percent)— second was organizational changes at 34 percent. As the pandemic wore on, people started to notice potential discrimination, like how often their own voice went unheard in video meetings (48 percent), or how much their colleagues' voices went unheard (57 percent), as stated in the *2021 Hybrid Workplace Report*.

All of this combined to create a setting for which the murder of George Floyd in the US would spark a worldwide movement and global protests for months. Those horrifying 9 minutes and 29 seconds launched ongoing conversations about critical issues like systemic oppression, privilege, and microaggressions. Workers across industries demanded that their leaders do "listening tours," increase training on issues of diversity and inclusion, take a stand on policies, and even weigh in on state and national matters.

One year after Floyd's murder, *USA Today* wrote "two-thirds of workers want their companies to speak out against racism" and quoted a study on over 2,000 workers planning to hold their organization accountable, with 54 percent stating they would consider quitting if their organization failed to take a stand.

Issues of equality are particularly important to Millennials, who are poised to become three-quarters of the workforce in the next couple of years. Gen Z is even more fervent in their support of issues of equality and the environment.

Some people found themselves in alignment with their organizations' values and actions, and others realized they needed to move on to another organization. A study by the American Staffing Association shows that 64 percent of Hispanics/Latinos and 49 percent of Blacks/African Americans said they planned to look for a new job within the next year, rates much higher than their White counterparts at 34 percent.

Political division and the climate crisis also played a role in rising resignations. Social media messages are designed to elicit strong emotions like anger and outrage. Inundated with a flow of divisive messages about everything from election results to mask mandates and vaccines, people were exhausting themselves with media when their emotional reserves were already depleted.

Nightly footage of the growing climate crisis added more to be worried about. All over the world, people were struggling to survive through tornados, floods, hurricanes, heat waves, droughts, fires, and polar vortex storms. What used to be natural disaster impacting someplace far away was now hitting close to home, with the very real consequences in terms of human life and the economy laid bare. It's estimated that climate change will cause a financial crisis more than double that created by the pandemic.

The world's papers were blazing with headlines like *National Geographic*'s "2021's Weather Disasters Brought Home the Reality of Climate Change" and *The Guardian*'s "The Climate Disaster Is Here." *The New York Times* ran a piece in February 23, 2023, titled "6 Podcasts to Help Tackle Your Climate Anxiety."

All of this contributed to people feeling exhausted, burned out, and scared. It's human nature to want to create a better life for ourselves and our families. To misinterpret the Great Resignation as just a temporary fight about working from home missed the larger reality. In her article for *Inc.*, Jessica Stillman states,

> *Workers aren't just looking for higher pay, more time off, or more days at home (though those things would surely help in the short term). They're actually questioning the whole meaning of the daily grind. Why do we put so much of ourselves into our careers? And are we getting a fair deal from our employers in return for all this stress and heartache? Holding onto employees then isn't just about scheduling. It's about showing them their work has meaning and that the company actually cares about them as human beings.*

These past three years have clarified our values and profoundly shifted what people want. Companies that thrive will move forward from this point in time, crafting a new future of work, one that we never could have contemplated before the pandemic began.

10. Entering Post-traumatic Growth

Trigger Warning: This chapter touches on the subject
of trauma, which some readers might find difficult.

Post-traumatic growth is the fourth pressure that accelerated and intensified our search for more purpose and meaning in our lives. Most of us have heard of post-traumatic stress, often in the term post-traumatic stress disorder or PTSD. Post-traumatic growth is the other way people can respond to difficult circumstances.

When humans experience trauma, we can respond in one of two ways. PTSD occurs when the body gets trapped in a cycle of reliving trauma, often through ongoing fight-flight-freeze cycles that may bring on anxiety, flashbacks, and depression. It's an injury because this is not a healing state of improvement but rather a stuck or maladaptive state, much like a wound that can't heal because infection remains.

I know this all too well because I have suffered from PTSD from childhood abuse. Those memories surfaced in my 30s and I experienced panic attacks for nearly a decade, becoming agoraphobic and rarely leaving my hometown. When I did try to go on vacation, you'd often find me curled in a fetal position on the bathroom floor just trying to manage the waves of adrenalin and fear.

I also know firsthand that for many it is possible to heal completely, even having been stuck for a long time. Luckily, through talk therapy and, finally, a few somatic healing sessions of EMDR (eye movement desensitization and reprocessing) and the brain-spotting technique (a deeper version of EMDR), I finally unlocked that cycle and have not had a panic attack since. I now travel often for speaking engagements and enjoy it thoroughly.

Another highly effective technique is Cognitive Processing Therapy (CPT) and trauma sufferers can see real and lasting relief after completing the ten-session series. Recently, there is compelling evidence around psychedelic-assisted therapy offering amazing results. Consider reading Michael Pollan's book *How to Change Your Mind: What the New Science of Psychedelics Teaches Us About Consciousness, Dying, Addiction, Depression, and Transcendence.*

Trauma is more common than you might expect. In the US alone, nearly two-thirds of men and half of women report experiencing at least one trauma during their lifetime. According to the Centers for Disease Control and Prevention, one in five people was molested as a child (one in six for men), and one in four was beaten by a parent. One in four women will be sexually assaulted during her lifetime. Nearly 25 percent of adults grew up with alcoholic parents.

The source of trauma can come in many forms making global trauma rates even higher:

- Military combat/war
- Refugee and hostage situations
- Natural disasters

- Accidents
- Medical conditions like cancer or AIDS
- Sexual assault/molestation
- Violent crime (physical assault, mass shooting, etc.)
- Losing a loved one
- Global pandemic

All of these sources of trauma are significant, but all except the pandemic are localized at the horrible moment in time to one family or region. When natural disasters hit, they are local and while others may see them on the news, it's not the same as looking out your window and seeing the devastation.

But this COVID-19 pandemic brought loss and devastation to every community. Never before has the global population experienced something so intense together. Previous pandemics did not move as fast because we were not connected by 100,000 flights per day. In addition, news traveled as spoken or written word, not high-definition images, available 24/7 on every device.

And while our bodies have not changed much, biologically, in the past few hundred years, our brains are not equipped to distinguish that what we see on the news may not be an immediate threat. We are wired to scan for and respond to danger. Our senses are always scanning, and our amygdala is always on alert.

Needless to say, we were not prepared to handle the sense of the danger the pandemic created. Our bodies reacted to the ongoing threat, night after night, month after month, depleting our surge capacity and leading to the incredible rise in burnout discussed in the previous chapter.

But many of us did not treat ourselves as trauma victims and may not recognize that we need help. Psychological experts are seeing the effects of this global trauma in the form of mental health issues like anxiety, depression, and other diseases of despair.

The World Health Organization put out a news release in March of 2022 with the headline, "COVID-19 Pandemic Triggers 25 Percent Increase in Prevalence of Anxiety and Depression Worldwide" and urged countries to increase their mental health services. Prescriptions for anxiety and depression also rose. According to insurance companies, pharmacy claims for mental health prescriptions rose nearly 10 percent, with 75 percent for antidepressants. While medicine is an important tool, it can sometimes manage the symptoms to the extent that people don't address the root cause; their need to heal from trauma.

According to the National Center for PTSD, most people will experience a trauma at some point in their lifetime. One response to trauma is to develop PTSD. Consider these statistics:

- On average, 6 out of every 100 people (or 6 percent of the population) will have PTSD at some point in their lives.
- Women are twice as likely to develop PTSD than men (8 percent of women versus 4 percent of men).
- 14 to 43 percent of children go through at least one trauma—3 to 15

percent of girls and 1 to 6 percent of boys develop PTSD as a result

- About 12 million adults in the US have PTSD during a given year, a small portion of those who have gone through a trauma.

A core feature of PTSD is "when recollections of the trauma become involuntary, intrusive, and unresolved." Essentially, people become stuck in a never-ending loop of reliving trauma without the ability to heal and move forward. If trauma survivors get the right healing support, they may recover completely, but many people avoid therapy or don't have access to insurance or providers. This is why many community organizations offer low-cost or sliding scale therapy.

The good news is that humans have another way to respond to trauma—what scientists call post-traumatic growth or PTG, a *positive* psychological change that results from struggling with a highly challenging life circumstance. And we are seeing a large part of the world population go through this healthy and adaptive response. It certainly explains the universal focus on more purpose and meaning.

Dr. Richard Tedeschi, from the University of North Carolina, coined the term "post-traumatic growth" along with his colleague, Dr. Lawrence Calhoun. Dr. Tedeschi says, "We're talking about a transformation—a challenge to people's core beliefs that causes them to become different than they were before...Studies support the notion that post-traumatic growth is common and universal across cultures."

PTG is different from resilience, which is the ability to bounce back quickly from trauma. In fact, Dr. Tedeschi says that people who do recover rapidly "aren't the ones likely to experience positive growth."

Fortunately, post-traumatic growth can occur on two levels: with a person, at the individual level, and at the level of the organization.

Personal Growth

Research reveals seven areas of growth for people at the individual level that tend to result from surviving trauma or adversity. Which of the following list have you experienced in the past couple of years?

1. Greater appreciation of life
This is a natural outcome because we can't help but notice the good things in our life, or the blessings that were previously unseen or undervalued. What are you now appreciating that you maybe didn't before?

2. Deepening of close relationships
This can happen in two ways: Going through a crisis naturally bonds those people who experience it together. In addition, relationships can be forged or strengthened when we lean on friends, families, or people in the helping professions for support. Who are you closer to or more bonded with now than a couple of years ago?

3. Increased compassion and altruism

Surviving trauma commonly gives us greater compassion for others and can move us into actions like donating money or volunteering your time to actively bring about change. Many survivors and families of victims of gun violence, for example, work on changing gun laws. Others suffering from rare diseases may donate funds or even start organizations dedicated to ending that disease.

4. New possibilities for a purpose in life

Exploring what feels meaningful to you is a natural outcome of post-traumatic growth. This element of post-traumatic growth is contributing to the surge of people around the world seeking more purpose. What new possibilities are you exploring for your own purpose?

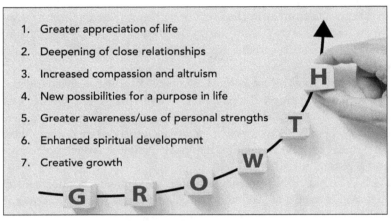

1. Greater appreciation of life
2. Deepening of close relationships
3. Increased compassion and altruism
4. New possibilities for a purpose in life
5. Greater awareness/use of personal strengths
6. Enhanced spiritual development
7. Creative growth

Post-traumatic growth at the individual level

5. Greater awareness/use of personal strengths

Going through difficulty often requires us to dig deep and use or find strengths we didn't know we had, leaving us with an increased sense of confidence in our ability to weather hard things. What are some of your newly developed or appreciated strengths?

6. Enhanced spiritual development

Traumatic events force us to ponder the "big questions" about our beliefs and values, so it's natural that people turn to spiritual matters or religious practices for guidance and comfort.

7. Creative growth

Increased creative growth comes from the disruption that trauma creates and the ways in which people have to innovate to more forward. It also comes from clarity around purpose or meaning. Interestingly, art therapy proves to be very effective in helping people process and heal trauma so there is a cyclical relationship. In what ways have you recently experienced creative growth?

Post-traumatic growth can give us hope that trauma, while both difficult and painful, can be a source of powerful growth allowing us to heal and thrive once more. In fact, it can even be the catalyst to becoming better than we were before—transformed in a powerful way.

When we go through trauma, it is common to hunger to return to how things used to be, before the trauma happened—trying to "return to normal" if you will. Yet, the hallmark of PTG is the path forward. Essentially using a process by which we're not only restored but achieve a *higher* level of functioning as a result of addressing and learning from a traumatic event.

Therapists and researchers have discovered that we can intentionally help people move to post-traumatic growth using a set of key tools and strategies. One study with cancer patients showed that they experienced statistically significant improvement in their post-traumatic growth and that growth was sustained one year later.

Research shows five ways post-traumatic growth can be facilitated naturally in therapy, making them a useful resource for survivors:

- **Education:** Understanding that trauma disrupts our core belief systems helps us heal. While it might confuse and frighten us, leading to anxiety and repetitive thinking, we should lean into learning as a tool for moving forward. We can explore what happened, how it impacts us, and more importantly, how to use the experience to craft a healthy new path.

- **Emotional regulation:** Being able to modulate the body's response and regulate our emotions is a significant tool in overcoming trauma. People can discover their window of tolerance and use various techniques to expand that window. Over time, people become confident in their ability to navigate challenges.

- **Disclosure:** Humans are biologically designed to process trauma through talking. Processing verbally helps us to relieve intense emotions and also shift debilitating thoughts to healthier ones. While we can process with loved ones, it's better to seek out a trained professional who knows how to provide appropriate support and without you feeling responsible for their reactions.

- **Narrative development:** A large part of healing and maximizing growth happens through transforming the story of what happened. At first, we must disclose it and feel it, but then we begin to make meaning from what happened. This allows us to ponder what good might come from an experience and how it might transform us.

- **Service:** According to Dr. Tedeschi, "People do better in the aftermath of trauma if they find work that benefits others." This can include helping those in their own circle or those who have been impacted by similar trauma. Focusing on others helps us facilitate our own healing.

How might you engage in these five ways? And how might you help others do the same? We all benefit when others are supported in healing from trauma, and you can play a direct role in helping your neighbors, coworkers, family, and friends.

Purpose Story 11:
Helping Others Heal Through Trauma
In 2018, I broke my neck in a motorcycle crash, which put me permanently in a wheelchair. The accident changed my life, and it also gave me a new purpose.

Prior to the crash, I was bartending and starting a new career in construction. I loved being a bartender and was really happy where I was at, but I knew I had to do more. So, after bartending and serving for many years, I decided to learn a new trade. I knew construction would help me out in my future especially if I ever wanted to be a homeowner.

Once I was paralyzed, I had to quickly adapt to my new way of life. I wanted to find ways to make things a little bit easier for myself and increase my independence. One of the reasons I have done well is because of the wonderful support I have from my family and my friends! You definitely find out who your real friends are after a traumatic event happens to you. I am very grateful for my old friends who stuck with me, and for all the new friends I have made since.

Exercise was a big part of my recovery and for my mental state. I now play wheelchair rugby and the physical aspect of the sport helped me get strong. But in addition, learning from others who were in wheelchairs really helped me gain my independence. We play competitively and I get to travel all around the country.

Learning from others made me realize that I could do the same and it is my new sense of purpose. I am now an ambassador for a spinal cord injury support group that covers central California all the way down to San Diego and is still growing every day. I also work and volunteer for a local rehabilitation hospital, serving as a peer mentor to others who are adapting to their injuries.

I learned to never give up. When you still want to live, you will put in all the effort. I try to educate and motivate all people, both in and not in wheelchairs. I am very excited for my future!

Organizational Growth

Like people, organizations may also go through post-traumatic growth. And, like people, there is often pressure to get through the trauma, perhaps using crisis-management techniques, to get "back to normal" as quickly as possible.

Ideally, however, they transform themselves to become better than they were before. One study, "Pandemic-driven Post-traumatic Growth for Organizations and Individuals" by Dr. Kristine Olson and Dr. Steve Southwick, from Yale School of Medicine, and Dr. Tait Shanafelt from Stanford University School of Medicine, looked at two hospital systems that were at the heart of a traumatic experience. One after Hurricane Katrina in New Orleans, where leaders were forced to make difficult decisions during an incredibly intense period, and the other a hospital system in Seattle, Washington, that was the epicenter for the first COVID-19 cases in the US.

They found that both hospital systems got through the crises by innovating, leaning on their strengths, and communicating openly. More importantly, after the crisis eased, they did not focus on returning to their old ways but instead used what they learned to further enhance their effectiveness.

"Ultimately, it is not the trauma that causes the growth, but rather how individuals and organizations interpret and respond to it," they said. "In facilitating post-traumatic growth, it may be possible to...create a more resilient healthcare workforce and stronger healthcare organizations."

They identified four steps that organizations can take to increase post-traumatic growth:

- **Deliberately reflect on the impact of the trauma and what can be learned from the experience.** Ask yourself, how can we become better as a result of what we went through?

- **Identify role models (people and/or functions) that grew through adversity.** Then ask, what did they do differently from the others? How did they lean into to growth?

- **See the opportunity to "reinvent" or catalyze change.** Ask yourself, how do we build upon our momentum to keep moving forward? What opportunity exists to transform ourselves?

- **Reconnect with people and values.** Relationships make work meaningful, so ask yourself, how can we create more connections? This is especially important after having to keep our distance for so long.

Post-traumatic growth refers to a process by which we're not only restored but achieve a *higher* level of functioning by addressing and learning from a traumatic event. Think about all the ways that businesses pivoted during the pandemic. Restaurants figured out how to serve hundreds of hungry customers through online ordering and contactless pickup. Organizations everywhere embraced new methods of sanitization and automation—even doorknobs were switched out for foot-activated latches. New online collaboration tools allowed people to work together from their living rooms as tech workers accomplished a decade's worth of digital transformation in a matter of months. This list goes on and on.

Consider how your organization might build upon what you have already done to continue to grow and improve.

Post-traumatic growth is a gift we have been given for healing from trauma. It is never too late to use the tools and strategies presented here to reflect on what you have been through and transform into something better than ever.

This section may have felt heavy but it's important. I'm seeing evidence of burnout and unhealed pandemic trauma in every organization I work with. It's important that we acknowledge that we have lived through an intense and unique time. The pandemic intensified a shift that was already in play and it's behind why so many of us are seeking more purpose in our lives. It also explains why you may be feeling so exhausted or apathetic.

So, pause and take care of yourself. We've been through a lot. Once I recognized that I was also experiencing burnout, I intentionally leaned into healing myself. I forced myself to do things I used to enjoy, even though I felt "meh" about them, and I started finding ways to play. I've been bitten by the pickleball bug and it has helped me so much. I also gave myself permission to chill out with comforting shows or books. I made a point of spending at least 3 days per week in nature (20 mins). I can report that these strategies work and I encourage you to use them too. While I am not a medical doctor, I hope you will consider this a "prescription" to lean into rest and healing.

Your Learning Journey
Take a few minutes to reflect on your own experiences with the four pressures of the pandemic.

- How has your life been shaped by loss and grief? What stages of grieving have you experienced?
- How did the lockdowns impact your life? Did you find yourself reflecting on your values and priorities?
- Have you experienced the three components of burnout (emotional exhaustion, lack of accomplishment, and depletion of empathy)? What have you noticed in yourself and others?
- Have you experienced post-traumatic growth as an individual? If so, which of the seven areas of growth (greater appreciation of life, deepening of close relationships, new possibilities for a purpose in life, enhanced spiritual development, increased compassion and altruism, creative growth, greater awareness/use of personal strengths) did you notice happening in your own life?
- Have the organizations you work with experienced post-traumatic growth? Why or why not?

III

YOUR JOURNEY
TO FIND PURPOSE

*"The purpose of life is to discover your gift. The work of life
is to develop it. The meaning of life is to give your gift away."*

David Viscott, author
*Finding Strength in Difficult Times:
A Book of Meditations*

11. You're on a Journey

There is a reason we are not born with a little message or map that tells us our purpose. Life is supposed to be a journey, part of the process of growing up and moving through adulthood. It's not meant to be easy but an ongoing series of events that give you more pieces to the puzzle. A quest of sorts.

Consider this an exploration, a process of discovery, like a maze or labyrinth combined with a treasure hunt. You'll find little gifts that boost you along the way and you'll also bump into roadblocks and obstacles. Sometimes the path will be straight and easy, other times you will hit a dead end and need to turn back to find the path forward.

I'm happy to report that people have developed many tools for you to use on your journey—tools to give you clues or hints that increase your clarity. Clarity can come in two forms: learning more about what your purpose *is* as well as learning what your purpose *is not*. That is important to remember because sometimes we might feel frustrated if we don't perceive that we are moving toward something. But learning what is not your purpose is valuable information and actually contributes to your forward movement.

In this section and section V, I have pulled together a variety of tools from a range of experts and each one has the potential to offer you something valuable for getting clarity around your purpose. I recommend you take each tool for a test run. Some will work and some won't but you can't find out unless you try. So, dedicate some time to exploring these resources and together we'll see where that leads you.

I also want to suggest that you to be very careful about who you share your discoveries with, especially at the beginning. Finding your sense of purpose is a tender and personal journey and many of us either want to share in our excitement or we feel we "should" share with our family and/or friends.

But it's a little bit like holding a tiny flame in your hand. If you have just nurtured it into being, one tiny puff can extinguish it. For example, if you share with someone and they have a less-than-excited response, it might douse your enthusiasm and make you question yourself. Or perhaps you have an overly critical parent or sibling or spouse—they could say something harsh, and the flame will go out.

I recommend that you go through this section and try the various tools to see what you learn. But keep it to yourself for a while until you are feeling more confident in your clarity. I also recommend that you journal about the questions and activities to help you process what you're thinking and feeling. I love this quote by Brad Wilcox, "A personal journal is an ideal environment in which to 'become.' It is a perfect place for you to think, feel, discover, expand, remember, and dream."

When you do feel ready to share, carefully pick and choose people who you know understand this tender moment and will support you. Exploring your sense of purpose is vulnerable. Bestselling author and the world's foremost expert on vulnerability Dr. Brené Brown actually defines vulnerability as courage in action. (If you have not yet watched her two TED talks, I highly recommend that you do.) Rather than sharing with everyone, she recommends that we only share with the people who have *earned* the right to our vulnerability. Meaning that they treat us with respect and kindness, creating a safe space for us to share without fear of judgment or ridicule.

Don't worry—you'll be able to share more freely later. But for now, hold that new, tiny flame carefully in your hands, and gently give it the puffs of oxygen it needs to grow.

I think it's helpful when we understand that we are not the only ones on this journey. Dr. Stephanie Shackelford and Bill Denzel wrote the 2021 book, *You on Purpose: Discover Your Calling and Create the Life You Were Meant to Live.* They conducted surveys with over 2,500 adults about the journey of finding one's purpose or calling. Here are some interesting findings:

- 57 percent of adults feel that understanding your calling is primarily a solo journey
- 86 percent agree with the statement that we can find wisdom and direction by looking within
- 55 percent of all people have done something to discover their calling or purpose in life
- 26 percent have not taken any steps (the rest were not sure)

Life Happens in Cycles

Sometimes people expect they will discover their purpose in one brilliant flash of insight, like being struck by lightning. And that once that happens, the newly discovered North Star will shine brightly and life will flow easily. Nope.

Even those blessed with discovering their North Star early and who live a life of great purpose have moments where it waxes and wanes, much like the moon. Its pull on us grows and shrinks like the moon, sometimes shining brightly and other times being completely dark.

Dr. Frederic Hudson studies adults and discovered that we move through an ongoing process of self-renewal, which occur in cycles. In his book, *The Adult Years: Mastering the Art of Self-Renewal,* he suggests that adults move through a series of life chapters that begin with dreams and plans, move to achievements and accomplishments, and then begin to decline, creating feelings of discord. As we move through them, our sense of purpose waxes and wanes too. So, it's important that you realize that a dip in clarity or losing joy in something that used to fulfill you is normal and natural. Humans are organic beings, part of nature, just like the trees you can see out your window. Trees don't forever flower or constantly produce fruit. They go through cycles of growth and productivity and then must shed their leaves and rest before blooming again.

Hudson found this to be true of humans too. A life chapter begins with dreams and plans, a time when we may feel that our purpose is clear. During this time, we set big goals and take action on our plans, until those come to fruition as achievements and accomplishments. This part of the cycle usually feels positive and productive, leaving us fulfilled.

But Hudson found that this period comes to an end. We tend to naturally move into a period where things begin to decline, which creates feelings of discord because things that used to be fulfilling may no longer be so, or the sense of purpose we so strongly felt before has waned. But there is no need to worry. Sometimes, we are just moving through the cycle and we will come around again.

As a life chapter ends, we move into what Hudson terms a "life transition," a time of internal renewal. At first, we focus on healing or recovering from the chapter's challenges, but then we start to set new goals and find a renewed sense of purpose. This cycle spans our personal and working lives, our years in retirement, and continues until we die.

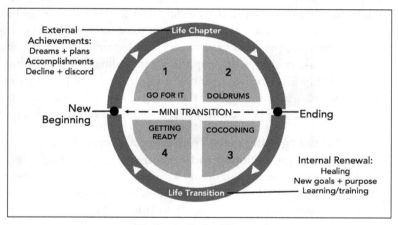

Hudson's Cycle of Renewal

Life chapters are about "doing" and life transitions are about "being." Each is broken into two phases, making four in total:

- **Phase 1 is the "go for it" phase** where we launch into a new adventure. This is a time of stability, where we feel a sense of purpose, and where we are focused and accomplishing our goals. This is often when we achieve something we have longed for, so it may feel like we have really arrived. It's generally a very creative time, where you feel fearless and even joyful. But at some point we hit a plateau and that moves us into Phase 2.

- **Phase 2 is called the "doldrums"** because we feel some level of disenchantment after our major achievement. Perhaps it didn't bring some of the things we thought it would, or now that it's been achieved, it doesn't feel as compelling. It's common to feel disappointment, stress, and even anger, depending on the situation. Hudson argues that at this phase we take one of two paths. We may enter a mini-transition, where we try and retool or restructure our current chapter. Here, people often turn to learning, as they arm themselves with new skills or information to make the mini-transition work. This is all about trying to improve what you have already launched and, for many, it can usher in a new "go for it" phase that brings renewed purpose and joy. Or, we may create an exit strategy so the chapter ends and we can move into the life transition and a state of "being."

- **Phase 3 of the model is "cocooning,"** a time of reflection and introspection. This period can feel a little scary as it requires both letting go of the old plan and patience while you wait for the new vision to emerge. Our next sense of purpose may not be visible yet, so we may experience a time when we feel directionless, but periods of waiting are normal. It might be unnerving but understanding that it's part of human biology makes it easier to embrace this phase with patience. Many people engage learning here for personal growth and development, perhaps going on retreats or taking classes that support their healing, contemplation, and rebirth. Many also turn to spiritual and mindfulness practices in this phase as well. At some point, the inner work pays off and people experience a turning point where they begin to have a new vision.

- **Phase 4 is the "getting ready"** phase, as you prepare for the next chapter. It's a time for exploring and experimenting while cultivating new ways of thinking, being, and doing. You experience a new acceptance of self, including strengths and vulnerabilities. This phase can also include a time of learning in order to get ready to launch the next chapter.

Purpose Story 12:
Transforming Addiction to Help Others
My struggle IS my success. Five years ago, I was burned out, mentally exhausted, and in a job I hated. I had climbed the corporate ladder for several years and, as a part of that journey, I was addicted to making more money, I was addicted to ambition, I was addicted to stimulants (Adderall) and as a result, I felt disconnected from the human experience.

So, I quit, taking two months off to travel and get clean. I paused. I got still. I went on a silent Vipassana meditation retreat for 11 days out in the desert where we meditated for 12 hours a day and didn't speak a word. I went inward in order to find my strength.

I learned what creates peace in my life and I learned what creates chaos in my life. The addictions, the depression, when not addressed, create chaos. Through meditation, exercise, a gratitude practice, journaling, cold showers, sending gratitude notes, and yoga. I have learned how to cultivate peace and a focused intention for my life.

Alchemy is turning base metals into gold. My purpose is to teach others how to turn adversity and struggle into resilience and strength. I would not have gotten this far if I wasn't willing to look in the mirror, take time off, and deal with the issues that have haunted me since childhood. It is an everyday battle, but it led me to my purpose.

My purpose is to educate, elevate, and liberate the body and mind of the masses through teaching, speaking, and coaching. The main factors that contributed to my struggle were addiction, trauma, and depression. These are the same factors that make me successful today as I have alchemized my pain into purpose and now I intend to show the world how to do the same!

I've taken everything I learned on this journey and created my own company where I serve individuals to large corporations by teaching yoga, meditation, and creating and presenting content on mental health, burnout, anxiety, and how to thrive through difficult times. My struggle IS my success.

Another way to look at the model is to think of the left side as phases of construction, where you rebuild yourself and your life, and the right side as phases of deconstruction, where you take apart your life and self-identity in preparation for reforming them. It's a bit like the caterpillar morphing into a butterfly, except we get to return to our cocoon state and reemerge in a new flight of transformation.

As creativity and leadership consultant Lisa Slavid puts it, "It's important to respect where you are in the cycle as each phase meets various needs, like reflecting, exploring, producing, etc. Many people can feel stuck in the 'doldrums' phase and it's typically a good time to seek support as you move through the reflecting, talking, and even grieving that are common to this phase."

I find Hudson's model useful because it helps me know that life is not an endless staircase, forever moving upward, only getting better. It's normal to have periods where you're unclear about what you want next, interspersed with periods when you achieve a dream and others where you feel disappointment afterward. Understanding this made me much more comfortable and able to embrace the natural cycles of human growth and development.

The tools in this section and section V can help you throughout all the phases of Hudson's model. But it's important to note where you are now so you can best support this part of your journey. Take a moment to reflect on Hudson's model and even journal about it. Looking back, when have you moved through the various phases? What have they felt like and what helped you navigate them? What phase of his model do you think you are in now? What signs or evidence are you noticing? According to Hudson, what should you be focusing on in the coming weeks?

12. The Stories We've Been Sold

Humans are wired to make meaning out of everything. We are born with brains designed to hear stories as important information. Our biology has not changed much in the past several hundred years, so we are particularly wired for story-telling, since this is how skills and wisdom were passed along when we lived in tribes on the plain.

While this part of our biology can be helpful, it can also cause problems. All of us have a story, or several stories, we tell ourselves about who we are and our potential. Some of you may know that story and others may find it's working along silently in the background but still strongly influencing your thoughts, feelings, and actions.

When I was a child, my mother told me I was unlovable. She even said she wished she'd had an abortion. Those words were said in anger but they were said multiple times and I took them in as truth. They shaped my beliefs about myself. I started tuning into her emotions, trying to figure out when she was getting upset, so I could fix it and earn her love. But I never could. I recently saw a post by influencer Ophelia Nichols, saying, "Sometimes our parents are our first bully."

As an adult, I realized my mother had a mental health issue, borderline personality disorder, which is especially harmful to family members. While she did the best she could and I have forgiven her, the truth is that she laid down that first story I would tell myself for years. Luckily, therapy helped me separate who I am from the stories I was sold. While my mother's story was certainly the most damaging, it was not the only one.

When I was in high school, I dreamed of becoming a marine biologist. What ended that dream was failing freshman chemistry—not because I couldn't earn a better grade, but because of the story my chemistry professor told me. After the first test, early in the term, I went to his office hours and asked for help so that I could improve. I had been the valedictorian in high school and believed that I just needed to learn how to study differently. He told me, and I quote, "Don't worry about it, honey. The A's are reserved for the men who are going to be engineers and scientists." I told him that I wanted to be a scientist too, a marine biologist. To which he replied, "You should pick a different major. You're not suited for that."

I left his office not outraged at the sexism I just experienced but defeated. I saw him as the expert who must know better than me, an 18-year-old first-generation college student. More importantly, he was the person who was supposed to help me and if he didn't think I was capable, who was I to argue? That two-minute conversation became part of my story—that I didn't have the skills to be a scientist. So, I changed my major and eventually graduated with my BA in sociology and communication.

This and other experiences as a young adult in the working world built a story in my mind. Beliefs of who I was, what I was capable of, and what people thought of me. You have a story in your head, too. I found it can be valuable to get to know that story. One journaling exercise I did in therapy was particularly revealing to me: I made a list of the beliefs I had about myself, or at least the ones I could identify. This was both positive things (I'm good with people, I have a funny sense of humor) and negative things (I'm not good at science, I am unlovable). I made a timeline on a sheet of paper and started filling in the moments that shaped me. Some of them were big and some of them were little.

It was really eye opening to see it as timeline. I could see where moments had changed the course of my path or where little moments became significant because I already had a belief in place that made them seem like confirmations rather than just the standalone moments they really were. These stories are like a pair of eyeglasses that color what we see. We constantly interpret our lives through our beliefs about ourselves.

Purpose Story 13:
From Engineer to Doctor
I was born to an Italian family in Brazil where my parents worked very hard—they lived by example, using their willpower to make dreams come true. My mother always told me that "Where there's a will, there's a way" and that "Happiness is where we put it, but we never put it where we reach it."

I graduated with a degree in agronomic engineering and practiced the profession for 5 years. I loved agronomy but something bigger was tormenting me—I always had a huge desire to study medicine. When I was 32, an opportunity arose to study medicine in Argentina through an exchange program. As I was single and had no children, I decided not to miss this opportunity. I sold everything I had and faced the challenge of moving to another country and becoming a student again. I graduated after six hard years of studying and today I work in a hospital emergency room and in a clinic providing primary and preventive healthcare.

I feel that if it weren't for persistence, discipline, humility, and a lot of effort, I wouldn't be here. I see myself as a fulfilled man and if I hadn't tried, I would not have achieved this dream.

I was in a comfortable situation with prestige and money, but I chose to drop everything and leave a life behind, because I had a very strong purpose and trust in God to take care of me. I always imagined myself as a doctor with a white coat. This purpose was born intrinsically from an immense desire to do something better and greater for humanity and to have a profession that I could practice until I am 80 years old, fighting for life in life.

I was moved by a very strong purpose and a clear objective. I then devised strategies on how to achieve this goal. Without struggle, sweat, sacrifice, luck, help from friendly people, hard work, this purpose would not have been completed.

Today I feel fulfilled personally and professionally. I'm married to my wonderful wife, and we have a 7-year-old daughter. I don't see myself working in another profession and I realized that what my mother said was true...Where there's a will, there's a way! But I learned that this power is in us and in the importance of believing in God and leaning on him in difficult situations.

Telling a New Story

I went on to earn my MA in mass media and a PhD in education, leadership, and organizations. Part of that was me following my own interests, but some part of it was also me trying to prove that professor and my mother wrong. I now synthesize research from neuroscientists and other leading scholars, writing books and providing leadership training to some of the world's biggest companies. I know now that I am smart enough to do well in freshman chemistry and could probably ace it if I took it again.

But I eventually found my sense of purpose, helping people and organizations rise to their potential. And I do this through sharing science-based principles and evidence-backed best practices.

The big question, though, is did I find my true purpose *despite* that chemistry professor or *because* of him?

I was taking a personal growth workshop when someone asked me, "What if everything that happens to us is designed to help us become who we're meant to be?"

WHAT?!? I could practically feel the circuits in my brain smoking as I contemplated this idea. I saw my timeline in my mind and several questions arose.

"What if I was born to a mother with borderline personality disorder
so I could get really good at reading others' emotions?"

"What if my chemistry professor pushed me toward a path
where I would study human potential?"

"What if my first marriage had to end so that I could find my true soulmate?"

"What if I had that crappy boss so that I'd finally launch my business?"

What an absolutely mind-blowing idea! I went home that night and pulled out my timeline. I laid it on the floor and looked at it with completely new eyes. There was clearly a pattern here. Every hard or negative experience had sent me toward a blessing or gift I later discovered on my journey.

And, I realized, every time I experienced something positive or wonderful, I couldn't have gotten there without the hard thing.

The workshop leader had challenged all of us to try on this idea that your life is always unfolding for your highest and best good. That a force is guiding and nudging you to find your purpose and the good you are meant to do.

I realize that this might sound like a spiritual belief that may or may not feel familiar or comfortable to you. But I'd like you to try it on for now and just entertain the idea. Whether or not you believe in a higher power, just take on the notion that your life is unfolding exactly as it should. And, more importantly, that you already have a lot of great hints about your purpose. Believe that your purpose is working hard to be found.

If you look at your story and timeline now, what looks different? In what ways are you being nudged (or even shoved) in a certain direction? What experiences or people (positive and negative) are in your path for a reason? How do they play a role in putting you on the right path? If you look at your life from this new lens, what hints and signs have you been perhaps missing or discounting?

Spend some time journaling and reflecting on this idea and just see what happens. Perhaps this tool of looking at your story and timeline has some important insight for you.

Note: This chapter is named after a song that helped me reclaim my story. Check out "Throw It All Away" by Toad the Wet Sprocket on the website www.lyricsondemand.com. My favorite lines are below.

Take the story you've been sold
The lies that justify the pain
The guilt that weighs upon your soul
And throw 'em all away!

Lyrics by Toad the Wet Sprocket

13. Clues from Your Résumé: Skills and Talents

One way to find clues to your purpose is to look over your experiences thus far and identify the skills you have developed. It doesn't matter if you use them today or even if you liked the job where you learned them. Our goal in this chapter is to make a list of all the skills you have gained through different life experiences.

Skills and Experiences

Let's start with your résumé. Turn each entry into a list of skills. Did you work with customers? Did you use certain software? Did you create something tangible? Did you do any public speaking? Did you edit or write content or marketing communications? Did you collaborate with others? Make a comprehensive list from your work experience, even those things that were not part of your official title. It's great to do this quickly, just throwing out a word or two to capture them.

Then expand to skills you picked up through non-work activities. What have you learned from your hobbies or interests? For example, I have taken several classes in the fabric arts (quilting, knitting, and collaging). I've also learned how to scuba dive and mountain bike. Some of these were fleeting interests that I don't even do anymore but I learned some skills, so they go on my list.

What have you picked up just from adulting, like making a budget or doing minor house repairs? I know how to do some basic spackling and painting, I'm good at baking, and I also know how to garden, make jam, and preserve foods. Boom, they are added to the list.

Again, don't worry whether you're good at it or love it—the goal is to just get down the big list. Have fun with it! Write it in a journal. Or start a wall of post-it notes and keep adding to it as you think of things.

Don't forget your childhood either. We often pick up skills in our youth that we later discount. For example, during the pandemic, my daughter became fascinated with crystals. On her own, she read at least five books on the subject and who knows how many websites, and watched hours of videos.

All that real knowledge is part of her journey. What is part of yours? Do you know a lot about trains or dinosaurs?

If you were a scout, what did you pick up? For example, I was a Girl Scout and between the badges and the marketing and selling of cookies each year, I gained many skills. My dad was an Eagle Scout and he credits many of those experiences for shaping the leader he became in the ski industry (you can read more in his book *My Life in Winters* by Mike Ewing).

Did you play a sport? Did you perform in the arts? What clubs did you join? And what after-school programs did you do? We live near the ocean, so surfing was a regular part of my daughter's summer activities. I grew up in the mountains and did a lot of skiing and skating as well as fly fishing, which I love and still do every summer. They go on the list.

Talents and Intelligences

Next, identify your natural talents or strengths. These are things that just come naturally to you, or you have always known how to do. For example, I have always been great with animals. It's not something I learned, per se, but it's just a consistent strength or experience I've had throughout my lifetime.

My husband is that way with all things tech. He just innately knows how tech works and can pick up any gadget and quickly figure it out. He's had a career in computers so his long list of skills would include various coding languages, software packages, and hardware. But he was drawn to that career because he's had a natural talent or intelligence since he was a little boy.

Many people enjoy taking the free strengths assessment that comes with the book *StrengthsFinder 2.0* or on the Gallup website (www.gallup.com/cliftonstrengths). They identify 34 strengths divided into four categories: executing, influencing, relationship building, and strategic thinking.

Remember Dr. Howard Gardner's multiple intelligences from chapter 4? Look over the descriptions again on pages 30 to 31. What intelligences do you exhibit? Don't be shy here—it is not boastful to claim your talents and intelligences. These are all potential clues, so take a moment to jot them down.

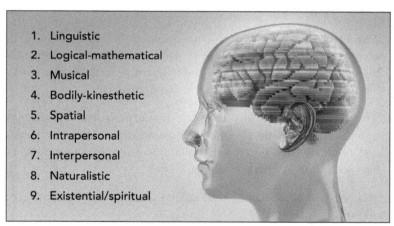

1. Linguistic
2. Logical-mathematical
3. Musical
4. Bodily-kinesthetic
5. Spatial
6. Intrapersonal
7. Interpersonal
8. Naturalistic
9. Existential/spiritual

The nine multiple intelligences

For example, as a child, when I skied or ice skated, I was just good at moving my body and learning by watching others. I picked up on new jumps and spins quicker than my peers, so I know I have bodily-kinesthetic intelligence. Because of my mom, I had to develop the ability to read her moods quickly, and as a result, I developed interpersonal intelligence.

Don't take this activity too seriously—the goal is just to quickly expand the list beyond what you're used to thinking about. It's a way to alter "the story" you might have about yourself and your abilities. This exercise should be fun and relatively quick.

In their book, *The Purpose Factor,* Brian and Gabrielle Bosché introduce the idea of your "natural advantage." They describe it as the natural role you tend to play in life and at work. To determine your type, they recommend asking yourself these three questions: As a kid, what role did you play in your family? What would you do all day if you didn't need money? And why do your friends come to you for advice?

They have identified five types of natural advantages:

- **The Builder:** You love to try new things. People come to you for your ability to craft strategy, provide direction, or create a plan. You enjoy starting projects/organizations/movements.

- **The Truth Teller:** You love to dig into issues and aren't afraid to speak your mind. People come to you for your ability to clarify issues and get to the truth. You enjoy challenging the status quo and are comfortable being strong willed or opinionated.

- **The Teacher:** You love to learn about how things work so you can share your insights with others. People come to you for your insight and to learn better ways of thinking, doing, or living. You enjoy helping others understand.

- **The Overseer:** You love to solve problems, get things organized, and/or support people. People come to you because you take care of them by helping them create a plan and you're attentive to their emotional needs. You enjoy being the person others can depend on.

- **The Recruiter:** You love to share your experiences and connect with others. People come to you for networking or to learn about what you've discovered. You're a natural influencer and enjoy bringing others into your world to share what you love.

Are you one type or do a couple resonate for you? Add your type(s) to your list as additional information.

Pleasures and Preferences

Once you have fleshed out the list as much as you can, it's time to add the layer of your pleasures and preferences because these matter too.

Often, we can get stuck doing things because we are good at them or have just invested a lot of time or money into them. But that doesn't mean that they are your purpose. Look at your pleasures and preferences to get a new perspective.

Go back through your list and mark the skills, talents, intelligences, and advantages that you like. Consider which ones have brought you pleasure, or even joy. Maybe highlight them with a certain color or mark them with a star. If you did the post-it note process, move them into their own area of the wall.

Purpose Story 14:

Just Because You're Good at It Doesn't Mean It's Your Purpose

I graduated from college with a degree in economics/accounting and a minor in computer science. My first job out of school was working as part of the finance team closing the books on $500 million per month in expenses. I worked there for five years and was super successful in the eyes of my different managers, however, I wasn't very happy. Just because you are good at something doesn't mean it will bring you fulfillment.

Accounting wasn't my thing. I found myself gravitating toward doing presentations and being in a place where I could help people grow and learn. I even volunteered to work with a local high school's junior achievement program. But we only know what we know and to me, education was being a high school teacher and I knew I didn't want to do that. Fate intervened and I came across the career planning book *What Color Is My Parachute?* Shortly thereafter I had a new direction...financial planning! I'd get to use my degree and teach people how to save and invest their money.

I soon found myself working in the financial planning industry. I attended their new employee training, and it wasn't long before I realized that I wouldn't be teaching or training clients any time soon. This job was all about sales! Make 10 calls to set 1 appointment and have 10 appointments to make one sale. I was not happy.

What did I do wrong? I had a direction that was aligned with my core beliefs, so why didn't the direction bring me fulfillment? I went back to the book and realized that I had short-changed the process of informational interviews. So off I went to talk to more people about their careers. I ended every interview with the question, "Who else do you know that uses the skills of _____?" They would give me a couple names. In 30 days, I talked to more than 30 people! Through those conversations, I discovered the field of organizational development.

Fast forward several years later and I was getting married. As a ceremonial process for myself, I went off on a solo camping trip and brought all my journals that I had written over the years. As I read through the pages I came upon this entry: "Today I met a super interesting guy. He works for 3M in their organizational development office, and he helped facilitate the process of developing Post-it notes, and he taught at a local university. One day I want to do that."

I was amazed because that's exactly what I was doing. I graduated with my master's degree in organizational behavior and started teaching part time. I was also managing the organizational development department for a medical device company!

Be careful what you wish for—when your purpose is clear it will become the reality.

Consider which ones put you in that flow state that Mihaly Csikszentmihalyi identified, where you lose track of time. He is one of the cofounders of positive psychology and author of *Flow: The Psychology of Optimal Experience*. His research found that optimal performance—that sweet spot where flow happens— lives at the intersection of the skills we have and challenges we face. If our skills are too high for the challenge, we experience boredom, routine, and loss of interest. But when the challenge is too high for our skills, we experience frustration, anxiety, and fear of failure.

When we're in flow, we are engaged, performing well, and fully immersed in what we are doing to the point that we lose track of time. This leads to feelings of ecstasy, motivation, and fulfillment. Csikszentmihalyi says, "The best moments in our lives are not the passive, receptive, relaxing times. The best moments usually occur if a person's body or mind is stretched to its limits in a voluntary effort to accomplish something difficult and worthwhile."

Flyfishing does that for me—it just puts me in sync with nature and the next thing I know, six hours have passed. You know what else puts me in a flow state? Building a presentation slide deck. Putting together the story arc and picking the images to take the learners on that journey is just so fun for me and, again, hours pass by quickly.

Also consider what you would like to do *more* of—your preferences, if you will. If you look at the list as all the options available to you, which ones do you love? If you had no limitations or expectations, what would you pick? Which ones call out to you?

I recommend taking a break at this point to just let it all sit for a bit. We're practicing the ways to induce insight from p. 29. Go for a quick walk, grab a snack, take a nap. Taking a break gives our brain space to noodle and form new connections. It can be a short break or a longer one if your life is busy. Tomorrow or the next day is fine too.

After you've had a break, come back and look at the list or the wall of post-its. Step back and look at the bigger picture. Do you see any patterns? Are they pointing you toward something? Are they moving you away from something? What do you notice?

If all these things (skills, talents, intelligences, and pleasures) are hints for you—messages from the universe or your purpose—what are they trying to say? Jot down your thoughts and observations. We're not looking for a big "aha!" moment here, just making room to see things in a new way.

Your Learning Journey

Take a few minutes to reflect on your own experiences with the concepts from this section.

- This section offered you a range of tools to explore. Which ones did you enjoy the most and why?
- What new insights did you gain about yourself?
- Looking at Hudson's model, what phase are you currently in?
- As you did the timeline activity, what stories have shaped how you see yourself? Which stories are not serving you or are interfering with your path to purpose?
- What new information did you gain about your skills, experiences, talents, and intelligences?
- What are some things you want to dig into more in the coming weeks? Set aside some time on your calendar to do that.

EXPLORING PURPOSE +
MEANINGFUL WORK

"Work gives you meaning and purpose, and life is empty without it."

Dr. Stephen Hawking (1942–2018),
astrophysicist and author,
Brief Answers to the Big Questions
and *The Theory of Everything*

14. Purpose and Meaning at Work

Given that we spend nearly one-third of our lives at work, it's no surprise that people view it as a major component in their quest for a sense of purpose in life. Behind sleeping, work comprises the next largest use of our time. Consider these statistics:

- One in five adults (19 percent) feel uncertain about their work and one in six (16 percent) feel trapped
- Nearly half (48 percent) feel stressed at work regularly and one-third feel overwhelmed at work
- 26 percent of all employees feel anxious about work (35 percent of Millennials and 40 percent of Gen Z workers)

Studies from many researchers over the past few decades show some consistent findings and frameworks that can help us all. What we know for sure is that meaning matters.

Meaning vs. Meaningful

Researchers distinguish meaning and meaningfulness as two different things.

- **Meaning is largely descriptive and is a mental representation of the relationships among things.** As we navigate our day, we naturally assign meaning to our experiences. For example, how would you answer if I ask you, "What is the meaning of work?" Some of you might say that it's how we earn a paycheck, others might say it's a series of jobs and promotions that make up a career, and others might say it's part of the economic system that provides goods and services to society.

   Meaning comes from what we are told by major influencers in our lives like our parents, teachers, and the media. They give us our first frameworks and definitions and an original set of values. My guess is that some of your views of work came from your parents' beliefs about, and experiences with, their own jobs.

- **Meaningfulness is evaluative—it's the amount of significance we give something.** We can think of it as a continuum with meaningful on one end and meaningless on the other. You can place various experiences on that continuum but it's *your* continuum, very personal, subjective, and unique to you.

MEANINGLESS ⟵——————————⟶ MEANINGFUL

So, what you define as meaningful work can be very different from another person, even when you hold a similar job or work at the same organization.

Because it's evaluative, it is also shaped by societal influences. In order to effectively explore this topic, we need to get clear on three concepts and how they are different:

- **Meaning OF work:** How you perceive the overall concept of work
- **Meaning IN work:** How meaningful that work is to you, specifically
- **Meaning AT work:** More narrowly defined as the context of that specific job in that particular organization

We are going to focus on meaning IN work—what makes work meaningful to people—but will explore meaning AT work in section VI.

Elements of Meaningful Work

Before we explore the large body of research on what makes work meaningful, take a few minutes right now to think back over your various jobs and careers. For the ones that were the most meaningful to you, what factors contributed to that evaluation? Take a moment to jot them down.

Studies about meaningful work began in the 1970s and have continued and increased over time—mirroring our human need for meaningful work and the desire of executives and human resource practitioners to find the formula that attracts and retains top talent.

Researchers found four main factors that represent the most robust or consistent findings (presented here in no particular order).

Job design

The first factor is job design, which includes the following elements:

- **Variety:** A range of tasks or skills so work does not become routine or boring

- **Autonomy:** Having some say or influence about how one approaches a task or the job

- **Challenge:** The role offers an opportunity to work at one's edge and helps you to grow or develop to your potential

- **Significance:** The task or role is perceived as having some benefit or meaning (as opposed to being pointless)

- **Status:** The work confers some level of status or influence

Workplace relationships

Several studies find that when we enjoy working with our colleagues it contributes to our sense of meaningful work. One researcher found that today's workers have "increasingly porous work-life boundaries," which means this second factor is taking on more significance over time.

Work can also create a powerful sense of belonging for people. Many find that recognition from their peers is an important element of meaningful work, as is "serving others" or work that impacts others, whether that is on a team, within an organization, or part of society as a whole.

Leadership and management

This third factor represents the influence that leaders and managers play in creating or undermining a sense of meaning that people find in their work.

- **Transformational leadership:** A particular style where leaders focus on inspiring employees to work toward a shared vision, as they celebrate efforts and catalyze change

- **Strong leader/member exchanges:** Frequent and transparent communication that builds rapport and trust

- **Manager/supervisor support:** A focus on authentic conversations and supporting employee success (another body of research indicates abusive or divisive managers directly reduce meaningfulness at work)

- **Manager recognition:** Studies show that recognition and celebrating accomplishments boost meaningfulness and contribute to employees feeling like efforts and time spent are worthwhile

As one study described it, "Managers are people who can destroy or challenge the attempts of individuals to find work meaningful."

Organization

Finally, we have the organizational level, where work is done to benefit the greater good through a self-transcendent or purpose-driven orientation. For example, organizations in healthcare, education, nonprofit work, spirituality, and the environment.

Benefits of Meaningful Work

Beyond a doubt, the plethora of studies showing robust results on the benefits of meaningful work demonstrate its importance for the well-being of people and organizations. We now have a clear picture that when people have meaningful work, good things increase, and challenging things decrease, as indicated by these compelling findings:

- **Attitudes:** Meaningful work is shown to increase attitudes like job satisfaction and enjoyment, commitment to the organization, engagement, and both intrinsic motivation and reward.

  As we learned in chapter 6, engagement is crucial for organizations. International research firm Gallup estimates that one disengaged employee costs an organization approximately $3,400 for every $10,000 or 34 percent of their salary.

- **Behaviors:** Researchers find that behaviors change when we have meaningful work, including lowered levels of absenteeism (tardiness or missing work) as well as intention to quit. Absenteeism alone yields significant savings for any organization. According to the US Centers for Disease Control, it costs employers $225.8 billion annually, or about $1,685 per employee. And the Society for Human Resource Management (SHRM) estimates that turnover costs 50 percent to 250 percent of annual salary plus benefits (the difference being how senior or technical the role).

- **Performance:** Meaningful work also boosts performance across a variety of measures, including customer satisfaction, knowledge sharing, creativity, and organizational citizenship behavior. Any improvement or productivity can yield significant results for organizations. Even a shift by 1 percent can yield results worth millions of dollars.

- **Well-being:** Having meaningful work reaps many rewards for individuals, including an increase in positive self-concept, life satisfaction, feelings of accomplishment, growth, happiness, work-to-family enrichment, and satisfaction in romantic relationships.

  Another study found when we experience meaningful work we experience that state of flow where time seems to stop, as opposed to meaningless work that feels like it's wasting our time and energy. Several studies show that meaningful work contributes to our overall well-being and leads to reductions in stress and depression levels.

  Considering the incredible damage caused by mental health struggles, ensuring that more people experience meaningful work could generate incredible benefits for organizations and society as a whole.

Models of Meaningful Work

From several researchers exploring meaningful work, six useful frameworks have emerged. As you read these summaries, consider which shed light on your current and past experiences.

Map of meaningful work

Let's start at the individual level and how we perceive or define meaningful work. Dr. Marjolein Lips-Wiersma, a professor at Auckland University of Technology in New Zealand, studies the nexus of meaningful work, sustainability, and well-being. She found four sources, or areas, that contribute to us feeling that work is meaningful:
- Developing and becoming our full self, which includes personal growth and being true to ourselves and our integrity
- Expressing our full potential through creating, influencing, using our strengths, and achieving our goals
- Unity with others by working together, sharing values, and having a sense of belonging
- Serving others by meeting the needs of humanity and making a difference

The four can be placed on two axes: one ranging from Self to Others and the other from Doing to Being. A meaningful life, then, is about finding the right balance, which is unique to each of us. In the center is our sense of purpose, or what inspires us. From her research, Lips-Wiersma created this map of meaningful work, which we can use in several ways.

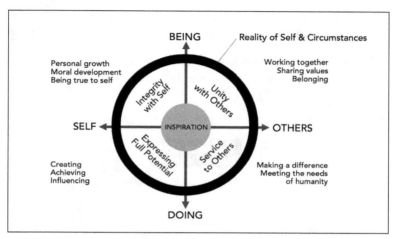

Lips-Wiersma's Map of Meaningful Work

First, she recommends reflecting on the past couple of weeks and placing your experiences in the various quadrants. What insight does it give you about how you are spending your time?

Next, is there an appropriate balance between self and others or is one more actively expressed? What about being and doing—are any adjustments needed? Finally, explore how your sense of purpose influences the four zones. Are the connections strong and clear or do you need to refocus anything?

Davin Salvagno, in his book *Finding Purpose at Work*, adds some more insights: "When we focus on our purpose, we fulfill our potential and experience high performance in all that we do, and we experience joy." He believes that the intersection of our potential and performance creates four zones. (1) When performance and potential are high, we are on purpose and experience joy. (2) When performance is high but potential is low, we experience indifference. (3) When our potential is high but our performance is low, we experience frustration and, (4) sadly, the outcome of low performance and low potential are feelings of depression. What feelings do you have in these four zones?

Meaningful work triangle
Dr. Neal Chalofsky, a renowned scholar in the study of meaningful work, has published many academic studies and authored the book, *Meaningful Workplaces: Reframing How and Where We Work*. His model emerged from a multiyear study and takes a larger view of meaningful work as the interplay between three areas:

- **Sense of self** is our path to self-actualization and includes our values, what we enjoy doing, our strengths, and what gives us a sense of purpose or meaning in our life.

- **The work itself** is the job and our path to excellence. It includes elements like how much autonomy or empowerment we have in our job, if we have opportunities to learn and grow that allow us to show mastery in our performance, and if it gives us a sense of fulfilling our purpose.

- **The sense of balance** is how we feel in terms of our time, involvement, satisfaction, and ability to manage the natural tensions of work and life, and also the job and our career.

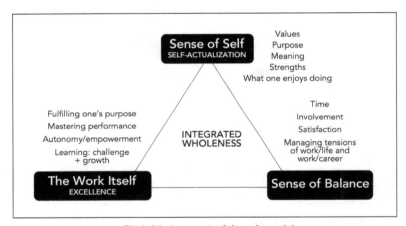

Chalofsky's meaningful work model

Ultimately, Dr. Chalofsky claims, meaningful work is about achieving integrated wholeness between these three parts of the triangle.

Again, you can treat the model as a tool for assessment. Take some notes about your experiences in the three parts of the triangle. What do you notice? Do any areas of your sense of self or the work itself need attention? What areas are strong? And how do you feel about the sense of balance? What is working and what needs to shift?

Multilevel factors
Meaningful work doesn't just happen out of the blue—it's the result of several factors. One cornerstone study was conducted by researchers from Purdue University, Colorado State University, Vrije Universiteit Amsterdam, and the University of Florida.

They identified four different levels at which meaningful work can be influenced: the individual, the job, the organization, and society. They synthesized the results of many different studies within each level and noted what factors positively influenced meaningful work and which ones detracted or decreased it.

For example, individual factors included disposition (positive attitude, conscientiousness, strengths), characteristics (intrinsic motivation, motivation for service, and greater good), and personal narratives (shared experiences, autonomy, and identity).

Job level factors include type, quality, and amount of work. This also included things like safe and fair conditions, and whether resources and development opportunities felt limited or restricted. Another factor was job design, including task significance, autonomy, and the ability to customize one's job thorough job crafting.

There were four factors at the organizational level:

- **Leadership:** Using transformational leadership practices, behaving ethically, communicating the organization's mission, and creating a sense of meaning

- **Culture:** This includes elements that support employees, are ethical in nature, and encourage innovation

- **Policies and practices:** Corporate social responsibility (CSR) and volunteering live here, as do HR practices that focus on engaging and developing employees

- **Social context of work:** Good or positive workplace relationships and a social and moral climate

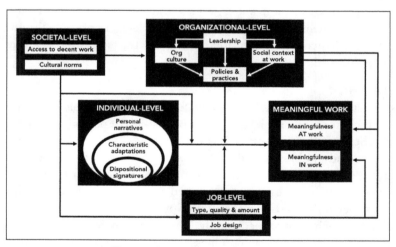

Factors that foster meaningful work

Finally, the societal level included whether people had access to "decent work," which included elements like access to healthcare, adequate compensation, and hours that allow for free time and rest. The other factor was cultural norms, which included whether there was an emphasis on, or pathway for, individual fulfillment and well-being.

This analysis allowed them to build a framework showing how these elements influence each other, so individuals and organizational leaders have a way to see and understand how these elements are interconnected, as well as starting places to introduce change or interrupt unproductive patterns. More importantly, we can explore the concept of "fit" between the person and the job, as well as the person and the organization. For example, a person might find great meaning in their job because they enjoy the tasks they work on and/or the people with whom they work. But they may still struggle because the organization's culture is insensitive to their needs. Consider these comments by the authors:

> *When individuals seeking greater challenge at work find themselves underemployed in their current job (that is, doing tasks or jobs that do not match their qualifications), they might experience lower work meaningfulness.*

> *Individuals high on prosocial motivation working in jobs that do not allow them to make an impact on the lives of beneficiaries (for example, coworkers, supervisors, clients, or customers) may also experience challenges in their work meaningfulness.*

> *Individuals concerned with the conservation and protection of the natural environment or with high moral identity are likely to experience greater meaningful work in organizations that implement CSR policies and practices.*

To summarize, meaningful work is an individual experience that tends to occur when someone's motivations, values, and goals are congruent with those of their environment (job, organization, and society). Look at the model and review which elements have contributed to and detracted from your experience of meaningful work.

Fit and flow model

Not surprisingly, many other researchers find that when people have a good fit between their needs and a job, as in either person-job or person-organization fit, they experience greater meaningful work.

Another study, published in the 2020 *Journal of Applied Psychology*, did a deeper dive into the impact of a poor fit between a person and the organization. The researchers wanted to test what happened when there was a misalignment between a person's needs for meaningful work and what they could access in their job, which they termed supply. They particularly focused on people's responses, assuming that meaningfulness would capture people's attention, and they would be aware and psychologically present to their experience and the work. The opposite reaction would be fatigue or a lack of desire for continuing the task at hand because it drained the person's energy.

They found that the match or fit consistently predicted people's responses. When our needs for meaningful work match the supply we have access to, people are highly attentive and engaged. But when the fit is wrong, we experience boredom (from too little meaning) or burnout (from too much supply). This implies there is an ideal zone or window where people gain the most benefit, like Goldilocks tasting the porridge that is "just right."

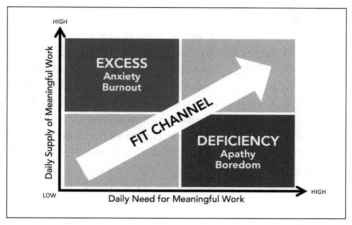

Fit and flow model of meaningful work.

Another study identified that meaningful work fit impacts our mental health, which exists on a continuum from languishing to flourishing with moderate mental health in the middle. It's clear that finding the right fit is critical for us to enjoy work and for our well-being.

LANGUISHING  FLOURISHING

The concept of meaning "fit" is relevant to our experience of the pandemic. Healthcare workers are known for having a high sense of purpose in their work and, generally, a good fit with their need for meaning (the ability to help people heal) and its supply (the regular load at a hospital or clinic). But the pandemic significantly overloaded the supply of meaning, especially in the early days before there were vaccines or treatments. Healthcare workers all over the world found themselves facing the extraordinarily difficult task of caring for people who were dying in record numbers and for which their normal skills and tools were woefully ineffective.

Many caregivers spoke of how disheartened and depressed they felt (languishing) along with the extremely high levels of burnout they experienced. Even a one-time event can be impactful. One ER nurse who worked during the 2017 mass shooting in Las Vegas said, "I loved being a nurse. But I just couldn't work in the ER anymore."

It's clear that the fit between a person's sense of purpose, their job, and their organization plays a vital role. Consider the fit you have had with previous jobs and organizations. Was there a balance between the supply and your own needs? If not, what was out of balance and how did that imbalance impact you?

Also consider the times you have been in the flow state. What does that tell you about the fit you were experiencing?

Spirituality at work
Many scholars focusing on religiosity and spirituality have explored this concept but a clear model has not yet emerged. The topic is just so broad. However, we do see an emergence of three common themes in the research so far: meaningful work, a sense of community, and the person's "inner life."

While scholars are not aligned around one shared definition, they are exploring potential benefits for employees, including intuition and creativity, honesty and trust, commitment, organizational performance, job satisfaction, intention to quit, organizational citizenship behavior, ethics, stress, and well-being.

Even though the research is still too varied to share a concrete model, those of you who identify as spiritual or religious may want to explore the research. I recommend the article "The What, Why, and How of Spirituality in the Workplace Revisited: A 14-year Update and Extension" by Dr. Jeff Houghton (West Virginia University), Dr. Chris Neck (Arizona State University), and Dr. Sukumarakurup Krishnakumar (Keck Graduate Institute), published in the *Journal of Management, Spirituality and Religion* (2016).

I also recommend these books written with a focus of spirituality:
- *Spirit at Work: Discovering the Spirituality in Leadership* by Jay Conger
- *The Purpose Driven Life: What on Earth Am I Here For?* by Rev. Rick Warren
- *Your Purpose Is Calling: Your Difference Is Your Destiny* by Dr. Dharius Daniels
- *You On Purpose: Discover Your Calling and Create the Life You Were Meant to Live* by Dr. Stephanie Shackelford and Bill Denzel
- *A Life at Work: The Joy of Discovering What You Were Born to Do* by Thomas Moore
- *Let Your Life Speak: Listening for the Voice of Vocation* by Parker Palmer
- *The Four Purposes of Life: Finding Meaning and Direction in a Changing World* by Dan Millman

Ikigai model
The last and most holistic model comes from Japan and represents a philosophy of life as well as a way to create meaningful work.

Ikigai (pronounced "eye-ka-guy") translates to "reason to live" or "reason for being." This concept is woven into the very fabric of Japanese culture and aligns directly with eudaimonic well-being. In fact, one study by Dr. Michiko Kumano explored how ikigai compared with another core value of shiawase, which aligns with happiness. She states, "This study verifies that, for Japanese, feeling shiawase is close to hedonic well-being and feeling ikigai is close to eudaimonic well-being."

Like the studies on purpose we reviewed, many scholars have explored ikigai's benefits. Studies included participants from Eastern and Western cultures, showing that it's not about the person's culture or ethnicity but whether they embrace the ikigai concept.

One 2022 study by Dr. Juliet Wilkes and colleagues, found that ikigai was positively correlated with participants' well-being and negatively correlated with depression and anxiety. Another study of 50,000 participants discovered that ikigai reduced risks for cardiovascular disease and its related mortality. A separate study found that ikigai reduces age-related dementia and cognitive decline.

Purpose Story 15:
The Path to Ikigai
I was a recruiting manager and had been leading my first team for a little over a year. I realized that my purpose and my work were not aligned, and every day I dreaded going to work. There were many aspects of people and branch management that I did not like. I took this time to take a step back and rate my job responsibilities based on what gave me the most joy and the least.

At the top of the list were coaching and developing my team, and I realized if I could do this at a larger scale I would be much more connected to my purpose. At the time I was also working for a nonprofit as a director, where I not only led a team but taught dance classes and had to come up with fun and creative ways to engage large groups of people on a regular basis. I started looking for opportunities to coach and develop others in fun and creative ways and this led me to take a step back in my career to join the learning and development team in my company. I immediately connected with my purpose and it showed through the way I facilitated classes and thought about the learner's journey. That step back in my career ended up being a gigantic leap forward because when my purpose connected to my work, my passion and commitment was clear to everyone around me.

When I was coaching or facilitating I felt and still feel myself go into "the zone." I could do what I'm doing for hours (and I often do). At the time when I was first discovering this, I would get excited about the challenges around coaching and creating memorable learning experiences, and that was a huge indicator to me that I should be doing more of that.

I actually didn't immediately move to learning and development. I first piloted the career of a college professor by becoming a research assistant. This helped clarify to me that it wasn't just about teaching, it was the act of spending the majority of my time helping others grow and develop that was core to my purpose. Turns out I don't get joy from doing research but taking the research that others do and making it digestible and using it to help others grow is more aligned with my purpose.

I would not be nearly as happy or successful as I am today if I hadn't taken the time to actually figure out my purpose and how to do more of it. It wasn't until recently that I had a manager who actually had a purpose conversation with me, and thinking about it now, I feel like this is going to be something even more important for leaders to do as the nature of management evolves. My purpose has thus evolved to not just coaching and developing others, but helping other leaders to do the same.

I don't have research to back this up, but I think often people get stuck believing that they can only have one purpose. This is just one example of a purpose I've found a way to live in my life. I have two businesses that each help me live another purpose I've discovered and connected for myself. My husband and I have put together a family crest to represent our values as a family and help members of the family connect their purpose to how they contribute to the family and the world. I find the concept of purpose, or ikigai in my culture, fascinating because it can connect so many aspects of our lives.

Finally, ikigai helps people heal from tragedy and loss. One study of the victims of the 2011 earthquake and resulting tsunami that devastated Japan—leaving 20,000 people dead and nearly 500,000 homeless—found that ikigai helped people cope with stress, grief, and trauma.

Dan Buettner, in his book *The Blue Zones: Lessons for Living from the People Who've Lived the Longest*, specifically calls out ikigai as a source for why Okinawans have such long life spans. Japan has seen its share of tragedy, especially during World War II, but ikigai allows a person to see beyond their current situation, even if it is fraught with misery, to look forward to the future.

While purpose or reason for being is at the heart of ikigai, from it springs many aspects of purpose in life, including meaningful work. And perhaps this model's greatest contribution is to expand the range of sources through which we all can find and express a sense of purpose.

The model is a Venn diagram where ikigai sprouts out into four overlapping areas: what you love (passion), what you are good at (talent), what the world needs (meaning), and what you can be paid for (vocation). These four areas create four intersections: (1) The intersection of what you love and what you are good at is play. (2) The intersection of what you are good at and what you can be paid for is your profession. (3) The intersection of what you can be paid for and what the world needs is your service. And (4) the intersection of what the world needs and what you love is your mission.

Finally, those four segments—play, profession, service, and mission—overlap to create four more intersections of challenges we'll face if we don't have ikigai, or purpose, at the center.

The goal is to live a life that has all of these elements so that you have a full and holistic sense of completeness. I especially like that our work life is one aspect but not the *only* aspect of a full life.

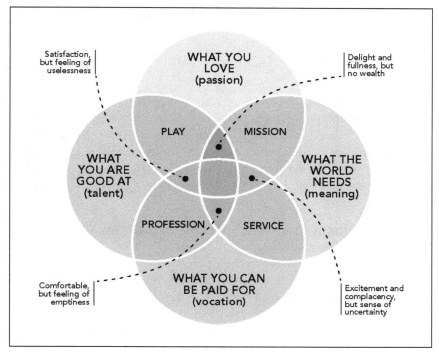

The ikigai model

I encourage you to use this diagram as a diagnostic tool and write down where your experiences land on the model. Consider the fullness of your life: work, hobbies and interests, volunteerism, family and friends, neighborhood and community, etc. What did you notice? What can you build? Are there any areas that need your attention?

Together, these six models give us a more complete picture of meaningful work and the role it plays in helping us develop a clear sense of our purpose in life. Use them to inform your reflection of past work experiences and to guide your choices around future work opportunities.

15. The 5 Paradoxes of Meaningful Work

Trigger Warning: This chapter touches on the subject
of suicide, which some readers might find difficult.

As we continue to explore the concepts of purpose, having a purpose in life, and meaningful work, we clearly see several myths and paradoxes at play. These can alter our perception of what is possible, and our own journey of discovery.

A paradox is when two seemingly opposite ideas are both true at the same time. The paradoxes of meaningful work arise so often in the research that the *Journal of Management Studies* devoted an entire issue to exploring them. As we look at the most common ones, consider which have impacted you over the course of your career.

Paradox #1: What we define as meaningful is personal, yet shaped by others.

We have already discovered that what we perceive to be meaningful, significant, or worthy is a deeply personal definition. And yet, those definitions are strongly influenced by others. Our families of origin and childhood cultures bathed us in messages about what jobs were worth doing and what careers were respected. That can create great challenges when we find ourselves unfulfilled by the path we were encouraged to pursue. Or worse, when we find great joy in the one that we were told to avoid.

Part of the journey to and through adulthood is developing *our own* set of values and beliefs based on our life experiences, so it's a natural part of the process to diverge from those who influenced us early on. But that doesn't mean it is easy or comfortable.

In addition, because of how history has unfolded thus far, all of us are influenced by societal values that are primarily male, white, Western, and Christian. This adds layers of value judgment onto careers. For example, jobs that have been gendered, labeled "women's work," like teaching or nursing.

Jobs have also been "mainstreamed" to fit the values of the predominant culture. Many children of immigrants feel pressure to pursue careers that their parents perceive will best set them up for success in the new homeland. The powerful pressure to assimilate pushes people away from their traditions to the careers that are seen as most profitable or respected in the new country.

Economic factors also play a role because of the wages or salaries assigned to jobs and even industries. Feeling that your work has value or worth in the eyes of others is shaped by many factors, including how much you are paid, the kind of support and benefits you receive, and the safety you feel.

Essential and nonessential workers
Even during the pandemic, employees were categorized as "essential" or "nonessential." "Essential" employees were pushed into an intensive time of high productivity, asked to work longer shifts in dangerous conditions. Getting

breaks and downtime was difficult, if not impossible. Many even chose to live separately from their family for fear of exposing them to the coronavirus.

While many essential workers felt that their work had purpose and meaning, the overwhelming pressures of the pandemic caused many to experience significant amounts of exhaustion, burnout, and other mental health challenges.

Those deemed "nonessential" experienced another kind of toll: Many were laid off entirely, losing income and medical insurance during a global health crisis. Many of those who kept their jobs still questioned their value under a label that suggests low level of importance. According to one study from the Netherlands, these labels affect people's perceptions of their own work: "The study found that employees who were not working during lockdown, or whose work hours were reduced sharply, perceived their job as contributing less to the greater good, identified less strongly with their organization, and experienced more job insecurity compared with those who retained a large percentage of their work activities." In addition, the longer people were in lockdown, these perceptions continued to grow.

Interestingly, the authors also found that when people felt that they didn't matter, the more they engaged in cyber-incivility against the organization and coworkers. Several studies show that experiencing incivility at work creates emotional exhaustion and decreases our motivation. While having a sense of meaningful work can buffer this effect, it can only do so much.

Feeling valued means that you matter and it further shapes what we perceive to be meaningful.

Paradox #2: We are each on our own path of fulfillment and self-actualization, yet it requires the support of others to make happen.

While finding and living one's purpose is largely about finding inner alignment, we often cannot get there without the support and even direct approval from influential people along the way, including parents, teachers, and managers.

If you knew at an early age your purpose was to work with animals, you'd still have the run the gauntlet of parental approval. ("That won't pay very much, so you should do something else.") Or teachers who might shape your view of your skills and options. ("That career requires a lot of math and science, which you're not good at. You should pick something else.") Or managers or bosses who evaluate your performance and set your career on a trajectory. ("We think you are better suited to this other role" or "We don't think you have management potential.")

Fulfilling one's purpose, then, is often a journey of fighting against all these forces rather than just tuning in and listening to what feels right. That fight can be exhausting and overwhelming, and may take decades.

Interestingly, research shows that while *all* the working generations seek purpose and meaning at work, they define it differently. One study by doctors Kelly Weeks and Catilin Schaffert found these differences in how members of the different generations define meaningful work. (Note: Members of Gen Z were not included because they were just entering the adult workforce when the study was conducted in 2018 but I have added definitions from a different study to this table.)

Generation	Definitions of Meaningful Work	
Gen Z (1997-2012)	Purpose Serving others and social good	Values-driven work cultures Equality and environment
Millennials (1981-1996)	Nice coworkers Serving others	Seeing lives improved Personal happiness
Gen X (1965-1980)	Working with good people Work-life balance	Pursue individual goals
Baby Boomers (1946-1964)	Success Helping others achieve goals	Reaching personal goals
Silent (1928-1945)	Challenging work Self satisfaction with work	Helping others Org values align with own values

Generational definitions of meaningful work

More importantly, the researchers found that members of each generation perceive the other generations negatively for not sharing the same view, and often held assumptions in error. For example, Millennials perceived that Baby Boomers "just work for money" while "helping others achieve their goals" is in the top three for Boomers. And Gen Xers perceived that Millennials "are more concerned with their personal life" when "serving others" and "seeing lives improved" were part of their top four.

These definitions and misperceptions can play out within families, among coworkers, and between managers/leaders and their employees, impacting how fulfilled we feel and how much we support others.

Paradox #3: We must find our own sense of meaning at work, yet leaders control the conditions.

Meaningful work, while defined by the employee, is heavily influenced and even controlled by the organization's leaders. They communicate whether a role or project is meaningful in numerous ways: It's given a title that indicates some aspect of meaning, as do the pay and benefits or resources. It's conveyed by where it sits in the organization's hierarchy, whether it warrants an office, and its level of influence on projects or budgets.

The organization's overall vision, mission, and values also play critical roles. Are they clearly articulated and easy to find? Do they even exist? And how easy is it for the employee to make a direct connection between their role or project and that vision?

A big part of finding meaning at work lives in the day-to-day interactions with your direct supervisor. Do they treat you with kindness and respect? Do they care about you as a person? Do they have the skills to create psychological safety? Or to coach you so you can reach your highest performance and fullest potential?

Policies and practices also matter. One aspect concerns corporate social responsibility (CSR), but other policies also matter. Are employees trusted to make decisions and given access to resources or do leaders view employees with suspicion? Are managers given training on how to provide coaching or build psychological safety? How often are managers evaluated and how is their success measured? If the organization is not analyzing employee engagement, turnover, and performance and tying them to the manager's performance, then they are not creating a culture of accountability.

All these factors contribute to an organization's overall culture and climate and are largely in the hands of the senior leaders. The good news is that leaders can take many actions to create a phenomenal workplace where employees are happy and fulfilled. We'll dig into this more in section VI.

As employees, it's our responsibility to know what we need to thrive and seek out the right fit as we apply and interview for a job. We'll explore more tools and strategies for finding the right fit in chapter 22. But we can only learn so much through that process. Once we start on our first day, we experience the *actual* organization and not just how it advertises itself to job seekers. It's on us to notice any discrepancies and our raise concerns. And, ultimately, to make the choice to leave if we need to.

Purpose Story 16:
Know When to Cut Your Losses
A couple years ago, I took a new job that perfectly aligned with my sense of purpose. I left a comfortable, well-paying job for something completely different, running an NGO in another country for almost no pay but with a mission that truly called to me.

For the previous 10 years, I funded my vacations by volunteering with medical and dental NGOs; so why not flip my life and live my vacation?

The team I was leading at the NGO was comprised of 25 foreign fellowships—staff who filled roles in logistics, medicine, pharmacy, and hospitality for multi-month assignments. Our daily work was to plan and execute medical clinics in remote villages spread out across an archipelago, providing acute illness/injury treatment, ongoing family planning, chronic disease management, and referrals to the Ministry of Health for conditions that needed more advanced intervention.

If this would have been the actual work, I would have "found my calling" and be living a life where my work and individual values aligned in harmony—advocating for and assisting a community to thrive in health. Instead, what I experienced was managing of an international team of short-term employees whose individual purpose was hedonistic and selfish in nature.

Each Sunday evening, as the team returned from the local tourist town to our base to prepare for the week, I was sure to have HR issues to address from the team's weekend escapades. The issues ranged from physical and sexual assault to arrests by the local police, or an injury from a drunken tumble out of a second-story window. During the week, while operating clinics, the team had a hard time adhering to World Health Organization standards of practice or conducting research.

Needless to say, I was not living my purpose. Instead, I was spending 90 percent of my time addressing the immature, unprofessional, and unethical behaviors of my colleagues.

I worked hard to communicate the misalignment with the board of directors. They said they heard the issues and would address them or support me doing what I could on my end. We developed an action plan and timeline to move the work toward the mission, but staff continued to undermine the efforts. I thought that if I was able to address the bad behavior by turning over the staff, new staff whose values aligned with mine would take their place and I could do the real work that the organization intended. But after six months of trying and no movement on the action plan, my purpose floated farther and farther away.

This experience helped put the context of insider versus outsider into context when it comes to community service. Being an outsider played a significant role in my feeling unsuccessful in this job. As an outsider, your role is to advocate and assist the inside community to lift themselves lest you run the risk of acting the "colonial white savior." But when everyone on our team did not see this view, the infighting and conflict took its toll to the detriment of the organization.

Ultimately, I had to make the difficult decision to leave the organization. My values are intact and my purpose to serve my community has never been stronger. It's just done in a different way than I envisioned when joining the NGO. But I learned that I was capable of some incredible things: making unpopular decisions, being the sole dissenting voice in a conversation, delivering tough messages and, maybe most importantly, that there are some key values I can't bend on like integrity, responsibility, and advocacy.

Paradox #4: We have an innate drive to seek meaningful work and purpose, yet this same drive can push us to harmful excesses.

I found it interesting that several researchers commented on "the dark side" of purpose, with many studies even using this term in their title.

One set of studies found that people who feel deeply connected to their sense of purpose, believing that it is their "calling," are willing to endure significant hardships, both physical and mental. For example, frequently overworking and not being able to create or hold appropriate boundaries. This leads to physical exhaustion and burnout, both of which harm physical and mental health.

Another study found that people with a deep sense of purpose have a high level of work devotion, but can be willing to accept poor, unsafe, or abusive working conditions in pursuit of making a difference. These can also lead to physical and mental harm and a decrease in overall well-being.

Not surprisingly, having a deep sense of purpose can sometimes take a toll on personal relationships. Dr. Carrie Oelberger found that overworking and the inability to hold work/life boundaries often creates conflicts about time and trust at home with loved ones. This can be worsened if the partner doesn't share the same value for, or find the same meaning in, the work. She states, "This disconnection-based conflict compounds the time- and trust-based conflict and engenders an emotionally agonizing situation—a context I call work-relationship turmoil." However, when the partner shares the same value in the work, it can foster emotional connection.

Finally, there is a significant body of research on the damage done when our sense of values or moral beliefs are violated. It's called moral injury or moral harm and it can lead to serious consequences. The National Center for PTSD has this to say:

> *In traumatic or unusually stressful circumstances, people may perpetrate, fail to prevent, or witness events that contradict deeply held moral beliefs and expectations. Moral injury is the distressing psychological, behavioral, social, and sometimes spiritual aftermath of exposure to such events.*

The hallmark reactions of moral injury are guilt, shame, disgust, and anger. Moral injury is the wound but it can manifest as PTSD, impacting physical and emotional well-being and even increasing the risk of suicide.

Moral injury can show up in many ways. It can harm a person's self-concept, driving negative self-talk of fault or failure. It can harm relationships by creating disconnection, loss of trust, "unforgivability," and ultimately severing ties. It can cause a range of difficult emotions and a loss of self-control or the ability to calm down. And it can lead to questioning our sense of good in the world or believing that life has no meaning.

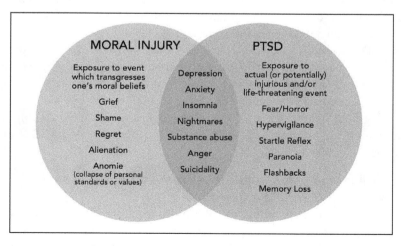

The relationship between moral injury and PTSD

Many purpose-driven careers have a risk for moral injury, including military service, social work, refugee/international aid work, teaching, and healthcare. For example, veterinarians have a high risk for moral injury because of the high rates at which they are asked to euthanize healthy animals. They also must euthanize animals for which they have provided long-term care and manage the grief of their clients, their staff, and themselves. This leads to a high rate of suicide among vets, as well as coworkers in nonclinical roles.

Many healthcare workers on the frontlines of the pandemic suffered moral injury. The deadly, fast-moving virus, coupled with a lack of resources (PPE, treatment options), led to daily difficult decisions and high death tolls.

One Duke University study found that during the pandemic healthcare workers had similar rates of moral injury as military combat veterans. Suicide among healthcare workers, particularly nurses, is also on the rise. Many healthcare organizations are focusing on employee mental health including reducing and preventing moral injury.

Having a lack of purpose can harm us too. As doctors Frank Martela and Anne Pessi wrote in an article for *Frontiers in Psychology*, "Human beings are hardwired to seek meaning and a lack of meaning is seen as a serious psychological deprivation associated with depression, mortality, and even suicide ideation."

While suicide rates have declined 5 percent since 2018 in the US, they had risen 36 percent from 2000 to 2018. During that period, suicidal thoughts and behaviors had doubled for 18- to 34-year-olds and tripled for youth under 18. Another area of concern is among middle-age white women whose rate of suicide increased 82 percent for those ages 45 to 54 and 92 percent for 55 to 64. Native Americans have the highest suicide rate of all groups in the US and men commit suicide at a rate of 4 times greater than women.

I realize this section is difficult to read so it feels important to remind us all to reach out for help when we are struggling. There are services, both local and national, like the US National Suicide and Crisis Lifeline at 988lifeline.org or the international website Befrienders.org.

Also, it's important to reach out and check on others, even if they appear to be doing fine. In fact, some of the people who are struggling the most are the ones who appear to be the happiest. Those same resources provide support to anyone concerned about someone else.

Finding and living a sense of purpose and meaningful work is important for our well-being but it must be balanced with appropriate boundaries and an abundance of support.

Paradox #5: Meaning and purpose create a pervasive sense of value, yet ebb and flow over time.

While our purpose might shine like the North Star, guiding us in a constant direction, there are days when it's covered by the clouds and harder to see. Or we're blown off course by strong winds, despite our desire and best intentions to stay on track. In particular, our experience of meaningful work can shift day by day, and even hour by hour, depending on the nature of the tasks, who we are working with, the organization's culture, and our own needs that day.

For example, I absolutely love researching and writing so I am quite happy as I type this sentence. But, tomorrow, I have to check all the citations to make sure they are accurately formatted. Ugh. Next week, I will deliver a keynote on my research, and I absolutely love connecting with an audience. But waking up at 3 a.m. to catch that flight east, not so much. Overall, my work is highly meaningful to me (I'm so grateful for that!), and that makes the annoying bits easier to manage. But if I had a high annoying-to-meaningful ratio, I might consider another path or make tweaks to my current one.

This is true for each of us. We must assess what we need to thrive and find the best ratio or mix for us. Living on purpose is not all rainbows and puppies 24/7—sometimes the work is hard and the challenges are overwhelming. But a strong sense of purpose and meaning carries you through.

Your own journey needs to include regular moments of assessment and reflection. When things are going well, take note of your emotions and what makes the work feel meaningful. Also consider how it expresses your sense of purpose. And when things dip, take an even closer look at what shifted. The levels we discussed in the last chapter are helpful:

- **Individual:** Is anything going on in your personal life that might be impacting how you're feeling?

- **Job:** Have your tasks or duties shifted? Has there been a change in the people you work with or the person you report to?

- **Organization:** Has there been a change in the organization's goals or future? Has a new leader brought a different tone to the culture?

- **Society:** Has something occurred on a larger level that is impacting norms, values, and priorities?

As we learned from Hudson's work in chapter 11, our sense of meaning and purpose goes through natural cycles over our lifetime, which influence how we feel about any particular job. I have seen this play out in my own life and Hudson's model has helped me separate a natural cycle of highs and lows from knowing when I need to take action. The burnout I felt from the pandemic put me into the "Doldrums" but I intentionally embraced cocooning and resting and I've cycled around to feeling on track again.

16. The 11 Myths of Purpose

As we grow up, we gain ideas about what purpose is and isn't. It's to be expected that along the way we all pick up a few misconceptions. Let's delve into the most common ones and see which have influenced you on your journey.

In his book, *The Purpose Economy*, Aaron Hurst identifies five common myths:

Myth #1: Your one purpose is about a worthy cause.

Hurst argues that our views about purpose have intertwined with the idea of a destiny. Storytelling has long followed the formula of the hero's journey. That the hero must find their one true purpose, the great and noble cause that will change the world. We've grown up with this idea that we each have one true purpose, just like we only have one true love.

It makes for a great movie or book plot, where life ties up neatly in 200 pages or 90 minutes. But in reality, there are lots of causes that need support, and many ways you can embrace purpose. "Purpose isn't a cause," he writes, "it is an approach to work and serving others. Purpose is a verb, not a noun."

Myth #2: Only the wealthy have the luxury of finding their purpose.

This myth perhaps again comes from media, as the stories we often see about people contributing to a cause are celebrities like movie stars and famous athletes. Leonardo DiCaprio and Zac Efron followed in Al Gore's shoes and are now ambassadors for the environment. Oprah Winfrey champions education for girls, even building her own school in South Africa. Princess Diana used her fame to break down the stigma of AIDS and Prince Harry is doing the same for mental health and veterans.

These are all wonderful efforts, but may lead us to believe that only the rich and famous can do purposeful work. Hurst shares data that purpose is inversely correlated with wealth, with the poorest Americans donating 3.2 percent of their income to charity while the wealthiest donate only 1.3 percent.

Everyone needs to have a sense of purpose and the path to purpose is open to all people.

Myth #3: Our purpose comes to us in a sudden revelation.

Again, this is influenced by media and the quick journey every hero must make to move the plot along. While this happens to a few people, it is more the exception than the norm, largely because most people don't just have one sense of purpose. We can have many over our lifetime and our life experiences contribute to the journey of discovery.

I had a clear sense of purpose when I was nine years old. I was going to be a competitive ice skater and win the Olympics. While I did skate for ten years, no medals are hanging on my wall. But wait! At 16, I realized I was born to work with the orcas at SeaWorld! After attending a show, I set my sights on becoming a marine biologist. While I did get a job at Sealand in British

Columbia, playing with the orcas and caring for the octopus, my marine biology degree never made it past freshman chemistry. And I've since learned things about the park industry that don't align with my values or ethics.

My sense of purpose became more clear after college and, since then, coalesced around helping others achieve their potential. But I have had many different jobs and worked for different types of organizations within that frame. Each one gave me some new skills as well as valuable information that informed my next choices.

My journey, it turns out, is pretty typical. We learn as we go and grow, changing over time. We're witnessing the reality of that right now with the pandemic forcing the world into a new reflection of what matters. It doesn't mean that people's sense of purpose was wrong before. It just means that we have been changed by facing our mortality and have entered a new phase of our lives. We just happen to be doing it together, which makes this a unique time in history.

Myth #4: Only some work generates purpose.

In his research, Hurst found that many people think only certain jobs truly bring a sense of purpose. As you can guess, they are the more visible or universally acknowledged "noble causes," like saving lives or fighting for justice. In fact, research shows that people believe many jobs, like administrative or janitorial work, could never possibly bring someone a sense of purpose.

But in reality, the majority (two-thirds) of people in *any* occupation, including administrative and janitorial roles, find purpose in it. Only about one-third see it as "only a job." Another study finds that 75 percent of people agree that we can find meaning in any type of work. As Hurst puts it, "What we do is not nearly as important as how we do it and what attitude we bring to the work. What we get from work has more to do with us than the work itself."

Remember, we can find purpose in many areas of our lives and our work is only one of them. Some people want to have the "just a job" experience so they can hold firm boundaries and fulfill their sense of purpose in their personal time. Others want to live and breathe their sense of purpose during those 40 to 50 hours per week and then just relax when they're off.

And as we learned in Myth #3, these desires can change over our lifetime, so we don't have to pick the perfect formula forever. Just ask yourself, what is the right formula for me now?

Myth #5: Living your purpose is easy.

Hurst's final myth is people believing that once they are living their purpose, everything will be easy. In reality, our purpose often asks us to dig deep and work hard. We will have to face difficult challenges and stumble along the way.

The good news is that when you have a sense of purpose, we perceive those challenges as less difficult, and those stumbles are easier to recover from. Having a North Star makes it easier to navigate the waves and winds simply because our eyes stay locked on where we are headed.

Other authors have also explored myths of purpose. In their book *The Purpose Factor* (2020), Brian and Gabrielle Bosché identified four others:

Myth #6: Purpose is about setting big goals.

You can't reach adulthood without learning about the value of setting and achieving goals. We set goals, translate them to our to-do lists, and even invest in fancy planners and apps to color code and track them. At work, we set goals and make sure they track to objectives and key results (OKRs) and key performance indicators (KPIs).

We even have an annual tradition of setting goals as New Year's resolutions. But the Boschés found that only 8 percent of people follow through, "That's 147 million people setting goals each January and 135 million giving up."

Goals are important and can certainly be a tool for getting things done. But achieving goals does not mean you have a sense of purpose. In fact, they state, "You can live an entire life of achievement and completely miss your purpose." They believe that purpose is about using what you have (skills, innate talents, and passion) to help others.

Myth #7: Pursuing passion is how your find purpose.

The Boschés state that 85 percent of people agree that to find your calling, you need to follow your passion. But they argue against that, claiming that the word passion has become synonymous with happiness or enjoyment. But really, passion is an intense emotion, defined as being barely controllable. While passion can certainly give you hints about your purpose, it's not the same as purpose. They define purpose as about who you can help.

Further, they argue that passion grows as you discover your purpose, gain experience, and develop your skills. They share examples of famously passionate people, like Walt Disney and Steve Jobs, who only became passionate over time, by pursuing their purpose. They state, "Passion is something that pulls you. When properly identified and given the time to grow, it inspires you. It drives you to do better, grow faster, and live longer."

Myth #8: You should find your purpose after you take care of your responsibilities.

This common myth keeps many people shackled with "shoulds" and "supposed tos." We tell ourselves, "I need to finish college first" or "I should get a higher paying salary" or "After the kids are older, I can look into that." Entire lives can pass waiting for the next good window until suddenly there is no time left.

The Boschés argue that we each have a purpose and to neglect it models to your family that "purpose is not compatible with life." Instead, they argue that you have a duty to discover your purpose and use it help others. It is not either/or but rather both/and.

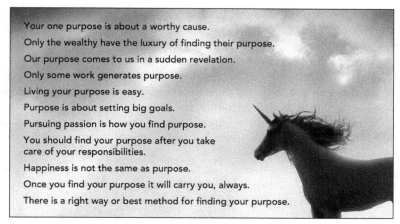

Your one purpose is about a worthy cause.

Only the wealthy have the luxury of finding their purpose.

Our purpose comes to us in a sudden revelation.

Only some work generates purpose.

Living your purpose is easy.

Purpose is about setting big goals.

Pursuing passion is how you find purpose.

You should find your purpose after you take care of your responsibilities.

Happiness is not the same as purpose.

Once you find your purpose it will carry you, always.

There is a right way or best method for finding your purpose.

The 11 myths of purpose

Myth #9: Happiness is not the same as purpose.

The Boschés find that as society has become more and more concerned with finding happiness, we are actually getting more miserable.

I found data that supports their claim. Recently, diseases of despair (anxiety, depression, substance abuse, and suicidal thoughts) have risen sharply. Twenty percent of Americans have some type of anxiety disorder and one-third (33 percent) of the world's population is struggling with loneliness.

As we learned in chapter 1, happiness and purpose are two distinct experiences that even show up in the brain differently. Happiness is that fleeting sense of joy that focuses on the self while purpose is that self-transcending experience of focusing on being of service to others. We need a balance of both in our lives. If we focus too much on happiness, we lose sight of the thing that brings us real fulfillment and peace.

Purpose Story 17:
Shifting the Trial-By-Fire Experience
I worked in the call centers at a dental company as a customer/technical service representative. When I started the job, I didn't care about the industry or what the company did—I just needed a job. The job was a far-cry from my ideal job. I felt stupid since we had to speak to doctors on the phone, and I felt less than qualified to give them any sort of information. The first six to eight months were miserable. It was trial by fire as I didn't know what I didn't know. It was as frustrating for me as it was for my customers. I considered quitting weekly. As I continued, I started embracing my curiosity, which helped me learn, master, and thrive in the most technical and fastest-growing department in the company. As I became more

competent, my day-to-day work felt easier and I began enjoying it. By the time I finished my sixth year with the company, I was handling the majority of the escalated calls and the most complex dental cases. I had dentists calling asking to speak to me only, over all the other registered dental assistants and dentists who worked with me.

At the same time, I observed the difficulties and stress that my coworkers experienced. I got the opportunity to train new employees. I didn't consider myself as much of a teacher, but to my surprise the trainees were really getting it. Given a few weeks of time, I could get anyone to speak coherently to dental cases.

Fast forward a few years and I get hired on as an instructional designer. One of the senior executives was pushing for a training program for new hires with the sole purpose of "one call resolution." The company's purpose finally aligned with my purpose! I saw an opportunity to help everyone get on the same page.

My boss knew about my previous work in the call centers and put me in charge of a small team to create the training program. We designed and implemented a six-week course for new hires that could take someone out of high school and teach them the interpersonal, software, dental, and specific technical skills to thrive at their job. Even though it was a massive pain in the ass to get this program up and running, I was driven by the knowledge that our new hires would never have to endure the trial-by-fire style learning that I experienced.

Following the launch of the program, I produced on-demand videos of the content for the rest of the company. I provided our legacy employees with the same learning opportunity as our new hires. I still receive messages from coworkers who are just now seeing these videos for the first time—they share their excitement about their new "aha!" moments.

I learned that having a shared purpose that's clearly communicated is so incredibly powerful. It made the work personally fulfilling for me and also allowed us to achieve more together.

From my research, I have identified two more myths to add to this list.

Myth #10: Once you find your purpose it will carry you, always.

The pandemic has shown us that this is not true. Even the most purpose-driven people can be pushed too hard, becoming exhausted and burned out. People living their calling can still experience a moral injury that changes their views. And all of us will be shaped by life's experiences and our own journeys toward and through purpose.

Again, you don't need a big epiphany or one noble cause. Just focus on where you are now and your next step. What is your sense of purpose now, for you, at this stage of your life and this moment in our history? Don't worry if you don't know, yet. We'll spend section V exploring more tools and strategies to help you gain some clarity.

Only time will reveal the whole picture of your journey to purpose, but you can trust that it will.

Myth #11: There is a right way or best method for finding your purpose.

There are lots of ways to explore and find your purpose. This book gives you some frameworks, tools, and strategies—you just need to try them out until you find the ones that work for you. I also encourage you to read some of the books I've mentioned so that you can benefit from their deeper dive into the various topics. These are from a more secular perspective—you'll find more spiritual books listed on p. 106:

- *The Purpose Factor: Extreme Clarity for Why You're Here and What to Do About It* by Brian and Gabrielle Bosché
- *Life On Purpose: How Living for What Matters Most Changes Everything* by Dr. Victor Strecher
- *The Purpose Economy: How Your Desire for Impact, Personal Growth, and Community Is Changing The World* by Aaron Hurst
- *The Path Made Clear: Discovering Your Life's Direction and Purpose* by Oprah Winfrey
- *What Color is Your Parachute? Your Guide to a Lifetime of Meaningful Work and Career Success* by Richard Bolles
- *From Strength to Strength: Finding Success, Happiness, and Deep Purpose in the Second Half of Life* by Dr. Arthur Brooks
- *Think Like a Monk: Train Your Mind for Peace and Purpose Every Day* by Jay Shetty
- *Awaken: The Path to Purpose, Inner Peace, and Healing* by Dr. Raj Sisodia

This section introduced you to robust research on meaningful work as well as paradoxes and myths about purpose. Hopefully, they give you information and context about your past experiences and help you as you look to the future.

Your Learning Journey

Take a few minutes to reflect on your own experiences with the concepts from this section.

- Thinking back over the various jobs and careers you've had, what factors contributed to it being meaningful to you?
- Reflect on the six models of meaningful work. Which ones gave you new insights about your own experiences? Write down some of the details.
- How have you experienced the five paradoxes of meaningful work? Have any been particularly impactful, positively or negatively?
- Which of the 11 myths have influenced your beliefs, purpose, and meaningful work?

CONTINUING YOUR JOURNEY
TO FIND PURPOSE

"I believe all of us are here on planet earth to learn how to give what we have been given. That's your job—to figure out how you're going to be used for a purpose greater than yourself."

Oprah Winfrey, author,
The Path Made Clear: Discovering
Your Life's Direction and Purpose

17. Clues from Yourself: Values and Emotions

Let's revisit the definition of purpose from chapter 1.

> *Purpose is an overarching sense of what matters in a person's life. It's driven by their* **core values** *and gives their life a sense of meaning. Purpose is self-transcendent where your actions result in service or benefit to others. Our sense of purpose acts as a North Star, even helping us know when we veered off the path and are no longer on purpose in our lives and work.*

Core values are our next place to explore. Values are individual beliefs that guide how people think, act, and feel. They are the source of how we move through the world, all day, every day. They influence where you work, what you buy, who you love, and what matters to you.

In my years of consulting, I have also found that one of the top three causes of workplace conflict is colleagues violating each other's core values. This is often unintentional, as we don't always walk around talking about them to other people, and we may not realize that our source of irritation or judgment for that coworker is really about our values and not their personality.

As we learned in chapter 15, violations to our core values can cause us anguish and even lead to moral injury. So yes, values matter. Your core values are already playing an important role in your life so let's spend a little time getting to know them.

Your Core Values

Knowing yourself, including your core values, is an important part of self-knowledge—one of the four areas that make up emotional intelligence or EQ. The others are self-control, awareness of others, and building relationships, according to Dr. Daniel Goleman's research on this topic.

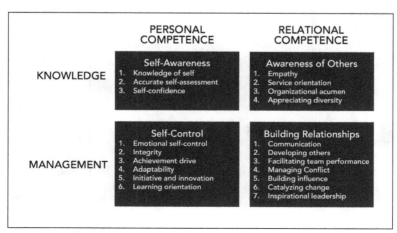

The four quadrants of emotional intelligence

One of the activities we do in my training on EQ is this exercise for discovering your core values. So, I'm going to guide you through it now.

Step 1: Define your core values
This activity is timed so that you must make quick choices. For this step, set a timer to 10 minutes. Using this list of common values, circle the ones that are most important to you, underline those that are somewhat important to you, and cross out any that are least important to you. There is no limit to the number you can have in each category, and you can add other values to the fourth column. Please note that all values are fine and crossing any out is not a judgment, we are just simply prioritizing the ones that are most important to *you*.

Acceptance	Effectiveness	Integrity	Recreation
Accountability	Efficiency	Intelligence	Reliability
Accuracy	Empathy	Intuition	Resourcefulness
Achievement/Success	Endurance	Joy	Respect
Adaptability	Enjoyment	Justice	Responsibility
Adventure	Equality	Kindness	Risk-taking
Autonomy	Excellence	Knowledge	Science
Balance	Expediency	Leadership	Security
Beauty	Fairness	Learning	Service
Boldness	Family	Love/Affection	Simplicity
Bravery	Fidelity	Loyalty	Sincerity
Camaraderie	Flexibility	Mastery	Spirituality/Faith
Challenge	Fortitude	Modesty	Stability
Collaboration	Freedom/Liberty	Nature	Status
Commitment	Friendship	Nonconformity	Strength
Communication	Generosity	Open-mindedness	Teamwork
Community	Grace	Optimism	Tolerance
Compassion	Gratitude	Originality	Trust
Competence	Growth	Passion	Truth
Competition	Happiness	Patience	Uniqueness
Consistency	Harmony	Perseverance	Unity
Control	Health	Persistence	Valor
Courage	Honesty	Playfulness	Variety
Creativity	Honor	Power	Vision
Curiosity	Humility	Practicality	Warmth
Decisiveness	Humor	Preparedness	Wealth
Dependability	Imagination	Productivity	Wisdom
Determination	Impartiality	Prosperity	Zeal
Dignity	Inclusion	Purpose	Other:
Discipline	Independence	Quality	Other:
Discretion	Individuality	Rationality	Other:
Diversity	Innovation	Recognition	Other:

After you finish, answer these questions:
- What did you notice as you did this activity?
- What strategies did you use to decide?
- Were you thinking of your work life, your home life, or your whole, integrated self?

(Note: For this exercise, I recommend the latter because we don't have a work body and a home body. But it's interesting to note what you initially chose. As you continue, think about the values that operate for your whole life.)

Step 2: Highlight your top 10 values

Now, set a timer for five minutes and get to your top 10 values. Highlight those and cross out the rest. Pretend that you can only have 10 values to guide the rest of your life. Which do you choose? After you finish, answer these questions: What did you notice as you did this activity? What strategies did you use to decide? I ask because people ultimately use some kind of strategy. I often hear statements like these:

"I picked the ones that I was raised to respect or honor the most."

"I picked the ones I try to live up to or want to be known for."

"I thought of them as subsets. If I pick passion, then I also get joy and happiness."

"I picked ones that really irritate me when I don't see them in others."

"I pictured my funeral and want these to be how I lived my life."

All strategies are valid—just notice what yours are. When you're ready, move to step 3.

Step 3: Choose your top five values

Set the timer for two minutes and get to your top five. Pretend you only have those five values to guide you for the rest of your life. What are they? Again, what did you notice and what strategies did you use decide? Take a moment to write them down. If you're doing this activity with others, share with each other.

Step 4: Assess how you express your top five core values

On the next page, write each value and list the activities you do that express that value in your life. Consider all aspects, including work, relationships, interests, hobbies, what/where you buy, etc. Based on what you list, estimate the percentage of your time each month that is spent on each value. The row can total more than 100 percent since some activities will express more than one value. The goal here is to get a sense of the distribution. Are all five of your core values getting equal expression? Are some underserved?

Value:	Value:	Value:	Value:	Value:
Expressed via:	Expressed via:	Expressed via:	Expressed via:	Expressed via:
% time	% time	% time	% time	% time

Answer these questions:

- Which values are the most expressed through your time and activities?
- Which are not sufficiently expressed? What can you do to change that?

Remember, you don't need to express all your values through work—some may be expressed through activities in your personal life or the causes you support with your time or money.

These are our top five values so when something that is core to who we are is not sufficiently expressed, we may feel emotions like frustration, anxiety, sadness, or even depression.

In addition, our integrity lives at the intersection between our values and our actions. Based on how you spend your time and the activities you do, what would others think are your top values?

Dr. Barry Posner and Dr. Jim Kouzes, authors of *The Leadership Challenge*, discovered that people evaluate their leaders based on how much their words and actions align. They argue that if you're a leader, you should share your core values and speak about them often. The research is clear that others don't necessarily need to agree with or even like your values, but they will perceive you as a better leader if you have integrity between your words and actions.

I think this same principle holds true for parents. Children watch what we do more than they listen to what we tell them is the right behavior. What lessons are your kids picking up about values, integrity, and priorities based on your words and actions?

The last reflection explores where your values come from. All of our values are sourced from somewhere. What life experiences, both positive and negative, contributed to your developing those values? Journal on the origin of each of your core values and see what becomes clear.

Emotions as Hints

Emotional intelligence is based on the notion that emotions are valuable data. They contribute critical information that helps us understand ourselves and others.

Coined by Dr. Daniel Goleman, the term emotional intelligence (EQ) can be likened to traditional intelligence or IQ, except EQ is about how smart we are with emotions and how effectively we manage ourselves and our relationships. Goleman's research launched a new movement in the world of business and management.

According to *Harvard Business Review*, EQ is twice as predictive of performance than IQ and accounts for 80 to 90 percent of competencies that differentiate top performers. The Center for Creative Leadership found 75 percent of careers are derailed for reasons related to emotional competencies. The Brandon Hall Group identified the top 10 digital-age competencies and EQ is the top skill, at number one.

The self-awareness component of EQ includes your ability to recognize emotions. One way to become better is to use the wheel of emotions. There are a few different versions out there but the "Feeling Wheel" by Dr. Gloria Wilcox offers a nice range of emotions and shows how the nuances spin out from the core emotions at the center.

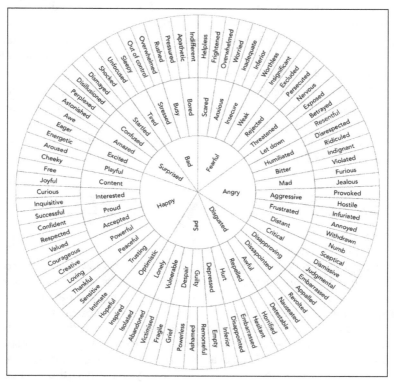

The wheel of emotions

Besides identifying your emotions, it's important to let yourself feel them, and find healthy ways to express them. For example, anger is an intense emotion. Do you recognize the signs of when you are getting angry? Where does it show up in your body? Anger is one of the emotions that we often suppress but it's important and healthy to let yourself feel intense emotions like anger or sadness.

The key is "healthy ways." Going for a run, screaming into a pillow, or punching a punching bag are all healthy forms of expressing anger. But hitting the table or wall when others are present or screaming at a coworker are not.

As we look at the role that emotions play in helping us find our sense of purpose, we can think of them as a compass of sorts, letting us know how aligned we are with our North Star.

People who have a strong sense of purpose know that when they veer too far off the path, heading west or south, their emotions will tell them. They will start to feel frustration, irritation, sadness, anxiety, or depression. And, conversely, when they are on the path and fully expressing their purpose—heading north, if you will—they will feel fulfillment, satisfaction, pride, happiness, and joy.

If we assume that your purpose already exists and it's just hidden from view, then your emotions become important hints that we should explore. Assume your compass is working but somehow the N was printed in invisible ink.

You already have some hints from chapter 13, when you thought about your skills and talents. Go back and review your preferences. Which ones gave you pleasure? If they are indicating the direction you should head, what do they say?

Now, let's walk around the wheel and fill in some information about what is related to each of the core emotions. Take a moment to identify the experiences that tend to make you feel sad, angry, scared, disgusted, bad, surprised, and happy. Remember, emotions are data. Your list might include valuable hints that will help you find your sense of purpose.

If you enjoy exploring emotions, I recommend Dr. Brené Brown's latest book, *Atlas of the Heart: Mapping Meaningful Connection and the Language of the Heart.*

Purpose Story 18:
Your Truth Will Catch Up to You Eventually
I have always been fascinated by human behavior and I wanted to become an educator from an early age. At university, I was set on a career in education and enrolled in the studies to prepare for the national exams in my country. My passion for education was based not on the subjects themselves but rather on the nature of the profession and the idea behind it: designing the ideal environment that is conducive to high performance.

Growing up between France and the United States, I moved over a dozen times and changed schools every two years. I had the chance to experience firsthand a wide variety of teaching methods. Because of this, my fields of interest have always gravitated around similar poles: the science of learning and how to optimize content structure and motivate people to enhance their performance.

But despite my clear passion, I shifted my studies towards more practical and lucrative business matters. After graduating, I was offered a job in a global financial firm that I couldn't refuse and moved to Luxembourg, one of the financial hearts of Europe, to work in the fund industry.

Throughout my time at that job, I kept thinking about the career I gave up in teaching and was endlessly distracted, daydreaming about ideas for classroom content and activities. At one point, I had enough and even applied for a position in a nearby Montessori school. The interview process was going great but at the last minute I ghosted them when they invited me for an on-site trial interview. I chickened out at the prospect of letting my finance career "go to waste."

At my finance job, I was clearly emotionally unsatisfied. This unhappiness came from a place of knowing that I was not in alignment with my passions and strengths, and I spent all my time trying to distract myself from the job that I did want. Perhaps if I didn't have such a clear idea of what I liked, I would not have felt the same gnawing to change. Social pressures were also a huge factor since, in my entourage, a lot of jobs were demeaned, and I didn't want to be perceived as lazy for choosing education.

I thought if I kept on working at it, eventually I would forget my love for teaching. I accepted a finance job in Switzerland, but after a couple years, I realized I was feeling burned out because I wasn't feeling any sense of purpose. My tasks felt meaningless and, at every new request I received from my managers, I felt irritation.

It took me a long time to be honest with myself and finally let myself follow the path that I always knew was for me. It felt like giving up a battle and I immediately felt a strange sense of calmness that comes with knowing where you're going in life.

It's better to be honest with yourself from the beginning and live your truth because it will always catch up with you eventually.

Spotlight on passion

Let's look at passion for a moment, because it can also give us some clues about our purpose. Brian and Gabrielle Bosché, in their book *The Purpose Factor*, claim that your passions are a clue in the sense that they call to you or pull you toward something. They call them "pull-passions" and they identify five types:

- **The Problem Solver:** The passion here is about solving big issues or global problems that impact lots of people. They enjoy tackling the issues that seem too big or too complicated to others.

- **The Need Satisfier:** The passion for this type is addressing the immediate and basic needs of a specific group of people. They work in a role of service, creating specific and measurable results for that one group.

- **The Hurt Healer:** The passion pull here is healing emotional or physical hurt for people who are in distress. They work in fields of healing and/or preventing physical and emotional pain.

- **The Desire Fulfiller:** This type is seeing a gap or hole where things could be done or done better. They seek to enhance enjoyment or the quality of life for others while using their skills and interests.

- **The Injustice Equalizer:** The passion pull is focused on equality and fixing past injustices. They can work on a range of issues but are interested in righting past wrongs.

They believe that people are primarily one type but I have experienced moving between them or combining them over the course of my own career and purpose journey. What about you? Which resonate for you and could that resonance be a hint?

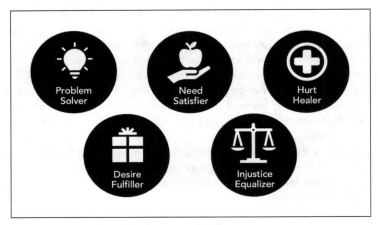

The five types of pull-passions

You may notice that these types have some commonalities with the purpose drivers that Aaron Hurst identified in his book, *The Purpose Economy.* You can find them at the end of chapter 1.

It's not uncommon to start working at one level of influence (individual, organization, or society) and as you find your sweet spot, gain in your own abilities, and grow your influence, to switch to working at a bigger level or faster pace.

The last thing I want to say about our emotions is that, because of the trauma of the pandemic and subsequent burnout, many of us are feeling what scientists call "emotional inflammation."

Psychologist Dr. Lise Van Susteren coauthored a book with Stacey Colino titled *Emotional Inflammation: Discover Your Triggers and Reclaim Your Equilibrium During Anxious Times.* They believe that it's a uniquely modern affliction, not unlike PTSD. We live in an age of hyperreactivity because our bodies are stuck in high alert, constantly hit with news that kicks off our survival biology.

They state, "If you've suffered from sleep problems, hyperreactivity, persistent grief, or inescapable worry about the future—especially triggered by the nonstop news cycle—then you're probably dealing with emotional inflammation."

They identify four main types of reactivity:

- **Nervous reactor:** You are likely to feel anxious, worried, fearful, or overwhelmed by many unnamed or ill-defined threats. You constantly feel that something is not right and spend your time being ready for anything.

- **Revved-up reactor:** You are likely in go-mode, feeling like there are a million things you need to get gone to stay on top of it all. Your pace can be fast, frantic, and incessant but it also brings you a sense of control. Focusing on "righting the wrongs of the world" can feel like a form of purpose.

- **Molten reactor:** You likely experience feelings of irritation, aggravation, and anger, often at the perceived shortcomings of others (greed, stupidity, ineptitude, etc.). You can feel moral outrage, particularly when your values are violated. Be careful to not suppress your anger or turn it inward, but channel it into something constructive.

- **Retreating reactor:** You likely respond to feelings of powerlessness, despair, or resignation by detaching, withdrawing, or numbing out. While that may be a useful coping mechanism in the short-term, it can increase your vulnerability to depression. Instead of pulling away, reach out for support and connection.

Do any of these types of reactivity resonate for you? If so, you may want to explore if you are stuck in a hyperreactive state. The good news is that the authors also offer some tips and strategies for regulating your emotions and learning to calm yourself. A web search for these terms will bring you other resources in your area. By using tools to alleviate the emotional inflammation, the hints from your emotions about your sense of purpose will become clearer and more consistent.

With that said, inspiration comes in many forms so it might just be your reactivity that points you in the right direction—use the totality of the activities in this section to give you a more balanced and holistic view. Take a moment to write own your observations and thoughts.

If you consider that your values and emotions contain important clues for your search for purpose, what are they trying to tell you?

18. Clues from Your Past: Wonders and Wounds

In my research, I read practically every book written on the concept of purpose and meaningful work. Nearly all of them mention that our past, and particularly our childhood, shapes our journey toward purpose. We're going to delve into the three areas most mentioned: when you experienced joy and curiosity, challenges you have overcome, and finding the tribe of people who support you.

Joy and Curiosity

Our early experiences with joy and curiosity are important. Sometimes those first memories of awe and wonder offer us great clues, especially if the fascination is still there.

Career advisors often tell clients to look to their early passions for clues. When we feel an early and pure love of something, it's worth revisiting in case your North Star was pinging for you at an early age. It often happens that many of us silence that ping after well-meaning parents and teachers tell us to set aside those "childish" things for more "appropriate" goals. To find yours, journal on these questions:

- What are your favorite childhood memories or experiences?
- What were you doing and how did it make you feel?
- What were you passionate about and/or awestruck by as a child?
- When do you remember feeling happiest in your childhood?
- When you were little, what did you want to be when you grew up?

Purpose Story 19:
Perseverance Across Borders
I grew up in Ukraine, where my passion for language learning started at an early age. I knew I wanted my work to be connected with foreign languages, so I graduated from the university as a teacher of English. I was sure this path was right for me. I had a sense of purpose and the necessary skills to do well. Unfortunately, being a teacher doesn't pay well in Ukraine, so I had to work extra hours.

Some years later, I married a Dutchman and moved to the Netherlands. To my big disappointment, my Ukrainian degree was not worth much in the Netherlands. I focused on my family for a few years, but I never lost touch with my passion for languages and teaching. When I decided to return to work, I wanted to pursue my purpose. I had to start from scratch, studying for two years to get another master's degree, graduating with flying colors, again.

I started looking for a job, but despite being well educated and experienced, I found the job search frustrating as a foreigner. My experience in Dutch education was next to zero, which apparently was a very important factor, not my skills or my teaching experience. However, when a position for an English teacher opened at a teacher training college, I immediately applied and was hired!

I now work with a team of dedicated colleagues, who are also nice and interesting people—those with a passion for teaching and a love for children. And the students we work with are some of the kindest and most fun people. The role I'm in allows me to promote the importance of good quality English lessons and the benefits that bi- and multilingualism bring.

What I do is meaningful and important both to me and the society. I'm finally using my potential and living my sense of purpose.

Overcoming Challenges

Another place to look for purpose is in the challenges we have faced over the years. As we learned in the last chapter, the authors of *The Purpose Factor* identified five types of passion pulls, which, they argue, come from our past, as part of our origin story. They define "origin story" as the series of events that most shape the way we see the world. This aligns with the exploration we did around our core values; they all come from somewhere, and both positive and negative experiences shape who we are.

As adults, we're all overcoming something. You cannot make it to adulthood without gaining some wounds and scars along the way, as nearly every book on purpose highlights. Thomas Moore, author of *A Life at Work: The Joy of Discovering What You Were Born to Do*, wrote a chapter titled "Reconciling with the Past." Dr. Stephanie Shackelford and Bill Denzel, in their book *You on Purpose* wrote a chapter titled "Pain Points: Finding Your Path Through Disappointment and Suffering." And Rick Warren, in his book *The Purpose-Driven Life*, wrote a chapter titled "Transformed by Trouble."

I share these because many of us can spend a lot of time avoiding the harder parts of our past but in our search for purpose, we may find that exploring them will give us great insight. Our challenges help us reframe our past and discover a more empowering story, which may even catapult us forward in our quest.

Few of us find opportunities to share our origin stories, and even if we do we still might not. Brian and Gabrielle Bosché say the four most common reasons are because (1) it doesn't feel appropriate, (2) we're afraid of rejection, (3) we haven't processed our story yet, or (4) we feel ashamed.

In her work on vulnerability, Dr. Brené Brown also talks a lot about shame. When we internalize a perceived characteristic, switching from guilt ("I did something to bad") to shame ("I am bad"), she argues that shame creates two negative messages we tell ourselves when we start to take a risk: "You're not good enough" and "Who do you think you are?" She calls them shame gremlins.

Hearing her say that in her TED really struck me. I've heard those voices in my head, many times, saying those exact words. And what's really frustrating is that they can keep us paralyzed from taking any action or moving forward.

When I initially considered writing a book, I was hit first by the "You're not good enough" message. It would undermine my motivation because it made me doubt whether I could write or, even if I did, could I write something good? This voice would keep me from trying for weeks at a time. And when I did write a little, it would rip me to shreds with critiques.

The truth is writing is messy, and it takes several drafts before the ideas in your head start to come across on paper. I struggled a lot but eventually got past that voice. But how many wonderful writers don't? How many wonderful works of art are lost to the world because the person was beaten down by that shame gremlin?

And the worst part is that if you get past that first gremlin, the next one pops up and asks, "Who do you think you are?" We've all heard that message as children, from teachers, parents, and other adults. It's the perfect phrase to shame a child into obedience, quiet, or whatever other behavior the adult demands.

We've all been raised with messages that having pride is bad, or confidence is boastful, or being smart/funny/pretty/kind is threatening. So, once I finally started writing, I kept hearing that voice and feeling like I was being too uppity to think that someone might want to hear my thoughts. It still happens. This is my fifth book, and that shame gremlin still popped up over the past few weeks. I share that to underscore that it's part of the human journey and, while frustrating, it is one that unites us all.

Fortunately, Dr. Brown's work taught me to recognize that gremlin for what it is—a message we were all given as children to keep us in our place. While I can't always silence it, I picture it my mind with a rather goofy appearance and a squeaky voice. That helps me to remember not to let it stop me.

Dr. Brown's concept of shame gremlins can be a helpful way to diminish their power, because shame can really cut us to our core. Especially if we experience a trauma and suffer a moral injury. As we learned in chapter 15, one aspect of moral injury is that we feel responsible, even on a small level, for what happened. We may suffer under an avalanche of "If onlys": If only I hadn't been there. If only I had said something. If only I had done X, Y, or Z."

Another researcher, Dr. Bessel Van Der Kolk, is one of the foremost minds on healing from trauma. He works with a lot of trauma survivors, especially military veterans, and wrote *The Body Keeps the Score: Brain, Mind, and Body in the Healing of Trauma*. He says that trauma, when left untreated, can keep people stuck in patterns that may harm them and their relationships. But he's found that the right combination of tools can help people heal and reclaim their lives.

We are designed with many mechanisms for healing ourselves, both physically and emotionally. The human body is always trying to move toward wholeness. Just think of the whole system of healing that kicks in when you cut your finger. Your body launches a bevy of mechanisms to stop the bleeding, close the wound, and eventually heal the skin. Bones can heal, lost blood is remade, and damaged nerves regenerate.

This is true of us psychologically as well. If you have experienced trauma, please read Dr. Van Der Kolk's uplifting, inspiring book, full of valuable resources to help you heal.

Trauma is more common than you think and, for many of us, our sense of purpose is birthed from trauma. Being aligned with our purpose can help us heal and we can become a powerful source for other people's healing as well.

The Boschés identify five common types of origin stories, where people are overcoming something from their past:

- **Trauma:** The person is overcoming a deeply impactful trauma, with most from a single event, though some people experience trauma over a series of years.

- **Loss:** The person is overcoming a loss that made them feel less than whole, such as the death of a loved one, the loss of a marriage, or a bankruptcy.

- **Betrayal:** The person is overcoming a violation of trust that has shaped how they see the world. Whether the betrayal occurred in one moment or over time, it has perhaps cost them something very important.

- **Rejection:** The person was rejected by someone important and has become afraid to show their true selves for fear of not being accepted. They seek acceptance in relationships but often feel unfulfilled.

- **Failure:** The person is overcoming a failure that they themselves caused—as a result, they are often struggling with a lot of shame and self-doubt.

The five common origin stories

Again, we can have experiences that are combinations of the above. Which types of overcoming are related to your origin story? And how might this new awareness give you a hint about your sense of purpose?

Dr. Dharius Daniels, in his book *Your Purpose Is Calling*, dedicates a section to exploring our "hurts, holes, and hazards." He asks three powerful questions that can help you process your past, and also shed light on your sense of purpose:

- **Where is the hurt?** He identifies hurt as something that was done *to you* that shouldn't have been. It injured you and caused you harm. He states, "Remember, it's common for us to push down or ignore emotional wounds until it seems like they go away—but they never actually go away. They just keep hurting."

- **Where are the holes?** Dr. Daniels identifies holes as something that should have been done *for you* but was not. Caregivers should meet our basic physical and emotional needs and, when they neglect or ignore us, it creates a different kind of wound, a hole. He asks you to consider what you always longed to receive and identify where you are leaking because the hole first needs to be patched up.

- **Where are the hazards?** He identifies hazards as the situations or circumstances that keep tripping you up in life. These tend to be patterns where the same thing comes up again and again and keeps getting in the way of your hopes and dreams.

I encourage you to journal on these questions and notice what feelings come up as you do. Be gentle with yourself as you do this exploration. Take time for some self-care after, like going for a walk, talking with a supportive friend, or enjoying a favorite comfort food.

It's also helpful if you get support from a licensed professional. Many health insurance benefits include sessions with therapists, social workers, coaches, or support groups. Some will work on a sliding fee scale to be accessible to everyone. Look into what you have access to—you can also search for local providers by typing "licensed therapist" or "certified life coach" into your search engine.

In his book *Awaken: The Path to Purpose, Inner Peace, and Healing*, Dr. Raj Sisodia states, "By committing to healing our traumas, we can amplify our positive impact on the world and leave behind a legacy of love and healing for future generations."

Finding Your Tribe

The final exploration of our past is the group of people who made a difference. Yes, there are people who harmed us but there have also been people who helped us. Let's focus on the latter to see what clues might be there.

While we are born to a family we are related to by blood, as we grow older, we can choose our family of the heart—those people who really get us and make us feel safe and loved. Let's explore a few questions about the people who have made a difference in your life.

- When you think about your happiest childhood memories, who was part of those experiences?
- Who has made you feel like you truly belong? What did they do to make you feel that way?
- Who did you look up to or admire and why?
- As an adult, who would you consider your family of the heart?
- Who has served as a mentor or cheerleader for you?

As you continue your journey to find your purpose, consider who you can turn to for support and encouragement. Again, timing is everything—you may want to hold that flame close until it feels strong enough and then choose wisely with whom you share it. But some of the people that you just journaled about might be contenders.

It has struck me in my life that the people I surround myself with shape my view of things. We talked in chapter 14 about how we learn what is meaningful. You could grow up in a home where being gay is judged and ridiculed and then grow up to find a community where it's respected and celebrated. You might go to a school where your passions are looked down upon by teachers and students but then grow up to find a vibrant community of adults who are passionate about it too.

If meaning is in the eye of the beholder, then it's important to surround yourself with people who share your point of view! Here are some questions to help you find your tribe:

- Who shares your passions, point of view, and potential purpose?
- Have you already met some of them? If so, how and where?
- How might you meet more people?
- Who do you wish you could meet?
- Are there any organizations in your town or state you should explore?
- What about professional or international organizations?
- Who do you want to be of service or support to?
- How might you find other people who care about the same community?

Joining organizations already serving a community you care about is a great way to meet your tribe. That experience can also give you clues that help you further clarify your purpose.

Take some time to explore the themes from this chapter. While it can be a little daunting to consider that the difficult things we've been through might hold clues for our sense of purpose, it can be comforting too. Especially when considering how far you have come and how high you can still climb. Look at what you have learned in this chapter and see what new insights you have on your path to purpose. What is becoming clear?

19. Finding Your Sweet Spot

Usually, our purpose does not strike us as a bolt of lightning. It's a journey with each year and experience bringing us more information. Things happen that shape us and we also try different things through our work, relationships, and interests.

It is a shared belief among most authors of books about purpose that you will be continually nudged and guided along your path. In this chapter, let's explore two things that will help you live your purpose: finding your sweet spot and learning life's lessons.

Finding Your Sweet Spot

For some people, finding a sense of purpose happens early in life, so they experience many years of feeling that they are on the right path, following their North Star.

For others, it takes time, even years, to find their purpose. In one study with over 2,500 adults, 76 percent agreed with the statement that you primarily find your purpose through trial and error.

Purpose Story 20:
A College Trip Turns into a Lifelong Career
As a college student, I studied abroad in Trinidad and Tobago. There, my eyes were opened for the first time to the vast disparity of wealth that exists in the world. (Coming from a comfortable middle class suburban upbringing, I had never been exposed to true poverty before.) I pledged to devote my life to evening out that wealth disparity in whatever way I could, fancying that I would become some kind of Robin Hood.

Shortly thereafter, I found philanthropy as a career path. Twenty years on, I have never left. I first worked to help small nonprofits raise money to support their missions. I went on to help large international universities raise money to increase scholarship access to first-generation college students. I then got a master's degree in philanthropy to get at the work even more deeply.

That led me to get two different philanthropy-focused startups off the ground in Texas and New Mexico. My career has been deeply aligned with my personal and professional passions. Some roles have been more "exactly right" for me than others, but I am proud to say that I have always stayed true to my path. I consider this to be a personal success story because I have always been able to keep my North Star in mind—making the world a better place, in whatever small way I can, through a career dedicated to philanthropy and the social sector.

When I take on a new role, I am looking for a combination of factors. Primarily, how much can I help this organization maximize the impact that it will have on the people it serves? Will it provide me with an outlet for growth and learning? Is it something that feels right in my gut and aligns with my sense of purpose? If a role will allow me to grow as a person, while building community and improving the lives that are served by the organization, then that is a professional win in my book.

Community building, whether implicitly or explicitly, has always been a central element of my work. I want people to feel connected to each other, which we know increases compassion and one's willingness to help one's "neighbor" in times of need. I want human bonds to be strengthened as a result of my work. I want people who have found material success in life to have the opportunity to share it with those who have struggled to make ends meet. (Primarily through the giving of their personal philanthropy to a community-serving organization.) I connect donors to organizations. I connect community members to one another. And I help organizations serve their communities better.

I excel at forming connections. I do this primarily by leading through my own vulnerability and openness. I strive to be honest and straightforward, no matter the situation; owning difficult moments and working through them as they arise. Maintaining my authenticity, genuinely caring about people, asking questions to help me understand them better, and LISTENING; above all, actively listening to what they have to say. I believe that we are all more alike than we are different, and that our similarities provide us with endless opportunity for connection.

I think this speaks to the time it takes for us to learn what our purpose is and then dial it into various drivers that Aaron Hurst mentions in his work. For the details, see chapter 1, but here's a quick review:

- WHO you want to impact: individuals, organizations, or society
- WHY you want to make an impact: karma and harmony
- HOW you can make an impact or your craft: community, human, structure, and knowledge.

Sometimes, you must try a few before you find your sweet spot, so while you may be doing good work, it may not feel like you are totally on purpose until those last pieces fall into place.

And then, of course, we change over time. In my twenties, I was lucky to find a sense of purpose that really mattered to me. I worked at a university and ran programs for first-year students. I didn't understand the real why at the time, but I was drawn to helping them successfully navigate the transition away from their families to their newfound independence. I was deeply invested in giving students information and skills to become their best selves.

I did that for twenty years and many of the programs I created were adopted by other colleges and universities around the world. I even wrote a textbook that many students in college read. What I didn't fully realize until partway through was that I was working on my *own* healing. My memories of childhood abuse had been suppressed, which is quite common, so when I first started doing the work I didn't recognize that by helping others I was slowly helping myself.

Those memories started rushing to the surface just before my 30th birthday. Out of the blue, I started having panic attacks that were really flashbacks— a common pattern for people who experience childhood trauma. That set me on my formal healing journey, working with therapists and eventually using some powerful healing techniques that unlock stored trauma like eye movement desensitization and reprocessing (EMDR), brain spotting, and cognitive processing therapy (CPT).

That is where I learned about the amygdala hijack and that our brain can go into a fight-flight-freeze response for reasons other than an immediate life-threatening situation. Learning about the amygdala hijack unlocked so many things for me and began my fascination with neuroscience. Years later, when I had the opportunity to do a TEDx talk, I thought, "If this is my only shot at 15 minutes of fame, I want to share that life-transforming information."

While our bodies are designed to heal, we can't really shortchange the process. Healing myself took time. My body had a certain amount of unshed tears that needed to be cried, and a certain amount of suppressed anger that needed to be expressed.

One of the things I have heard other adults worry about is that if they start exploring the difficult parts of their life, that they may not be able to stop crying. I understand that feeling. While it can seem safer to keep all that stuff bottled up tightly inside with the cork firmly in place, the problem is that it's still in there doing damage, physically and emotionally. And it does not stay neatly tucked away—it comes leaking out in our relationships and jobs and it comes blasting out in moments when we are triggered.

I can't recommend enough the power of leaning into healing. It helped me so much. Therapy helped me talk about things and learn some new patterns. And a few key workshops helped me learn how to express my backlog of emotions in healthy ways. I found the work of Dr. Chérie Carter-Scott to be especially powerful. Her Inner Negotiation workshop changed my life and may have even saved it.

Once I started processing those feelings and experiences, I did cry. A lot. But I found appropriate times to do it and I didn't just fall apart like I thought I might. Certainly, in my therapist's office but also whenever I rode my bike. For some reason, this allowed feelings and memories to come up, so I rode my bike three or four times a week and cried on almost every ride. I allowed myself to remember things and express my true feelings. And you know what? I eventually stopped crying. I eventually shed that last backlogged tear and it felt good.

My reactions to life's events stabilized to more normal and healthy responses. I wasn't so devastated by the news, and I wasn't so angry when people pushed my hot buttons. I better understood my needs and wants and started building healthier relationships and having more fun. It doesn't mean my memories are gone or that I don't have feelings about them, but my body shifted out of the ongoing state of survival (a hallmark of PTSD) and returned to a healthy, normal state of functioning where I can regulate my emotions.

My story is not unique—the book *The Body Keeps the Score* is filled with stories just like mine, of lives restored through the power of healing. We all know someone who experienced trauma, children and adults alike. I believe the more we can share this information, the more we can create the world we want to live in because unhealed trauma lies is at the heart of so many hurtful human actions and policies.

But you know what happened once I was better? My work became less fulfilling. I still liked it, but I didn't love it with the same passion I had the previous twenty years. That surprised me because I thought I had found my life's purpose; that I had my forever career. But our sense of purpose can and does shift over time. For me, my healing allowed me to feel a sense of closure about working with college-age students and start to explore newer passions and fine-tune my purpose for the next phase of my life.

The pandemic similarly impacted many people around the world—it created time for reflection, which allowed them to ponder their values and priorities. Some people are launching into entirely new directions and others are making some small tweaks to get better aligned with the current versions of themselves.

I can't underscore enough that your purpose is there, trying to find you just like you are trying to find it. We are wired to live lives of purpose and so your biology and other forces will keep nudging, and sometimes shoving, you in the right direction.

Lessons Are Repeated Until Learned

One concept that really helped me is from Dr. Chérie Carter-Scott's book *If Life Is a Game, These Are the Rules: Ten Rules for Being Human.*

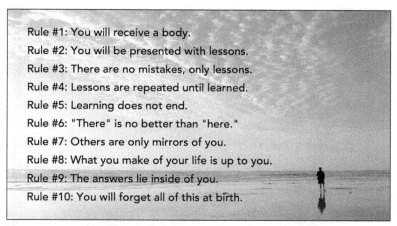

Rule #1: You will receive a body.

Rule #2: You will be presented with lessons.

Rule #3: There are no mistakes, only lessons.

Rule #4: Lessons are repeated until learned.

Rule #5: Learning does not end.

Rule #6: "There" is no better than "here."

Rule #7: Others are only mirrors of you.

Rule #8: What you make of your life is up to you.

Rule #9: The answers lie inside of you.

Rule #10: You will forget all of this at birth.

The ten rules for being human

All 10 are great but Rule #4 really spoke to me: "Lessons are repeated until learned." I started getting better at noticing when I was repeating a pattern or having the same experience show up again and again. I started seeing that as information and looking for the lesson I needed to learn. Many of my lessons were nudging me where I needed to go.

Author Dan Millman also highlighted this concept in his book *The Four Purposes of Life: Finding Meaning and Direction in a Changing World*. He argues that we have multiple purposes in life, which helps me not feel so focused on finding the "one" thing:

- **Learning life's lessons:** Millman states, "Earth is a perfect school.... You aren't here on earth merely to strive for success; you're here to learn—and daily life is guaranteed to teach you all you need in order to grow, and evolve, and awaken to your higher purpose here." He goes on to say that when we don't learn the lessons, they get harder. Oprah Winfrey noticed a similar phenomenon:

  > *The universe speaks to us, always, first in whispers. And if you don't pay attention to the whisper, it gets louder and louder and louder. I say it's like getting thumped upside the head. If you don't pay attention to that, it's like getting a brick upside your head. You don't pay attention to that— the brick wall falls down. That is the pattern that I see in my life and so many other people's lives. And so, I ask people, 'What are the whispers? What's whispering to you now?'*

- **Finding your career and calling:** Millman defines your career as a service you perform, trading your time, effort, skills, etc. for income and other benefits. Whereas your calling is your drive, interest, or passion that is usually of a higher order. It feels something you must do; it touches you deeply, absorbing you and you're not always sure why. These don't always have to be the same thing and many people have satisfying careers but live their calling through other ways, like their relationships, hobbies, volunteering, or creative endeavors. As long as it ultimately serves others, it's a calling, and that's what differentiates it from your pleasurable activities.

- **Discovering your life path:** Millman found that we also have a life path, a hidden calling of our highest potential that is the real reason we are here. It undergirds our innate drives, challenges, and gifts and, for some people, this can remain unseen or obscure. He introduces a system to help determine which of the nine life paths you're supposed to lead: creativity, cooperation, expression, stability, freedom, vision, trust, recognition, and integrity.

  Whether or not those resonate for you, the idea here is to consider a broader concept that brings all the various life experiences and choices into a cohesive whole with a deeper sense of purpose.

- **Attending to the arising moment:** The last of Millman's four purposes is about being fully present to this moment, the now. Millman has a long history with the power of mindfulness practices and wrote books like *The Way of the Peaceful Warrior* and *Everyday Enlightenment*. Ultimately, we need to learn to live in the present moment, not stressing about the past or worrying about the future. That skill or practice is a vital part of living a purposeful life.

Millman is not the only one who holds this view. Other thought leaders on the power of mindfulness include Eckhart Tolle, the author of *The Power of Now*, and *A New Earth: Awakening to Your Life's Purpose*. If you'd like to learn more about the impressive scientific research about the benefits of mindfulness, my favorite book is *Altered Traits: Science Reveals How Meditation Changes Your Mind, Brain, and Body* by Dr. Daniel Goleman and Dr. Richard Davidson. They share amazing data on the power of mindfulness practices including its ability to

- reduce reactivity of the amygdala, making us less reactive to triggers,
- increase our resilience to stressors, including our ability to recover from difficult experiences,
- reduce unconscious bias,
- decrease inflammation,
- slow the aging process, making us physically younger than we are in years, and
- ease pain, anxiety, and depression to the same level as prescription drugs.

As we close this chapter, consider what might be a repeating lesson in your life and if there is something you are being called to learn. Explore the information you have gained so far about your purpose drivers. What have experiences shown you about your sweet spot?

My career continues to evolve but my sense of purpose is now crystal clear. I am here to help people and organizations rise to their potential. Some of you recognize this as my tagline—it's actually my core purpose. How I do that shifted over the years and continues to evolve. But that is the golden thread that ties it altogether. Now, when I feel my sense of purpose wane, I first have a little patience in case I am just feeling tired or moving through one of Hudson's phases. But if it continues to wane, it means that it's time to take stock again, see what lessons or insights have popped up, and how they are propelling me to the next phase of my journey.

20. Avoiding the 6 Purpose Derailers

Part of our journey to finding our purpose is also avoiding things that can derail us from our path or snuff out our sense of purpose. While we look at the six most common ones, reflect on which ones have impacted you over the years.

1. Ignoring the Messages

From what I can tell, the people who don't live a life of purpose are the ones who ignore the messages they are getting about their purpose or failing to learn the lessons. This often happens because the truth of their purpose goes against what their family or society believes is the right thing.

After all, if your purpose is to create art but your family told you that was a worthless pursuit, or at least not a practical one, it can be difficult to honor the light of that North Star. Honoring your purpose might upset or disappoint people. Or it might mean you make less money. Or it might mean you have to step away from years invested in education or career growth.

So, it's no wonder that some people try to ignore the message and keep following the initial plan. Dr. Dharius Daniels writes about the danger of conformity in his book *Your Purpose Is Calling*:

> *This push toward conformity starts during childhood, and it's usually quite subtle. We feel it without feeling it. We're shaped by it without any idea that we're being shaped by it. Before long, we get pushed away from the uniquely designed individuals every one of us was created to be…Pushing us to move away from our authentic selves and toward what everyone else desires.*

2. Exhaustion and Burnout

As we've learned from the pandemic, overwork, exhaustion, and burnout can take a heavy toll. If they are not recognized and corrected early, you can lose a sense of purpose that used to drive you. While sometimes burnout can nudge us to a new and better purpose, it's important to realize that you should also protect your purpose by making sure you don't push yourself to exhaustion.

Dr. Saundra Dalton-Smith's work on the types of rest has been particularly valuable to me in recovering from burnout and restoring my sense of purpose. You can learn more by watching her TEDx talk but here's a quick summary of the seven types she identifies:

- **Physical rest:** This includes all forms of sleep, including naps, massages, and active rest like yoga.

- **Mental rest:** Taking a break from thinking about work or life's worries. This can include taking a quick walk or vegging out with some TV.

- **Sensory rest:** This involves creating a calm and tranquil environment so we can get a break from all the sensory input (visual, auditory, olfactory, and kinesthetic) that we are barraged with every day, including unplugging from our digital devices.

- **Creative rest:** This is not about doing art or being good at it; creative rest is any activity that you do for enjoyment that lets you express yourself. It can also include appreciating beauty and art, and surrounding yourself with things that inspire you.

- **Emotional rest:** This happens when we take a break from people pleasing and just focus on being authentically ourselves. For some, this happens alone or with pets; for others it may include trusted friends.

- **Social rest:** We rest socially when we hang out with people who genuinely care about us and get who we are. After spending time with people you can socially reset with, you will likely feel recharged rather than drained.

- **Spiritual rest:** However you define "spiritual" for yourself, this type of rest includes things that open your heart, connect you with a sense of community, and give you a sense of purpose. For some this includes a religious tradition or a practice like prayer or mindfulness.

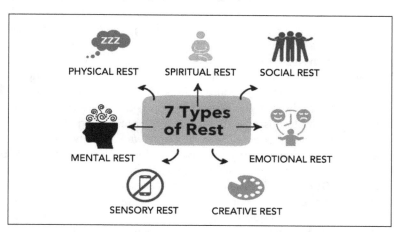

The seven types of rest

3. Too Many Commitments

Having too many commitments can get in the way of honoring our purpose too. Raising young children or helping sick family members can take a lot of time and focus and so, sometimes, purpose must take a back seat for a while. This choice can be hard and the right thing at the same time. But it doesn't mean that your North Star is gone. You're just heading in another direction for a bit, and sometimes these detours eventually give us valuable information that informs and strengthens our sense of purpose.

The important thing here is not to keep waiting or pushing it off. "Until the kids go to elementary school" can become "Until the kids graduate from high school," which can become, "After I retire" and then, the next thing you know, you're nearing 70. That's not to say that you still can't pursue your passion at 70, but do consider how much time you want left available to invest in this thing that's so important to you.

Purpose Story 21:
The Birthday Wakeup Call
While at my 48th birthday party, I realized I wanted a change of pace. I'd been in retail and nonprofit management for many years, but it was clear that I was burning out. It was like hitting a brick wall and I just couldn't do it anymore.

I realized I was not very happy with my life, but I had recently met a massage therapist who seemed so happy with hers. She made her own hours, worked with her hands, and I wanted to have a life like hers.

So, at my birthday party, I made the decision to go back to school and study massage at my local community college. I'd always been a hands-on person. For my whole life, I'd enjoyed things like knitting and gardening so massage seemed like it would be a good fit.

It was a great move, but also a little challenging. Most of the students were in their 20s and 30s, and when I walked in the door the first day, most of the students thought I was the instructor! I had to reprogram my brain and renew my skills to keep up with the program's pace. But during those classes, a lightbulb went off. I thought, "Oh my gosh! I should have chosen this years ago!" I realized it was perfect for me and it made me very happy.

I discovered that massage therapy is my true calling. Massage is a powerful tool that helps people. Seeing people walk into my office stressed and overwhelmed changed my outlook on life. Seeing people walk out feeling relaxed and refreshed gave me a sense of purpose.

I'm in my 60s now and still a practicing massage therapist (MT), seeing at least 10 clients every week. I actively look for modalities that I think will help my clients, so I continue to learn and grow. That led me to move into instruction and teaching other massage therapists. I love being part of their journey to this profession. Over the years I have had many causal reunions with former students and instructors. This journey has been a joy and a challenge. But I loved (almost) every minute of it!

4. Believing We Have to "Earn" It

Another purpose killer is when we hold pursuing our purpose as a reward that we must earn. For example, some people think, "I can only do that once I lose 20 pounds" or "finish that degree" or "pay off my debt." Media influencer Elyse Myers has a wonderful message about this. She says,

I need you to know that you are allowed to love yourself exactly as you are right now. No exceptions. Wholly and completely love yourself. Because you're brilliant. You're not a project that needs to be fixed. You don't need to be reinvented. You don't need to lose 15 pounds or get a new wardrobe. You don't need to be loved back by another person to be worth your own love. You have permission to love yourself today, not put it off until you reach that goal. You're worthy of being loved. Especially by you.

5. Turning Pleasure into Work

Remember, we need both types of well-being: hedonic (happiness) and eudaimonic (purpose/meaning). Sometimes, when doing something gives us feelings of pleasure or passion, we can think that it must be our purpose too. But that's not necessarily true. Some things are just meant to be fun and give you that feeling of joy.

I've been guilty of this myself, especially when I discover a new craft or hobby. I immediately dive in and start making things for others. At first, it's all good and I'm having fun making things for family and friends. But then the entrepreneurial part of my brain kicks in and I start to think about turning them into a business, like selling them on Etsy. I can't tell you how many times I have taken something fun and turned it into work, along with the pressure of deadlines and pleasing people.

It's one of those patterns or lessons that kept repeating until I finally learned it. But I know I'm not alone in this. I've seen many media influencers start posting about their pleasure/passion and, at first, it leads to followers and likes and opportunities. But then, it can quickly grow into a full-fledged business that they may not have really wanted.

For example, at the beginning of the pandemic, this one mom started posting her videos about her cookie decorating hobby. They were quite good and led to many orders and opportunities. But, recently, she did a post of how she now must get up at 5 a.m. to bake the hundreds of cookies people ordered. She made a very efficient process for mass production but still ends her day late at night. I could just hear the exhaustion in her voice as she signed off, "And then I get up tomorrow to do it all again."

Now, obviously, every passion comes with highs and lows and if it was only that one post, I wouldn't comment on it. But I have seen the joy slowly become work, and what was once the fun expression of creativity become the pressure to meet people's expectations.

Notice if this is something you should keep an eye out for. Do you want to turn your passion into a business? What will you gain and lose by doing that? Can you get the support and help you need as you grow so it stays enjoyable? And do you have the skills to set healthy boundaries with yourself and your customers? Perhaps most importantly, how will you find a new, pressure-free source for fun and creativity?

6. Opening Yourself to Others' Opinions

Another thing that happened to this cookie creator is that she started getting really nasty comments on her social media channels. Not just opinions about her art but about her personality and her appearance, and a whole host of things that had nothing to do with her posts.

While there were lots of positive and supportive posts, we are biologically wired to give more weight to negative comments. It's part of our survival biology as a tribal species to ensure that we are not in danger of getting ousted by the tribe. (I write about this in depth in my book, *Wired to Connect*, if you wish to learn more.) People can tell us, "Just ignore the negative people and focus on the positive ones" but that is asking us to go against hundreds of years of neurological makeup. Not easy to do. Or, more accurately, impossible to do.

These days, the internet is full of computer-driven bots that are programmed to deliver hurtful and hateful messages, and then there are those mean-spirited people who hide behind online anonymity to say cruel things to others. Many of them are hurt people who are releasing their own pain on others. But while we can know this conceptually, when we are the target of that hate, our body is still going to respond as it would to a legitimate threat.

One story that really struck me was by writer Lindy West, who was horribly trolled by one particular man after her father died. He even created an account in her father's name and sent her the most terrible messages of cruelty. But she took it upon herself to find him. She tracked him down and confronted him. You can listen to their conversation on the podcast, *This American Life*, episode 545, titled "If you don't have anything nice to say, SAY IT IN ALL CAPS."

It's a captivating discussion where he shares why he did it. After talking with him, Lindy goes on to say, "Trolls still waste my time and tax my mental health on a daily basis. But honestly, I don't wish them any pain. Their pain is what got us here in the first place. That's what I learned from my troll."

People in pain can be toxic because they are ultimately threatened by people who are happy or confident or living a life of purpose. Instead of cheering others on and working on themselves, they tend to tear others down.

Toxic people are everywhere, and it's important to protect yourself from them when you can. Especially if you are just starting to explore your purpose. Remember, we're holding that tiny flame in our hands at first, so tend it vigilantly. Until it's a strong, roaring fire, it can get doused by a friend's insensitive comment, even an inadvertent one, much less that passive-aggressive comment from a parent or nasty spewing of an internet troll.

Dr. Brené Brown shares her own journey of dealing with trolls. After her first TEDx talk went viral in 2010, she was impacted by horrible comments about her appearance, her marriage, and even her children. It threw her into a state of distress until she figured out how to manage it. She speaks about it in her interview with Oprah Winfrey on *Super Soul Sunday* as well as in her book *Daring Greatly: How the Courage to Be Vulnerable Transforms the Way We Live, Love,*

Parent, and Lead. She found this quote by Theodore Roosevelt, known as "The Man in the Arena" from his speech on citizenship. In her 2012 TED Talk, she summarized it like this:

> *It is not the critic who counts. It is not the man who sits and points out how the doer of deeds could have done things better and how he falls and stumbles. The credit goes to the man in the arena whose face is marred with dust and blood and sweat. But when he's in the arena, at best, he wins, and at worst, he loses, but when he fails, when he loses, he does so daring greatly.*

Remember, she recommends that when we're being vulnerable we protect ourselves from people who have not earned the right to have an opinion about us. Consider how you can create the right boundaries and safety measures to protect yourself from harmful opinions and hurtful comments.

Living Our Purpose Forward

Remember, we're not expecting that bolt of lightning where you get immediate clarity on your sense of purpose, nor that once you find a sense of purpose it will be the one thing you do forever. We're just focused on right now. Who you are now and what is resonating now. The rest will be revealed with time, as you have new experiences and grow along the way.

I hope you try all the new tools for exploring your sense of purpose and that you will discover at least a few that resonate for you, now, in this phase of your life. But remember, we move through cycles and evolve over time, so it can still be helpful to revisit this book in the future. You may find that a tool that doesn't resonate for you now will be very useful in the future.

Once you home in on your sense of purpose and you have some clarity, you'll need to do some general maintenance. Keep looking at your compass and paying attention to your emotions. You'll want to notice when you're veering off the path and need to course correct. Some side roads are worth traveling and others are distractions.

Also pay attention to the signs. I have found that I have such a strong force of will that I can push through a lot of obstacles, often to my detriment. Sometimes, the universe is sending me signals and if I ignore them in my focus of getting things done, I can actually delay a shift I was supposed to make.

The good news (even though it doesn't intuitively sound like it) is that when we ignore those whispers, they don't go away. They will come again and get louder. But as I have lived my life, I have gotten better at tuning into the whispers and the signs and paying attention to them sooner so that they don't have to hit me upside the head.

Another thing I would recommend is to express your values in a few different ways. Your job or career is just one avenue of many—but consider these:

- Job/career
- Your relationships

- Hobbies and activities
- Supporting the efforts of other organizations through volunteering your time or donating your money
- How and where you shop
- Professional associations
- Leaders you follow/support
- How you vote

By expressing your sense of purpose in a few different ways, you increase your chance of feeling fulfilled and being of service. If you get a new manager at work who is not supportive, you will still have the benefit of feeling fulfilled through other channels. If you experience a loss in your relationships, other avenues of your purpose can sustain you.

Finally, don't forget to have fun. Purpose is important and makes our lives worth living but it is supposed to be balanced with happiness. It's vital to your well-being to enjoy life, play, and have fun—so don't let those things get lost along the way.

Your Learning Journey

Take a few minutes to reflect on your own experiences with the concepts from this section.

- This section offers a range of tools to explore. Which ones did you enjoy the most and why?
- What are your core values? Share any new insights you gained about how you express your values and if any need more attention.
- How hints are your feelings and emotions giving you? What type of emotional reactivity (nervous, revved-up, molten, and retreating) do you experience most often?
- Share what you discovered about your joys and curiosities.
- What challenges (trauma, loss, betrayal, rejection, and failure) are you overcoming? How can you boost your healing?
- What patterns or lessons are repeating in your life? What do you need to learn from them?
- Have you experienced any of the 6 purpose derailers? What can you do to get back on track?
- Share your plan for getting more of the 7 types of rest in the coming weeks. Make sure you put this on your calendar.

BUILDING PURPOSE-DRIVEN ORGANIZATIONS

"Never underestimate the power of a small group of committed people to change the world. In fact, it is the only thing that ever has."

Margaret Mead,
author and anthropologist

21. The Continuum of Purpose-Driven Organizations

In the past, I would have considered purpose-driven companies as inspiring examples of what is possible but would remain the minority of business models. But after doing the research for this book, I am firmly convinced that they are becoming, and will soon be, the norm for how business is done on this planet. And not because CEOs are leading the charge (although many are) but because employees and consumers are demanding nothing less.

The momentum is now too strong to suppress. The entire human population is forever changed by the pandemic. The profound shifts we have made as individuals and societies simply cannot be undone. In addition, Gen Z and Gen Alpha are extraordinarily committed to pushing us forward.

In this chapter, we'll explore this bold new world of purpose-driven businesses, what distinguishes them from others and the benefits of creating them. In the remaining chapters, I'll offer strategies for employees, leaders, and managers for maximizing their role in this exciting new world.

The Continuum of Purpose

Using the term "purpose" to describe a business is not new. In fact, all business and organizations have a purpose of some type—they each exist to accomplish some goal and to thrive financially so they can continue to exist.

But the scope of that purpose has evolved dramatically in the past decade. And, just like human consciousness has been rising and accelerating (as we discussed in chapter 6), so has the idea of the purpose-driven organization.

In *Reinventing Organizations,* Frederic Laloux documents the shift of organizations from orange and green consciousness to the emergence of teal in 2014. Here is a quick summary of what differentiates these levels:

- **Orange/Achievement:** These organizations focus on profit and growth with the goal of beating the competition and providing great value to their financial shareholders. Innovation is the key to staying ahead so this stage has driven much of modern capitalism. Leaders use management by objectives (MBOs) or key performance indicators (KPIs) to measure effectiveness and success. Leaders use command and control on what the organization does but middle management has more freedom on how it gets done.

- **Green/Pluralistic:** These organizations seek to stay competitive by harnessing employee motivation and engagement. The definition of stakeholder expands beyond financial shareholders to include customers and employees. Green organizations focus on creating values-driven cultures, often offering a range of perks and benefits. In addition, there is a feeling of "family" within the organization and leaders seek employee input and strive to create an empowering environment.

- **Teal/Evolutionary:** Teal organizations started emerging in 2000 and not all were start-ups. Laloux found several organizations, ranging in size from 600 to 40,000 employees and across a wide range of industries, including apparel, manufacturing, technology, and healthcare. Teal organizations are seen as living systems with directions of their own that need to be listened to. This shifts the organizational structure from one of hierarchy to more localized and collaborative teams, which ushers in new models of decision-making, job responsibilities, and performance management. The definition of stakeholder expands beyond customers and employees to include communities and the environment, which alters how "costs" are determined and how success is measured. Known as holacracy, key breakthroughs include self-management, wholeness, and authenticity.

I describe these stages in more detail in my 2016 book *Wired to Resist* where I state: "There are levels of human consciousness beyond teal including turquoise, indigo, and purple/violet. As more and more humans express those levels, we will see them make their way into human society and organizations decades from now."

What myself and many other researchers could not anticipate were the extraordinary events that would soon occur, causing a massive leap forward in both human consciousness and what we want from organizations. But here we are and it's exciting.

Raj Sisodia studies purpose-driven organizations, documenting their rise since 2000 and tracking their continued outstanding financial performance. In the book *The Healing Organization: Awakening the Conscience of Business to Help Save the World*, Sisodia and co-author Michael Gelb articulate four stages of purpose-focused businesses that exist on a continuum:

> *A traditional business might say: "Here is an opportunity to make money by exploiting a need or gap in the marketplace." A business with a slightly more advanced mindset says, "Here is an opportunity to make money by exploiting a need or gap in the marketplace, and we will initiate some corporate social responsibility initiatives and employee wellness programs to help mitigate the suffering we cause. And we will throw some money at a few charities." A more evolved conscious business leader says, "Here's an opportunity to make a profit while serving customer needs and the needs of all stakeholders, including our communities and the environment." A Healing Organization says, "Our quest is to alleviate suffering and elevate joy. We serve the needs of all our stakeholders, including our employees, customers, communities, and the environment. We seek to continually improve the lives of all stakeholders while making a profit so that we can continue to grow and bring healing to the world.*

They go on to highlight 18 organizations that operate as healing organizations, which share these qualities:

- Their employees love coming to work
- Their customers are passionately loyal
- They have a strong and positive impact on the communities they serve
- They preserve and restore the ecosystems in which they operate

Other data supports this notion that profit-only is a thing of the past. McKinsey found that only 7 percent of Fortune 500 CEOs believe their companies should "mainly focus on making profits and not be distracted by social goals." The new norm is the "triple bottom line," which Harvard Business School calls the three Ps: profit, people, and the planet. This philosophy is at the heart of most current MBA programs. As we see in the above diagram, the triple bottom line covers three of the four stages on the continuum.

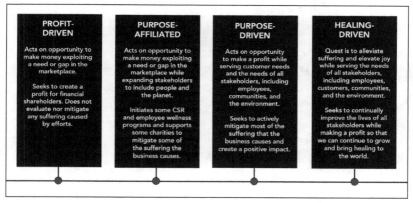

PROFIT-DRIVEN	PURPOSE-AFFILIATED	PURPOSE-DRIVEN	HEALING-DRIVEN
Acts on opportunity to make money exploiting a need or gap in the marketplace. Seeks to create a profit for financial shareholders. Does not evaluate nor mitigate any suffering caused by efforts.	Acts on opportunity to make money exploiting a need or gap in the marketplace while expanding stakeholders to include people and the planet. Initiates some CSR and employee wellness programs and supports some charities to mitigate some of the suffering the business causes.	Acts on opportunity to make a profit while serving customer needs and the needs of all stakeholders, including employees, communities, and the environment. Seeks to actively mitigate most of the suffering that the business causes and create a positive impact.	Quest is to alleviate suffering and elevate joy while serving the needs of all stakeholders, including employees, customers, communities, and the environment. Seeks to continually improve the lives of all stakeholders while making a profit so that we can continue to grow and bring healing to the world.

Continuum of purpose-driven organizations

Laloux and Sisodia's research identifies that more and more organizations are exhibiting teal consciousness and that we are now seeing the first signs of indigo consciousness. Some of these organizations were already teal and have accelerated their journey and others rapidly made the shift from their previous status as orange or green organizations.

- **Indigo/Transcendent:** The hallmarks of indigo consciousness include self-transcendence with our sense of purpose and meaning focused on being of service to others. This comes from an understanding that all things are connected, along with greater compassion for, and even cherishing of, others. Stakeholders now include suppliers, families of employees and customers, and more holistic views of communities and the environment. In addition, the tone changes from "do no harm" to focusing on ending suffering and creating healing. This shift naturally initiates a breakdown of old paradigms, philosophies, and structures as many were birthed from previous consciousnesses and are no longer compatible with the new level of evolution.

We can already see evidence of this shift at play. All the major business researchers—McKinsey, Deloitte, Gallup, and Gartner—recently published reports or feature articles on purpose-driven organizations.

Simultaneously, there is a big focus on well-being and thriving or flourishing. The US Surgeon General's 2022 report titled *Workplace Mental Health and Well-Being* released a new framework that identifies five essential elements: protection from harm, connection and community, work-life harmony, mattering at work, and opportunity for growth.

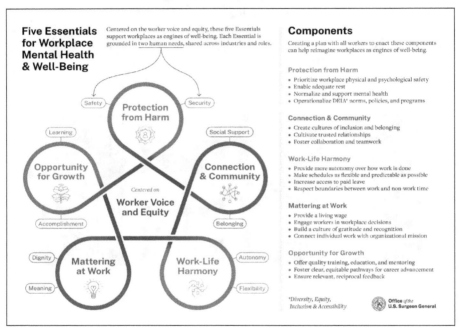

The five essentials for workplace mental health and well-being

Gallup has also turned their attention to well-being and now measures thriving along with engagement. They argue that well-being includes the following five elements:

- **Meaningful work/career well-being:** Liking what you do each day and being motivated to achieve your goals

- **Physical well-being:** Having good health and enough energy to get things done daily

- **Social well-being:** Having supportive relationships and love in your life

- **Financial well-being:** Earning a living wage and managing your economic life to reduce stress and increase security

- **Community well-being:** Liking where you live, feeling safe, and having pride in your community

Hallmarks of Purpose-Driven Organizations

According to several researchers, purpose-driven and/or healing organizations present five hallmarks:

1. Expanding the stakeholder model

Every expert on purpose-driven organizations mentions expanding beyond financial shareholders to include multiple stakeholders that must include communities (people) and the environment (planet). *Harvard Business Review*'s Paul Polman and Andrew Winston define purpose-driven organizations as those that "improve well-being for everyone it impacts and at all scales—every product, every operation, every region and country, and for every stakeholder, including employees, suppliers, communities, customers, and even future generations and the planet itself."

These efforts can range from trying to actively reduce or offset the organization's carbon footprint to radically transforming business practices and even industries. For example, several clothing retail companies like H&M, Nike, Kering, and PVH created the Global Fashion Agenda, a nonprofit organization that focuses on sustainable fashion. They are addressing everything from how and where materials are sourced to their use of plastics and packaging and creating closed-loop recycling.

2. Putting employees first

Many sources argue that employees must be considered the *first* stakeholder since so much of the organization's ability to achieve its goals relies on an engaged and thriving workforce—including paying a living wage, ensuring physical and psychological safety, and other key elements of thriving and well-being.

This is a smart move because Deloitte found that when choosing a brand, 28 percent of consumers look at how the company treats their employees. Gallup's research has long shown that engaged employees are more productive, loyal, and innovative, driving up financial performance and customer experience.

Purpose-driven companies are ending the philosophy that the "customer is always right" to better protect employees from abusive customers. Several airline and hospital executives have taken a firmer line since the pandemic created a rash of hostile and abusive behavior by passengers and patients alike.

3. Investing in making a genuine difference

Gone are the days when organizations could make a cursory effort to look concerned about purpose. In *The Purpose Economy,* Aaron Hurst explains that many companies used cause-based marketing "to infuse their products with purpose" by partnering with a nonprofit and "drafting off of their purpose." For example, a company might donate a portion of their proceeds to a nonprofit organization or sponsor a fundraising event.

After drafting, organizations might shift to more direct actions like initiating a corporate social responsibility practice, or launching a donation-matching program for employees. While these are positive practices, they become problematic when the organization undermines those same advances with their own sourcing and production practices. Today's employees and consumers want more authentic investment, where the goal is real and sustained change. Millennials and Gen Z employees and consumers are particularly sensitive to hypocrisy and will not hesitate to call it out publicly, using social media and protests to raise awareness and apply pressure.

To choose their list of the 100 most purposeful brands each year, the Purpose Power Index looks at four elements:

- **Beyond profits:** Has a higher purpose that's bigger than just making money for shareholders
- **Improving lives:** Improves the lives of people and their communities
- **Better society:** Does things to not just benefit shareholders, employees, or customers but society as a whole
- **Better world:** Is committed to changing the world for the better

They also solicit the opinions of consumers and employees to determine who makes the cut. It is not uncommon to see organizations tackle a range of issues "like waste disposal, water quality, access to healthcare, and even police violence."

4. Measuring results and creating accountability
To ensure that their efforts are driving critical results, purpose-driven organizations invest in measuring and tracking their progress as well as creating cultures of accountability. As researchers at Deloitte put it,

> *Much like what a foundation is to a house, a conductor is to an orchestra, and a canvas is to an artist's masterpiece—a clear purpose is everything to an organization. It is an organization's soul and identity, providing both a platform to build upon and a mirror to reflect its existence in the world. It articulates why an organization exists, what problems it is here to solve, and who it wants to be to each human it touches through its work.*

Executives are setting meaningful goals, tracking progress, and creating accountability. For example, cleaning product company, Seventh Generation, is aiming to be a zero-waste company by 2025. They built sustainability targets into the incentive system for their entire workforce.

Benefits of Purpose-Driven Organizations
The data is also clear that purpose-driven organizations experience many benefits, the most prominent being the following:

Financial growth
In Deloitte's global study, purpose-driven companies enjoyed higher market share gains than their competitors and grew three times faster. *Harvard Business*

Review found nearly 60 percent experienced growth over a three-year period, compared to only 40 percent for companies with less clear purpose.

The nonprofit organizations Torrey Project and Conscious Capitalism find that purpose-driven companies consistently outperform their counterparts by as much as 15 to 1. Consider this compelling data:

Cumulative Returns	5 years	10 years	15 years	20 years
S&P 500	86%	96%	301%	269%
Good to Great companies	106%	54%	234%	422%
Non-US Firms of Endearment	49%	93%	961%	1,509%
US Firms of Endearment	109%	231%	901%	2,077%

Performance of purpose-driven organizations against S&P 500

Part of this is due to real financial rewards for being purpose-driven. While there might be initial costs to make changes—for example, to a more sustainable or renewable source of energy—those investments offer a good return, including increased market share and/or consumer loyalty.

Organizations can reap other financial benefits as well. For example, Danone, a multinational French food corporation, was able to secure cheaper capital from a syndicate of banks that prioritized organizations meeting certain environmental, social, and governance (ESG) goals.

Consumer loyalty
When choosing a brand, 20 percent of consumers look at how the company treats the environment, and 19 percent look at what the company is doing to support the community. This gives consumers a sense of meaning and purpose with their purchasing decisions. Becoming a purpose-driven company can generate new revenue and also protect against loss. McKinsey found that nearly half of consumers (47 percent) will stop buying or even actively boycott a brand's products if they are disappointed with their stance on a social issue. Nearly 20 percent are lost for good to your competitors.

Employee retention
This desire for meaning and purpose holds true for employees as well. McKinsey finds that because the majority of employees feel disengaged, they are "agitating for decisions and behaviors that they can be proud to stand behind and gravitating toward companies that have a clear, unequivocal, and positive impact on the world." Today's employees are willing to stage boycotts and

protests, leverage social media, and petition their leaders and elected officials to create change.

In addition, they are more selective about where they work. Before they apply or accept a job, two-thirds of Millennials look at a company's stance on social and environmental issues.

Executives that strive to build a purpose-driven organization tend to also invest in building positive workplace cultures. They see marked advantages over their competitors who don't and can attract and retain high-performing workers even amidst talent shortages.

Purpose Story 22:
Daring to Lead
My most profound and recent experience was when I was working for a retail brand, managing their eCommerce customer service team. Shortly before COVID hit, we partnered with a huge UK fashion house and became a shared services hub for multiple brands. It was a big shift for all of us.

Then we all went into lockdown, which was hard on everyone. After a few months of listening to my colleagues' concerns, I did something bold for our company culture. This action took quite a bit of courage on my part: I scheduled a meeting with the CEO and executive team and requested that once a month we stop for an hour or so and do a workshop on Brené Brown's book *Dare to Lead*.

At that time, we did not have any professional development programs in place. It would not be required by anyone, but an invitation to grow through difficult times. It felt very vulnerable, especially to propose something about being better leaders to the leadership team, but I felt it was something that we all needed.

My request was accepted and they even financed the books and materials we needed. Most of the company came, and together we created a safe space to process each of our different experiences with the current company changes. We rose above our fears of the unknown, together.

When I resigned from that company to become a coach, every single person wrote to me, thanking me for opening the door to the workshop opportunity. All I had done was set the table with a few simple tools and sat back and watched these amazing humans take flight. I can guarantee that some of those participants will do that same thing for others during the course of their careers.

I believe that experience exemplifies what happens when we are faced with an opportunity to fulfill our purpose—in spite of our human fear, we are motivated to reach for our North Star no matter what the cost.

Looking back, it was an egoless decision. Perceived personal or professional judgments did not hold me back from asking for what was needed. It seemed like such a big deal then, but now as I write this it does not sound as profound as it felt. My sense of purpose was to develop others to be the best leaders in their own unique way. What really caused me to act was a conversation I had with a colleague who said, "We have the opportunity to be the leaders we would want." I just provided the HOW to the WHAT.

I did what the book encouraged—I dared to lead by getting vulnerable and leading by example. The workshop had an impact because the people I worked with still talk about it years later. You never know the impact you have on others, especially when you speak your truth, act your truth, and respond from the heart.

Sustainable business

The above benefits of financial growth, consumer loyalty, and employee retention exist, of course, in parallel with the real benefit of building a world that promotes your own business sustainability. Consider this headline from the *Wall Street Journal*: "PG&E: The First Climate-Change Bankruptcy, Probably Not the Last."

Climate change drove a decade-long drought in California. In 2017, PG&E power lines triggered 17 major wildfires and destroyed nearly 200,000 acres. The damage spread over eight counties and killed 22 people—making it the most deadly and destructive fire season on record.

My family, and thousands of others, were evacuated and that was before the resulting mudslides tore through our community, killing another 23 people in 2018. PG&E faced $30 billion in liabilities leading it to seek bankruptcy.

California was not the only state suffering. The National Centers for Environmental Information tracked wildfires along with three tropical cyclones, eight severe storms, two inland floods, a crop freeze, and droughts. All are rooted in climate change and all cost businesses and their owners more than $300 million in damages, lost inventory, buildings and facilities, staffing, and insurance, to name a few.

Dr. Bruce Usher at Columbia Business School studies climate change and investing. He identifies three climate-related risks that will cause more businesses to fail in the future:

- **Physical risks:** These include damage to business facilities and properties or lawsuits and financial liabilities (like PG&E faced).

- **Policy-related risks:** Government agencies will pass new regulations to change behavior by businesses and consumers alike, which will cost financially when adopted.

- **Technological risks:** Certain products and ways of business will become obsolete, and companies will need to adapt or close their doors. While the shift away from fossil fuels and combustible engines points to a world of more electric vehicles, there is another man-made sustainability crises. For example, China is home to more than 90 percent of the rare earth metals used in a wide variety of electronics. They claim those will be mined out in as little as 20 years.

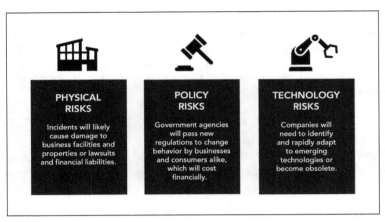

The three types of climate-related risks

We're also facing a climate-driven crisis with animal species. The Living Planet Index (LPI) monitors the world's populations of mammals, birds, fish, reptiles, and amphibians. According to their 2022 report, there is an average decline of 69 percent in species populations since 1970. Think about that—we have lost nearly 70 percent of the earth's species populations in just 53 years! Latin America shows the greatest regional decline (94 percent), while freshwater species populations have seen the greatest overall global decline (83 percent).

Scientists at the UN Convention on Biological Diversity recently concluded that, "Every day, up to 150 species may go extinct. This means as many as 10 percent of species a decade." The five major causes of extinction are habitat loss, introduced species, pollution, population growth, and overconsumption (hunting).

Humans are suffering too. While extreme poverty has been declining around the world over the past generation, the pandemic also pushed millions into extreme poverty. Nearly half of the world's population lives on less than $6.85 per day, and three billion people cannot afford a healthy diet. The good news is we have the ability to end world poverty and many countries are making progress. But this issue impacts us all: poverty influences access to, and quality of, healthcare and greatly contributes to disease progression as well as how we can respond to a global pandemic.

The power of purpose-driven organizations is not just about creating meaningful work, although that certainly creates a transcending experience for many. Purpose-driven organizations are the avenue by which we create a better world for us all to live in. As Feike Sijbesma, former CEO of DSM, says, "You cannot be successful, nor call yourself successful, in a society that fails."

22. Strategies for Employees to Create Meaningful Work

Finding meaningful work is critical to your health and well-being. The following tips and tools can help you find the right match as you seek new employment or enhance the experience you have at your current organization. I also recommend reading the next chapters on managers and leaders to further guide your exploration.

1. Get clear on what you want.

This will come from the reflection you have done throughout this book and what you learned about your sense of purpose, your skills and talents, your pleasures and preferences, etc. Doing that exploration arms you with deep knowledge about yourself, which will help you find the right fit.

2. Set a good bar.

Needing to find a job can create a lot of pressure, especially if bills are coming due. But it's important to set a good bar because it will help you be more discerning and not settle. Instead of saying, "I need to a job that pays me X amount," strongly claim, "I want a job where I have meaningful work, feel supported and fulfilled, am paid well, enjoy my colleagues, and can have pride about our impact in the world." You deserve those things and, by setting them as your goal, you will be more discerning.

I swear, sometimes, I think the universe is listening. I have had the experience of shifting my expectations and better options suddenly start showing up. Setting that type of goal gives you a lens by which you apply and interview, and it will help you see where things may not align.

3. Look for purpose-driven organizations.

Your chances of finding meaningful work go up when you work at purpose-driven organizations. Before you apply, do some research. Use published lists about, and books on, purpose-driven organizations to create a list of places to apply.

Once you identify some possible places to work, look on the website for their vision, mission, and value statements. This is good information to have when you interview anyway but it also helps you decide if you want to apply there. You might also want to search for stories about the impact they have on customers. Do the customers like the product and service they get? Are employees making a difference in the lives of the people they serve?

Also explore their corporate social responsibility (CSR) practices. How and where do they support the local community? What kind of philanthropy do they engage in? And do they support their employees in giving back? What role are they playing with social issues like equality and the environment?

4. Research the senior leaders.

Your next step is to research the people leading that organization. This is important because a new president or CEO can quickly ruin a great culture. Make sure that the people who created the aspects of the organization that you like are still in charge. If it's a small organization, it might be the original founder or president; if it's large, it might be a team of senior executives. Search the website and LinkedIn to learn what you can about them.

In particular, you want to know how long they have been there and anything you can about their leadership style or philosophy. Sometimes bios or videos sharing their thoughts can be found online. Sometimes there are press releases, briefings, interviews, or videotaped meetings where you can learn more or even see them in action. Sometimes, you have to read between the lines, like looking at their past companies and what people said about them there.

Glassdoor.com has some useful information about how an executive is perceived. But be warned: much like Yelp, Glassdoor manipulates companies into paying for their service. Both Yelp and Glassdoor will withhold the positive comments so that more negative views are prominent and will only balance them once the company or restaurant pays a monthly fee. So, don't trust Glassdoor completely but let them add some additional flavor to things you are discovering elsewhere.

In addition to the senior leaders, look at the leader of the function where you will be working. This person will set the tone for the culture you experience on a regular basis so learn all you can about them.

5. Explore how they treat their employees.

This is a really important part of your process and you should do a bit before you even decide to apply. Here are some things to look for:

Your best sources are previous employees, so ask around and see if you know anyone who has worked there or someone who has a connection. LinkedIn is another good place to look.

How does the organization talk about employees on their website or materials? Do they use language that indicates that employees are an important part of their community or another cog in their machine? Do they sound sincere or patronizing?

Organizations that want to attract and retain good employees publicize their perks and benefits. Healthcare is a common benefit but the better packages include vision and dental coverage. Do you get paid time off? Do they demonstrate that they care about families with paid leave, family days or events, and pet insurance? Look at how they talk about wellness and well-being. What do they offer to help people thrive?

You may not be able to discover all the answers before you apply but try to learn what you can throughout the interview process.

6. Discover how they support their managers.

Another critical element of purpose-driven organizations is that they provide training and support to their managers. As the source of how safe, respected, and supported people feel, your manager will have the most influence over your daily experience at the organization. Make sure that the organization provides training and support to their managers and supervisors.

In addition, learn about your direct manager. These questions are best directed to the HR person who runs your hiring process. Some things to ask:

- How long have they been there?
- Have they gone through training?
- How do they measure manager success and create accountability? For example, do they measure employee engagement? How are the scores for this team? And what is the turnover like in this department?
- Why did the person leave the role you are applying for?

Again, whether or not you get direct answers for each question, try to piece together a picture. Especially if you notice people deflecting the question or dropping eye contact as they answer you.

7. Observe how they treat you as a candidate.

The application and interview process will also tell you a lot about the organization. Do they set you up for success with clear communication and accurate information? Do they talk positively about the organization and its purpose in the world? Pay attention to how you are treated and the tone of your interactions. They should be warm and friendly, and make you excited to work there. If they are failing at that, it is not likely to get better once you accept the job.

Purpose Story 23:
Enduring Through the Pandemic
I was hired as an instructional designer and joined the team with a strong sense of purpose and desire to help others better understand how to create impactful adult learning. I quickly learned the trainers were set in their ways and not interested in discovering the value of learning science or new tools.

After a year, I was told my role was shifting to recruiter. I could recruit new talent and train them on adult learning theory. I didn't want to be a recruiter, but the pandemic had just hit and I was concerned about the job market, so I stayed on doing something I knew nothing about. For two long years, I tried to love it but it simply never filled my cup. I had very little support from my team and felt more and more alone.

I tried to create change. I told my supervisor I didn't like recruiting—to be clear, I was successful in my work. I hired talent, I trained them, and they still work for the company. I talked to my supervisor and the chief people officer about moving into a role more suited to my skill set. I asked about taking over our internal training program when the people who ran it left, but I was denied. I tried hard to find ways to bring my skills and passion to the workplace.

At some point, I was told I was now in charge of onboarding too. Never was I asked, I was told. I tried to find purpose there. For 90 days, I'd do my best to onboard a new hire and teach them what it meant to make quality content. The problem was we only hired content creators once or twice a year, and therefore, I was left with too many days that had no purpose. I had no direction, no guidance, and no team to collaborate with. The concept of Ikigai comes to mind. I was making money, but had no purpose, which left me feeling dissatisfied and useless. I needed more.

I wouldn't say I fell into depression, but I would say I was certainly depressed about my job, my position, and what I was doing with my life. I found other outlets outside of work to ensure my mental health was nurtured—I upped my gratitude practice and increased my time spent mediating. Both helped stave off the depression in an otherwise lonely time in my life. But I persevered and I can't say enough how excited I am to feel purpose again....

Throughout this entire struggle, I searched for jobs. I wanted a job with purpose and I'm happy to say that role has arrived. I'm now the Talent Development Partner with a global company that cultivates and maintains a strong culture. I can feel in my heart that it is what I need. Even during the interview process, I felt the passion rise up from within just talking about the role. I feel energized. I feel alive.

8. Ask questions because interviewing is a two-way process.

It's easy to feel that you need to do everything you can to impress interviewers but that doesn't mean they shouldn't be trying to impress you too. Interviewing is a two-way street and while they are asking you questions to see if you are a good fit, you should be asking questions to see if they are a good fit for you.

At the end of every interview, they will ask you if you have any questions, and honestly, this is an important part of the interview. Having been part of hiring hundreds of people over the years, I'm always surprised if someone doesn't take advantage of that opportunity.

In addition to learning about how they engage in being a purpose-driven organization, here are some questions to consider asking:

- Tell me why you like working here?
- What inspires you when things are challenging?
- Do you offer training and development to employees?
- What kinds of topics do you offer and how does one get to participate?
- Please tell me more about how the work of this role or the team contributes to the organization's overall vision and mission? How can we measure our contributions' impact?

9. Negotiate the offer.

Once you get the job offer, negotiate the terms to better support your needs. They cannot withdraw an offer just because you ask for something—the worst that can happen is they don't adjust it. Request the compensation that reflects your experience and the perks or benefits that will make you feel supported. You can only do one round of this so do your research before the offer arrives. Consider elements like financial compensation, bonus rates, stock options, flexible work schedule, expanded benefits, additional days of vacation, and access to professional development like conferences, classes, etc.

10. Attend new-hire orientation or onboarding.

This is an important part of how the organization welcomes you and sets you up for success. Use this time to learn about the organization, meet key support people, and start building your relationships. Take notes and ask questions along the way.

11. Set up a 30-60-90 day plan and a mentor.

The best managers will think through how to best onramp you to the team and projects. The most common form is a 30-60-90-day plan. If they have not prepared one for you, ask for it, so you have a document that articulates their expectations, to better measure your success. Another best practice is to assign a mentor or buddy to a new hire—an experienced employee to guide and offer support. If your manager does not assign a mentor to you, ask for one or find your own among the more senior members of the team.

Set up your cadence of regular meetings with your manager. When you are new, you should meet at least once per week and more frequently is common. You might then switch to every other week, or monthly. In addition, it's great to have quarterly performance check-ins that build up to the annual performance review.

12. Join employee resource groups and volunteer opportunities.

Many organizations now offer employee resource groups (ERGs) or other opportunities to connect with people around important issues. In addition, the organization may offer activities around volunteering and community involvement. Learn what is available and join ones that resonate for you.

13. Take advantage of learning and development (L&D).

Discover what L&D options exist for you and use them. You'll get support for growing your skills, which helps you in the current role and sets you up for future opportunities. Plus, L&D is usually run by people with experience cultivating potential, so you may find support that your manager cannot provide.

14. If there are issues, speak up.

Everyone starts a new job engaged but, over time, things happen to take the blush off the rose. Some may be things you need to live with. Others should be addressed, but this will only happen if you raise the issue. Your manager is your starting place. Share what is happening and make a clear request for what you need or the support you want. Your manager should listen to you respectfully.

If you don't get what you need, you might want to ask people in L&D. They tend to have a good view of what is available in the organization and it's not the same as "reporting" something to HR. Perhaps there is someone higher in your function—many executives have an open-door policy or they have a chief of staff you can speak with. Maybe there a committee is already working on that very issue and you can help shape the solution.

If not, and you still believe in the organization, explore how you can move to a different area. Some organizations offer internal job moves and you can also apply for open jobs. I've even had success pitching an idea and creating a new role for myself.

15. Don't wait to too long to leave.

If the organization is not the right fit for you, don't wait too long to leave. Each day that you are in the wrong fit, or worse, an unsupportive or toxic culture, harm is happening. It creates worry, stress, and burnout, all of which have real implications for your physical and emotional health. If your efforts have not made a difference, they are not going to magically start. Spend your energy on finding a better fit.

16. Consider working for yourself.

Sometimes, the best way to create meaningful work and live your sense of purpose is to work for yourself. This may seem scary, but every business was founded by someone who felt similarly—they realized that they had something to offer that couldn't happen inside someone else's organization.

Starting a business is easier than you think, and your local chamber of commerce and community college will have great resources on how to do so. Many offer classes, and it can be fun joining the community of business owners. Remember, your life is unfolding exactly as it should so if you have struggled in finding the right place to work, it may be because your purpose is to create it.

Purpose Story 24:
Believe in Yourself
Success happens when you keep going and never give up in what you believe in. When I started my coaching business 10 years ago, I was told that my business would not survive. But here I am!

When I started my business, I helped people with their resumes for free—yes, for free. Then I started charging minimally. My next step was to get certified as a coach. I paid money that I did not have, meaning I charged it to my credit card, because I simply believed in myself. I took the 12-month coaching course and became certified as a life and career coach. At first, business was slow and I wanted to give up, but I kept saying to myself, "Someone needs my help." I kept pushing because my purpose is to coach the working woman on how to have work/life harmony in her life.

Through it all, I kept believing in myself. I think the biggest part of my coaching business being successful is that I am the example that people can follow. I believe in coaching and I have a coach. I believe in the practice and I believe in the results. I practice what I preach and teach.

My sense of purpose comes from my life story, what I have been through, and what I have continue to overcome. I'm not special. If I can do it, anyone can. The mind is the obstacle—if we change the way we think, we can do anything.

Even now, as I'm getting my PhD, I continue to have work/life harmony. I put a pause on some of my coaching business activities so that I could focus on this new goal. As hard as it was, I had to do it because I recognize that I am human. I continue to practice what I preach, overcoming obstacles and living my best life while doing it. And that is exactly what I coach others to do. Let's just say, I love what I do!

We spend more time at work than we do sleeping so it's important that you find where you flourish. You deserve to spend that one-third of your life doing something you love. I hope you use these various strategies to ensure that you live your purpose and have meaningful work.

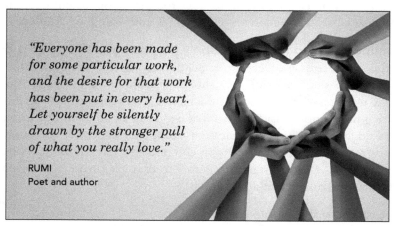

"*Everyone has been made for some particular work, and the desire for that work has been put in every heart. Let yourself be silently drawn by the stronger pull of what you really love.*"

RUMI
Poet and author

Rumi on meaningful work

23. Strategies for Managers to Enliven Purpose in Their People

While leaders set the tone for a purpose-driven organization, managers are the ones who bring it to life. Or bury it.

We already discussed the damage that poor managers do but in this chapter we'll focus on the incredible power that managers have to enliven purpose and shape meaningful work for their people. Consider these findings:

- Gallup found that managers account for 70 percent of the variance in employee engagement.
- *Harvard Business Review* discovered that management techniques explain nearly 20 percent of the difference between the highest- and lowest-performing employees.
- Every 10 percent increase in a manager's effectiveness yields a 14 percent increase in employee productivity.

Managers matter. Being a great manager is about making the critical pivot from star performer to facilitator. Your success is now measured by your people's success. Your focus now is to create the conditions for them to do *their* best work.

If you manage others, I recommend trying out these strategies to enliven purpose and enhance your employees' experience of meaningful work. Notice that many of these speak to the five areas of well-being from the Surgeon General's report in chapter 21: protection from harm, opportunity for growth, mattering at work, connection and community, and work-life harmony.

1. Communicate your organization's purpose and the good it does.

Hopefully your senior leaders are regularly sharing the purpose, vision, and mission but, if not, you definitely should. Ensure communication makes it from the top of the organization to the people who report to you. Spend time discussing the purpose, vision, and mission in team and one-on-one meetings.

Pass along important communications from your leaders. If you can, watch all-hands meetings together as a group and discuss what you learn. Make sure your people get access to senior leaders. For example, invite an executive to have a coffee discussion with your group.

2. Get to know the whole person.

Spend time getting to know each of your people. Build rapport so you can have authentic conversations to learn about what makes work meaningful to them. Discover their dreams and what gives them stress. Ask where they are on their journey to finding their own individual sense of purpose. Ask how they like to be supervised and what makes them feel appreciated. Be willing to share as well—the most authentic and open relationships are reciprocal. Consider reading *The Dream Manager* by Mathew Kelly.

3. Help your people discover their sense of purpose.

If some of your people are unclear about their purpose, provide opportunities to support them. Encourage people to utilize this book and others that guide people through a discovery process. See if your organization's learning program offers relevant workshops and resources.

4. Help your people find alignment between their role and the organization's purpose.

Spend time talking with them individually about their roles. Explain how their daily activities connect to your department's important work and how this, in turn, supports the organization's purpose and its impact in the world. Ideally, you would do this with all your employees. It's especially impactful when you are recruiting, hiring, and onboarding new team members.

5. Shine a light on successes to build pride.

People can feel their work is more meaningful when they see the impact of their role and/or organization. Make a point of regularly sharing success stories. Feature stories from your customers—ask your marketing department if they have any to pass along to your team. Highlight your own team's successes as well as other teams or projects in your organization. Look at the impact they are having in the community. Better yet, do this as a team—have people take turns finding things to share. Together, these things can build pride in where you work.

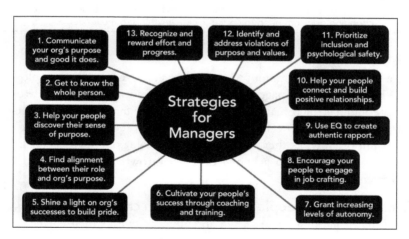

Strategies for managers

6. Cultivate your people's success through coaching and training.

Everyone wants the opportunity to learn, grow, and improve. To help them do this effectively, develop your coaching skills. Take any coaching classes or manager training available to you. Read the book *Help Them Grow or Watch Them Go: Career Conversations Organizations Need and Employees Want* by Beverly Kaye and Julie Giulioni or enroll in a coaching program.

7. Grant increasing levels of autonomy.

Autonomy is a key factor in helping people feeling their work is meaningful and fulfilling. Did you know there are eight levels of autonomy you can grant an employee? Ross Weber discovered that the levels are differentiated by who does the analysis, who makes the decision, and who takes the action.

1	The delegate has no autonomy in this lowest level. Delegate looks into the problem, gathers the information, and gives it to the leader/manager who makes the decision and takes the action.
2	Delegate explores the alternatives available, noting the pros and cons of each option. The delegate presents this analysis to the leader, who decides what to do and takes the action.
3	Delegate explores the options and makes a decision, recommending a course of action to the manager. The leader approves the decision and takes the action.
4	Delegate explores options and makes decision about a course of action, but delays implementation until the leader approves. At that point the delegate takes the action.
5	Delegate informs the manager of his or her plans and can take the action unless the leader says not to.
6	Delegate takes the action and informs the leader after the fact what was done and how it turned out.
7	Delegate takes the action and only communicates with the leader if the action was not successful.
8	The delegate has complete autonomy in this highest level. Delegate takes the action and does not need to communicate anything to the leader.

The eight levels of autonomy

As a manager, be clear about what level you are granting your employee, so you are both on the same page. If they get less autonomy than they were expecting, they could feel micromanaged; if you grant more than they expect, they may not step up the way you need them to or they might feel set up to struggle.

Most importantly, as they demonstrate success at one level, grant increasing levels of autonomy to acknowledge their growth and encourage further development.

8. Encourage your people to engage in job crafting.

Job crafting or hacking occurs when an employee tweaks their current role or duties to better align with their skills and interests. For example, a marketing coordinator in a tech firm took on as much event planning as she could, even though it wasn't originally part of her job. She explains, "I do it because I enjoy it, and I'm good at it. I've become the go-to person for event planning."

Similarly, a maintenance technician in a manufacturing company also crafted his job. He says, "When I first came here, we started using the new, higher-speed equipment. Then lots of new guys came in, so I started helping them learn the ropes. Now it's just expected that I train the new guys. I did this in my previous job, so I have experience with it, and I like it because I'm able to help and work with guys from different backgrounds."

You can hear in both examples that they have made their work more personally meaningful, giving them a sense of pride. Ask your people about their strengths, passions, and preferences and encourage them to help you cocreate a great job with them.

Purpose Story 25:
Creating Purpose for Your Team
Having worked in Learning & Development for many years, I understand the value of purpose for individuals and how it deepens connection for a team. Unfortunately, we don't always land in organizations that understand this importance and we've got to make the best of a situation.

A few years back I was in such a situation. I was leading the Learning & Development function for a mid-sized organization, but quite frankly it was a bit of a mess. There were a lot of silos and infighting across teams. I really wanted to make as much of an impact in this organization as possible as I saw the opportunity ahead of us.

Within my first year, we had built a development framework for the organization from scratch, and I slowly built/hired my team. Once we were all in place, I could feel that it would be easy for the team to get lost in the chaos of the larger organization if we didn't have the right anchor. As a team, we went through an exercise to define our own mission, vision, purpose, and values. Our values aligned with the organizational values, but with an added layer of nuance that was unique to the work we did for the organization.

Once we finalized it within our team, we published it to the organization to provide an exemplar of how a team or organization could create a North Star. We also published it as a way to hold ourselves accountable. While our impact within the organization was limited, it's what kept our team together and provided grounding and direction for our work.

The organization eventually went through a series of transformations and the team disbanded. However, we still have monthly "team meetings" to keep each other up to date on what we're working on and offer help as others need it. The purpose we defined together as a collective is something that persists today, even though we're not all working in the same organization. It really demonstrates the value and bond that collective purpose can create.

9. Use emotional intelligence to create authentic rapport.

When you do your job well, employees will share with you how they are really feeling and what they need. Develop your emotional intelligence skills so you can better understand them and create authentic rapport. I encourage you to explore the variety of books and trainings on emotional intelligence, particularly those by Daniel Goleman, the father of emotional intelligence. I also have video courses on LinkedIn Learning on EQ and related topics.

10. Help employees connect and build positive relationships.

A major component of meaningful work is feeling camaraderie with our colleagues. Design work environments and experiences that help people connect with their coworkers. Encourage casual events and invest in both team building and team training, as they are different but crucial for group success. You might want to check out my brain-based training for tips on how to build high-performing teams (see page 215).

11. Prioritize creating inclusion and psychological safety.

The research is clear—inclusion and psychological safety are the cornerstones of high-performing teams and also part of how you demonstrate the well-being of "protection from harm." I go into depth about this in *Wired to Connect* and I also recommend you read Harvard professor, Dr. Amy Edmondson's book *Teaming: How Organizations Learn, Innovate, and Compete in the Knowledge Economy*.

12. Identify and address violations of purpose and values.

You'll find this strategy also listed in chapter 23 as a responsibility of senior leaders. But the truth is that you will more likely be able to see the violations of the organization's purpose, vision, and values. It's vital that you address them as soon as you can because perceived hypocrisy is the most damaging to employee engagement and retention. You need to walk the talk yourself.

13. Recognize and reward both effort and progress.

Part of what makes work feel meaningful is when others recognize our contributions. As a manager, take time to acknowledge each person's strengths and their contributions to the project and team. Make a point of celebrating milestones and project completions. Research shows that these casual rituals of celebration contribute greatly to people feeling like they and their work matters.

In addition, be sure to reward effort and progress. Your team can be working very hard, and we can tend to focus on where we are behind or how much there is to do. But by rewarding effort and progress, you keep everyone motivated, and on the path to learning and growing.

If you need further motivation, consider this quote from Patrick Lencioni's book *Three Signs of a Miserable Job: A Fable for Managers*:

> *Here's the thing...And I think you probably know this deep down inside. You have an opportunity to make a substantial difference in your employee's life. And in the lives of the other people you manage. There is probably no other person in the world right now, other than their spouses, who is going to do as much to determine these people's sense of accomplishment and peace of mind.*

24. Strategies for Leaders to Build Purpose-Driven Organizations

Harvard's Dr. Ranjay Gulati, author of *Deep Purpose: The Heart and Soul of High-Performance Companies*, identifies four ways in which purpose galvanizes organizations and drives outstanding performance and growth.

- **Directional:** Purpose serves as a North Star, guiding strategic direction, day-to-day decisions, and goals for innovation.
- **Relational:** Purpose helps you build credibility and trust with stakeholders, supporting the development of long-term relationships.
- **Reputational:** Purpose enables you establish loyalty and trust with customers, employees, partners, and communities.
- **Motivational:** Purpose elevates the value of the work, which inspires employees, customers, stakeholders, and even your industry.

It's clear that building a purpose-driven organization offers powerful benefits to that organization and every part of its ecosystem, from people to the planet. But how do leaders go about doing it? Many organizations have succeeded by following a series of interdependent actions and this chapter includes several proven strategies to guide your efforts. For such important work, many leaders accelerated their journey by engaging a consultant to help navigate the steps, create the right cadence, and ensure accountability.

1. Expand your stakeholder orientation.

The cornerstone of a purpose-driven or healing organization is to expand your definition of key stakeholders. At a minimum, you should include these critical groups (in this order): employees, customers, community, environment/planet, vendors/suppliers, investors, and other key influencers like government agencies, unions, activists, and competitors.

Try framing each relationship with the question: How do we create a win-win partnership where everyone flourishes?

Your business will sit at the center of this ecosystem of stakeholder, social issues, and the environment. Presumably, your competitors and even other industries sit within the same ecosystem. One of the ways you can distinguish yourself is getting to know your stakeholders better and ensuring that each group is flourishing.

Getting to know your stakeholders takes time and you'll want to put together a team of passionate people in your organization to lead these efforts. This is not a "one and done" journey—you are building the relationships and processes that will create long-term and beneficial partnerships with each of these groups.

2. Listen deeply and seek to understand stakeholder views.

Your next step is to set up listening sessions and to arrive with humility. It's not a time to share your views or pitch a plan. Your goal is to gain information that will help you understand the needs of this stakeholder group. This process takes time and, depending on the size of your group, might require a variety of modalities or formats.

For example, Nordea Bank spent over six months listening to more than 7,000 people. They used online surveys, workshops, and over 1,500 coffee discussions. One leader stated, "We discussed deeply why people had joined us, why they stayed, and what they see as impact for a financial institution."

From the range of possible questions to ask, focus on learning more about their needs and what it means to them to flourish. Learn where they are struggling or suffering, too, even if it has nothing directly to do with your business.

As you listen, remember to embrace the messenger, especially when what they share is difficult to hear. This is the beginning of building rapport with this group of stakeholders and how you respond to critiques and suggestions will tell them a lot about your credibility and their ability to trust you. As you listen, keep notes on what you are learning, and periodically meet with your team to share what you're hearing.

Finally, be sure to explore what they value in terms of social and environmental impact. If you need some examples, I recommend the book *Conscious Capitalism Field Guide: Tools for Transforming Your Organization*.

3. Find your business ikigai.

At the end of chapter 14, we introduced you to the ikigai model for exploring your personal sense of purpose. You can adapt this model to help your organization develop its purpose too. The categories shift slightly but the spirit remains the same. (See the image for the changes.)

- The intersection of what the world needs and what you care about now becomes your vision, which will touch your employee and customer stakeholders. Other organizations, in your industry and others, may have similar visions.
- The intersection of what you care about and what you're good at becomes your mission as you identify how your unique strengths and advantages align with your employee and supplier/vendor stakeholders.
- The intersection of what you are good at and what people will pay for becomes your offering—the product or service you bring to the world. Remember, it is likely that your competitors offer a similar product or service to a similar group of customers. Consider how you can distinguish your business by excelling in the other parts of this model. For example, outperforming your competitors in how you treat employees or care for the environment can help you earn an distinct advantage, enticing some of their customers to switch to your product or service.
- Finally, we have the intersection of what people will pay for and what the world needs—a kind of value proposition. Harvard professor Clayton Christenson referred to them as "jobs to be done." He says, "People don't simply buy products or services, they 'hire' them to make progress

in specific circumstances." This is where you can decide what you can uniquely bring to the need.

As mentioned, consumer priorities have shifted dramatically to include making progress with social and environmental issues. Study after study shows that consumers want more than just their individual needs met. They now look at a brand's environmental impact, its stance on social issues, and how it treats its employees when choosing what to buy. One study found that two-thirds of consumers (and 91 percent of Millennials) would switch to a purpose-driven company. If a brand is socially responsible, Gen Z is 85 percent more likely to trust a brand, 84 percent more likely to buy their products, and 82 percent more likely to recommend them to others.

Business ikigai at the center of the ecosystem of stakeholders

We can now think of "what the world needs" as automatically including a positive impact on equality and the environment. Consumers don't want to choose between who is the less bad, they want to invest in something that makes them feel good—that makes them feel they are doing something meaningful with their purchase.

Raj Sisodia, author of *The Healing Organization*, says that taking a holistic approach to business "looks at social, environmental, and financial performance simultaneously rather than sequentially." Researchers at Deloitte find that purpose-driven companies go beyond their role of offering a product or service and develop programs that have a social or environmental impact.

When we put your business ikigai in the center of our stakeholder ecosystem, we begin to have a holistic model that makes sense for our new world.

4. Set ambitious goals and measure your progress.
Now is the time to engage in self-assessment, measuring your current state and overall social and environmental impact. This can be challenging for a couple of reasons. First, you may not have easy access to the data; and, second, the analysis might shock you. For example, Starbucks discovered that dairy products accounted for one-fifth of their total carbon footprint. Researchers at Gallup argue that metrics also "highlight disconnects in how employees and customers perceive your purpose—so leaders can address lethal brand incongruity."

Start where you can and add on from there. All efforts are valuable and some will make sense to accomplish first, as they will create a positive domino effect. Here are some common actions with increasing levels of impact:

- Donate revenue, products, or services directly to those in need
- Enable employee volunteering to local community partners and projects
- Leverage revenue, talents, and resources to support nonprofit partners and community projects
- Pledge to minimize organizational or industrial impacts in the future with a five- or ten-year road map, complete with milestones
- Create and offer education on important topics to employees, consumers, and community members
- Design policies and procedures that align with your values and purpose
- Take strong action to minimize organizational or industrial impacts
- Offer a platform for activists or leaders to share their perspectives
- Fund research and development (R&D) projects to find solutions to social and environmental issues
- Lobby politicians for support in relevant legislation issues
- Transform your industry's practices to drive larger impact

Many organizations find it helpful to start with an established framework such as the United Nations' Sustainable Development Goals or the Global Reporting Initiative. Using these frameworks gives you access to ongoing research on these topics, a host of well-designed resources and materials, and an active community already engaging in these meaningful conversations.

One of the exciting benefits of becoming a purpose-driven organization is that you can launch what is known as the "wheel of change." Dr. Rebecca Henderson, who teaches sustainable business strategy at Harvard Business School, describes it this way:

> *The wheel of change begins to turn when a company makes a business case to solve an issue, such as global climate change. Changes in strategy, business initiatives, and leadership style not only work to address the problem but often force*

competitors to follow suit—especially if they produce successful results. This ramps up the wheel's speed. Consumers sense this shift and demand more sustainable products or services that align with the company's purpose to combat climate change, despite potentially higher price tags. Ultimately, the market shift becomes self-sustaining, with all leading firms in the industry driving progress.

One example of the wheel of change in action started with Alaska Airlines. Like many airlines, they started making changes to become greener and lower their carbon footprint. They engaged in an aggressive campaign to reduce inflight waste and have recycled nearly 2,000 tons of materials. They were one of the first airlines to install split-scimitar winglets on their fleet, saving 34,000 tons of fuel annually since 2013. As they shared these successes with consumers, it drove conversations that pushed other airlines.

But their leadership on alternative fuels is having the biggest influence on the industry. They have heavily invested in alternative biojet fuels, particularly renewable options made from timber harvest like stumps and branches, laying the groundwork for industry-wide adoption. The Dow Jones Sustainability Index ranks Alaska Airlines as the most sustainable airline in North America.

Sometimes, executives worry that such changes will cost too much financially but most efforts pay for themselves and often yield big gains in increased market share and brand loyalty. According to Dr. Rebecca Henderson,

The shareholder value model of capitalism pressures many managers to maximize profits due to perceived legal obligations. However, companies can legally sacrifice short-term profits with the promise of long-term success. When well executed, purpose-driven decisions can build high levels of trust between team members, companies within the same industry, and, more importantly, key stakeholders.

For example, CVS Pharmacy was the first drugstore to stop selling tobacco products. They felt this was an important move given that their purpose was about helping people achieve better health. Instead of just removing the products, they used the opportunity to help people quit smoking through educational campaigns and quitting aids like nicotine patches. While they lost $2 billion in cigarette sales, they experienced 10 percent growth in revenue as people began to see their brand as having integrity with healthcare.

Another example is Patagonia's commitment to repairing apparel so that consumers wear it longer. This created positive pressure for other companies to follow suit, causing a massive reduction in apparel waste.

Yvon Chouinard, Patagonia's founder, has continued to drive change. Rather than sell the $3 billion company or take it public, he created a trust to ensure that the annual profits (~$100 million per year) are used to "combat climate change and protect undeveloped land around the globe."

Identify which goals make sense for your business and various stakeholders. And don't be afraid to partner with other organizations like universities, government agencies, and even competitors. Collaboration is how small changes become significant shifts that make a measurable impact.

5. Articulate an inspiring vision.

Once you get clear about your purpose and how you will help all the stakeholders flourish, articulate it as an inspiring vision and share it widely. According to PwC, nearly 80 percent of leaders believe that purpose is central to their organization's success yet less than half of employees know what it is.

A shared vision is how you get everyone aligned and excited about what an organization can accomplish. According to a study by McKinsey, 82 percent of employees feel that it's important to have a purpose and 72 percent believe it should count more than profit. But only 42 percent felt that their organization's purpose statements drove impact.

Work with your leaders and stakeholders to craft something that articulates your vision and then share it widely. It should connect to your strategic goals as well as the day-to-day work, informing business decisions, undergirding policies and practices, and being how you measure success.

6. Enable success by creating the right climate and culture.

As we explored in chapter 5, climate and culture are both critical to your organization's success. Climate comprises the actions, channels, and tools to support your purpose organization. A culture of purpose is in place when those resources and resulting actions become a *daily* part of the organization.

Deloitte's researchers found that "consistency between the externally facing purpose-led brand and the internal employee experience of purpose is critical, and companies need to ensure that they effectively integrate purpose and draw on the workforce's ideas in their business strategy." This is why treating your employees as your first stakeholder is a cornerstone of success.

You'll have already involved employees in your listening tour as stakeholders, and also in crafting your vision. Now it's time to walk your talk. Ensure that the employee experience is imbued with purpose from the moment they consider applying to work at your organization to their last day when they become your alumni. Your benefits package should reflect your concern for your people. Make sure they have access to affordable healthcare, including vision, dental, and mental health support. Be generous with parent/family leave options and wellness programs.

Listen to their hopes and dreams and find ways to enable their goals. For example, many employees struggle with financial health. Obviously, paying a living wage is a critical part of this but so, too, are offering learning programs on financial well-being like budgeting, home ownership, and financial planning. It's especially important to explore if you have a split employee experience with your hourly workers or those in certain roles struggling while others are thriving.

For example, when PayPal's CEO Dan Schulman learned that 25,000 of their entry-level workers were struggling to make ends meet, he took action. The company's purpose is to improve the financial health of customers, so to have employees struggling violated their core values as an organization. The leadership team set a goal of increasing the net disposable income of their employees and then significantly lowered the cost of health insurance, raised wages, and gave their employees critical financial skills through learning programs.

In addition to hitting your own targets for environmental wellness, be sure your employees and customers have access to education and tools that help them do the same. Set expectations that they participate in making a difference. Make sure your corporate social responsibility practices include supporting employees to act on their own sense of purpose. Many organizations now grant a certain amount of time off every month for volunteering and match their employees' donations to nonprofit organizations.

This kind of policy strengthens your ties with the local community as well. For example, the Timberland apparel company encourages all employees to be "earthkeepers," both at work (by creating sustainable products) and also through protecting the outdoors. They organize two company-wide days of service per year, Earth Day in April and Serv-a-palooza in the fall.

Offer training and development opportunities so that people can grow a range of skills and competencies. Offer tuition reimbursement and expand it beyond just college programs. Investing in learning will pay off because "the opportunity to learn and grow" is often a top-three factor for today's employees when deciding where to work. Not having enough opportunities is also a top reason why they leave.

7. Invest in creating great managers.

The most common reason employees leave? A bad boss. In fact, 57 percent of workers say they quit a job because of a poor manager and one in four dreads going to work. The majority of employees (84 percent) say poorly trained managers create a lot of unnecessary stress and 50 percent feel their own performance would improve if their boss received the right kind of training.

Investing in manager training is critical to your success. Your employees' experience of your organization's purpose, your leadership, and your culture lives in the daily words and actions of their manager. Consider these tips:

- **Pick the right people to lead others:** Organizations often promote top performers into manager roles. Gallup estimates that only 1 in 10 people have the talent to effectively manage others and, worse, organizations select the wrong candidate 82 percent of the time! "Bad managers cost businesses billions of dollars each year, and having too many of them can bring down a company." Instead, focus on the people who know how to create the right conditions for others to thrive.

- **Offer manager training early and regularly:** Leading others can be learned. Give managers the skills and tools they need to succeed. At a minimum, training should include coaching, emotional intelligence, project management, and how to create psychologically safe and inclusive environments. Several studies show that manager training more than pays for itself in increased productivity and employee retention.

- **Measure manager impact and create accountability:** Track key metrics like employee engagement, thriving, turnover, and productivity, and hold managers accountable for these markers of team success, not just their own productivity. Many people can become great leaders with the right training and support. But if someone is not able to step up to the plate, don't hesitate to move them back to a nonsupervisory role. Recognize and reward your managers who are doing well.

- **Remove abusive and/or toxic managers immediately:** Leading others is a privilege and if managers engage in any kind of abuse, harassment, or bullying, they should be removed from the role immediately. Researchers estimate that 20 to 30 percent of managers engage in toxic behavior. You already have evidence of your organization's problematic managers—just look at your engagement data, filed complaints, and exit surveys. Every day you leave a toxic manager in place undermines your credibility and erodes your employees' trust.

- **Create two paths to excellence:** Making management the only path to promotions and raises is a mistake. Not everyone is suited to leading others, so if you create another path, for example, "master craftsperson," you can reward top performers with more advanced projects without putting them in a role that does more harm than good.

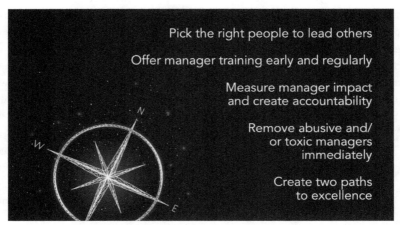

Pick the right people to lead others

Offer manager training early and regularly

Measure manager impact and create accountability

Remove abusive and/ or toxic managers immediately

Create two paths to excellence

Creating great managers leads to success

8. Celebrate progress and effort.

As you make progress on your purpose, vision, and ambitious goals, make sure you celebrate along the way. Raj Sisodia argues that maintaining a visible commitment by measuring your goals "creates pride, enthusiasm, and optimism among employees and other stakeholders."

All people want to be part of something meaningful, so be sure you keep your purpose front and center all year. And don't just focus on big successes—celebrate effort and progress too, to inspire people to feel part of the journey. Small movements matter on big issues, so find ways to track progress and the effort going into making a difference.

Weave your purpose and progress into all-hands meetings, organization-wide communications, and quarterly reviews. Spotlight projects and teams. Share impact stories so that everyone can see the effect of their collective efforts.

9. Learn from failures and adjust.

While celebrating your successes is important, so is learning from your failures. You will fail. Achieving great things is a slow process and the path to success requires taking risks and making mistakes. It's how we learn from those mistakes that really matters, whether it accelerates progress or undermines motivation. Think of the word FAIL as an acronym for "first attempt in learning."

Be transparent. Don't harm your credibility by only offering a one-sided view of mistakes or trying to sweep them under the rug. You have a great opportunity to model true innovation.

Perhaps you need to adjust your strategy or actions. Perhaps you have an opportunity to partner with another organization. Perhaps you need to tweak your approach, the resources you've allocated, or how you've framed the solution.

Take the time to assess what happened, harvesting lessons learned so you can do better. Talking about and learning from failure is how we create excellence. As we learned in chapter 5, psychological safety is critical for creativity and innovation (not to mention performance in general). Make it safe for your people to share their questions, concerns, critiques, and mistakes. This will not only help you get better at achieving your ambitious goals, it will also help you succeed in all other parts of the business.

10. Create impeccable trust, integrity, and accountability.

For your purpose efforts to succeed, you must build impeccable trust with each of your stakeholders. This doesn't happen overnight. Trust is earned through interactions, as we show we are dependable over time. Demonstrate your integrity by walking your talk—living the consistent alignment between your words and actions that helps people know they can trust you.

For example, the CEO of H&M, Helena Helmersson, used to be their chief sustainability officer, so she opened up their supply chain to rival brands in order to accelerate *all* of their sustainability, coordinating partnerships with other apparel retailers to form the Global Fashion Agenda.

Be consistent and persistent. Many of your stakeholders have been part of other organizations where leaders launched change initiatives just to watch them stall out. They will naturally have some skepticism until you establish your credibility. By showing up consistently and not giving up when things get hard, you build trust and establish your integrity as a leader.

You must also create a culture of accountability where everyone is held to certain standards. Accountability means expectations are clearly set and metrics are measured with appropriate recognition and consequences. Consider how you can create accountability from the top executives through to frontline workers and then around the various stakeholders. For example, in Costa Rica, the FIFCO brewery is working hard to reverse its initial impact on the land by healing previous damage and becoming an active steward of the environment. CEO Ramon Mendiola established that 40 percent of FIFCO's leadership compensation is linked to achieving the company's environmental and social goals.

As you lead, make sure you are building a pipeline of passionate and committed leaders to keep progress moving forward. Be careful who you choose for critical roles on the executive team and ensure that they share the same commitment to your purpose. They need to believe in collaboration because many of your efforts will require them to work across the organization to succeed. For example, McKinsey recommends the following efforts among top leaders:

- **Chief Executive Officer (CEO):** Identify the purpose and build it into all aspects of your culture, ensuring that employees find meaning in their day-to-day work.

- **Chief Marketing Officer (CMO):** Represent your customers' values and purpose priorities to the other executives and craft the messaging around your brand's purpose and intended impact; help other executives communicate messaging effectively to their teams.

- **Chief Financial Officer (CFO):** Measure and track metrics around your purpose and communicate progress to various stakeholders.

- **Chief Information Officer (CIO):** Identify which data is relevant and how it can be leveraged for authentic storytelling around impact.

- **Chief People Officer (CPO):** Embed the organization's purpose into hiring, onboarding, and training, and how managers lead their teams.

I cannot stress enough the importance of the right leadership team. Committed and enthusiastic leaders generate a climate of positivity and camaraderie that spreads through an entire organization. Even one leader can do damage in a very short amount of time. Be sure you have a strong succession plan in place and that senior leaders are held to standards through clear accountability metrics. If things are going off course, address them immediately.

Finally, identify and address violations of your organization's purpose and values. Perceived hypocrisy seems to be the most damaging to engagement and retention, according to researchers at McKinsey:

If a person showed up believing the organization stood for one thing...and then the organization violated this, it was just that, a violation. It had significant downticks in the person's willingness to stay, their engagement, their involvement. You'd see a direct link to performance. Also, for most people, that creates so much dissonance that they usually leave.

These violations can happen many different ways. One is if your own internal operations undermine your vision and purpose. For example, a company that touts its commitment to the environment while sourcing from suppliers with horrible environmental records. Another is if the leaders or executive team don't uphold the same vision and values they are asking others to uphold. This signals to everyone that these efforts don't matter and it can quickly domino to bigger problems. Another is if you don't take action against problematic behavior. For example, if your company says it is committed to equal rights issues but doesn't have zero-tolerance policy in place for workplace harassment and bullying.

Purpose Story 26:

When a Change in Leadership Ruins the Culture

When I started working in my role as a senior executive, I was thrilled to join the team. I applied because a new chief information officer had joined a few months before and was creating an exciting vision of what we could accomplish. He'd been successful at his previous company, and I wanted to be part of the changes he was driving.

It turned out to be the best decision. He created a positive team environment and we worked hard to accomplish those big goals. He set high standards and then supported us with great leadership training and the autonomy to make decisions, and he had our backs when we faced challenges. Those five years were the best professional experience of my career—I felt part of a great team that was transforming the business and we could see our impact across the entire organization.

Then he left to accept a great role and another "leader" came in. It was astounding how quickly he killed the culture. Within a few short months, he created a culture of fear, shutting down ideas that didn't align with his own views. We were a team of multidisciplinary experts, but he didn't bother to learn about our areas—instead, he instated plans that we knew would undermine all we had accomplished.

Our teams had worked so hard during the pandemic to pivot all the company's work to online tools and virtual meetings. People had put in extraordinary amounts of overtime and the outgoing CIO had approved well-earned bonuses and raises. The new CIO cancelled those rewards and we started to watch our best people leave, some who'd been there for many years and were outstanding performers. I did my best to advocate for my team, but I dreaded going to work each day, especially knowing that there was not much I could do. Many of us went to the CEO, raising our concerns but by the time he finally listened, too much damage had been done. In less than twelve months, one bad leader destroyed a purpose-driven culture and chased away our best people, me among them. It will be years before the department recovers.

Collectively, these 10 strategies give leaders a process to follow as you build a purpose-driven organization. If you need support, engage an executive coach or a consulting firm to support and guide your actions. It takes time and effort but those investments will more than payoff in the long run. You may also find value in reading these books:

- *Reinventing Organizations: A Guide to Creating Organizations Inspired by the Next Stage of Human Consciousness* by Frederic Laloux
- *The Healing Organization: Awakening the Conscience of Business to Help Save the World* by Dr. Raj Sisodia and Michael Gelb
- *Deep Purpose: The Heart and Soul of High-Performance Companies* by Dr. Ranjay Gulati
- *Firms of Endearment: How World-Class Companies Profit from Passion and Purpose* by Dr. Raj Sisodia, David Wolfe, and Dr. Jag Sheth
- *Wellbeing At Work: How to Build Resilient and Thriving Teams* by Jim Clifton and Dr. Jim Harter
- *Conscious Capitalism Field Guide: Tools for Transforming Your Organization* by Dr. Raj Sisodia, Timothy Henry, and Thomas Eckschmidt

Looking to the future

The recent leap forward in AI technology, like ChatGPT, are revolutionizing how work is done. Several experts predict that 40 to 70 percent of jobs could be automated in the next 10 years. As *Forbes* author Deborah claims, "Suffice it to say that ChatGPT, the Metaverse, and many other work- and life-altering technologies we'll see in the years ahead will send us on a wild ride." Savvy leaders will adapt and innovate at record speeds.

In researching this topic, I found several informative and well-written articles. And discovered at the end, the author was ChatGPT! Don't worry, I actually wrote every page of this book. But I am pondering what my next book might look like if AI is doing research, drafting chapters, creating graphics, and formatting citations. I'm reminded of that iconic scene in the movie *Hidden Figures*. When the IBM 7090 computer arrived at NASA, capable of 24,000 calculations per second (woefully slow by today's standards), the human computers didn't lose their jobs. They pivoted to newly created jobs, coding that IBM and checking its accuracy. If I'm freed up from the time-consuming administrative aspects of book publishing, will I write more and publish faster? Will I get to go even deeper and produce better work? Will I spend more time at the beach sipping piña coladas? I suspect it will be a combination of all three.

I'm struck by the fact that November 2022 saw the arrival of two significant moments: ChatGPT was released and the world's population hit 8 billion (predicted to hit 10.4 billion by 2086). Undoubtedly, AI and other technologies will change how people spend their time, freeing up energy to invest in other efforts. As human consciousness continues to rise, increasing our desire for purpose-driven work and meaningful lives, we will lean more into doing social good and healing the planet.

As a result, purpose-driven organizations will continue to grow and expand, drastically changing currently accepted tenants of capitalism and profit. Efforts like universal basic income (UBI), access to quality healthcare, and sustainable/healing business are getting significant traction and we already have the tools to end hunger, disease, and poverty.

We stand at the dawn of an exciting new world of work and humanity. How will you lead your organization and your industry to be part of this transformation? I find inspiration in Octavia Butler's words, "Purpose unifies us... strengthens our efforts...and offers us greatness."

"Purpose
Unifies us:
It focuses our dreams,
Guides our plans,
Strengthens our efforts.
Purpose
Defines us,
Shapes us,
And offers us
Greatness."
OCTAVIA BUTLER
Author, *Parable of the Talents*

Octavia Butler on our search for purpose

25. Conclusion: Final Thoughts on Purpose

As we come to the end of this book, I hope you are as amazed as I am by the alignment among all the different sources. As I read over 50 published books and 500+ research studies, and as I reviewed the latest reports from global consulting firms and observed the themes and issues arising in the many organizations I consult with, I was struck again and again by how in sync it all was—and continues to be! None of my previous books have had this kind of alignment and it's a real indication of how powerful and pivotal this moment in time is for us all.

This alignment continued as people from around the world submitted their stories about purpose. They represented a wide range of backgrounds and ages working in a variety of industries. When my team first handed me the collection of anonymized entries, I read them in one sitting. I was touched by the vulnerability people shared as they wrote about both the challenges and blessings they faced on their journey to finding purpose.

I was also inspired by the consistent evidence that our purpose is trying to find us as much as we are trying to find it. We are not only biologically wired for purpose, but it's clear to me that it WILL happen as long as you're willing to seek it. We are destined to find our purpose.

It's also clear that when we get derailed from our path, it's because we're focusing too much on other people's expectations. For those who listened to the shame gremlins and the messages of "shoulds" and "ought tos" (myself included), we can spend time wandering around with someone else's compass. It might be pointing north for them, but it's sending us in the wrong direction. It's time to hand it back so you can focus on your own path.

You have your own compass inside of you, pointing to your North Star, and it's been there all along. My hope is that the tools and strategies I've shared help to make your compass easier to find, to read, and to follow. Trust it and trust yourself. Your body and biology are your allies—they will nudge you with emotions. Your purpose will send you hints and lessons. Your job is to pay attention and trust in the process.

The good news is that you are not alone in this journey. Human consciousness is rising and with it comes a momentum that is pushing us forward, collectively and individually.

It's boosted by the force of will that Gen Z and Gen Alpha demonstrate every day. They are more empathetic and connected than previous generations. They are also fearless and impervious to other people's opinions. If you're a parent or a teacher, you've probably already experienced this—when you try to hand them your compass, they forcefully hand it right back. It's both impressive and a bit intimidating because they have a confidence at a young age that many of us spend our adult years trying to find. They are fiercely committed to creating a world of equality and caring. I'm inspired by them and believe we should all do our best to support and protect them.

I'm on this journey with you. I, too, am forever changed by the past few years. At first, I was afraid and felt lost in feeling out of control. But then I focused on others and looked for ways I could help. That gave me both peace and happiness. It also reminded me how powerful learning is. How it creates a shared experience of growing and reaching to become better, together.

That enlivened me! I had already been working on my Brain Aware Leader training program but I experienced a burst of creativity during the lockdowns as I connected with learners from all over the world. I leaned in and found myself being more productive than I had in a long time. Ideas were sparking and I found that incredible sweet spot of flow. For me and my team, building that training became our purpose during that difficult time.

It has gone on to win awards and drive results in all kinds of organizations, and of course I am proud of that. But the real joy came in following my North Star to be of service to others. I feel the same way about this book. It has been a privilege to do the research and to synthesize the findings for you here. I love to see readers interacting with my books! If you have a photo to share, please feel free to tag me on social media. Thank you for the gift of your time in reading it.

Synthesize Your Learning Journey into Action

As we conclude, look over your notes from the various learning journeys in this book. You should now have a robust understanding of purpose and meaningful work. Take a moment to finalize your notes and create an action plan that will unfold over the next few weeks and months.

- Reflect on the continuum on p. 159 and share the type of organization you are currently working in. Is it the right match for you?
- As an employee, which strategies do you want to use in the coming weeks to boost your own sense of purpose and meaningful work?
- If you are in a leadership role, what are some actions you can take in the next 30, 60, and 90 days that will uplevel your team or organization in terms of purpose and meaningful work?
- What are your three to five biggest takeaways from this book?
- What are some actions you can take in the next 30, 60, and 90 days that will help you further clarify or live your sense of purpose?
- Consider how you might share some of what you have learned with colleagues and leaders in your organization. For additional resources and training materials to help you, visit BrittAndreatta.com/Training.

REFERENCES + RESOURCES

Introduction

Dostoyevsky, F. (1879). The brothers Karamazov. *The Russian Messenger*.

Horovitz, B. (2022, May 13). Young people seek jobs with a higher purpose. *Time*. https://time.com/6176169/what-young-workers-want-in-jobs/

McFall, M. (2022, June 23). Council post: Employees want purpose at work: How to deliver on this priority. *Forbes*. https://www.forbes.com/sites/forbesbusinesscouncil/2022/06/22/employees-want-purpose-at-work-how-to-deliver-on-this-priority/

Browley, J. (2023, February 3). Finding purpose at work and the growing need for corporate values. *Essence*. https://www.essence.com/news/money-career/amazon-aws-finding-purpose-at-work/

Keohane, J. (2022, January 11). Everyone wants meaningful work. But what does that really look like? *Entrepreneur*. https://www.entrepreneur.com/magazine/entrepreneur/2022/01

Hurst, A. (2019). *The purpose economy: How your desire for impact, personal growth and community is changing the world* (3rd ed.). Boise, ID: Elevate.

Andreatta, B. (2017). *Wired to resist: The brain science of why change fails and a new model for driving success*. Santa Barbara, CA: 7th Mind Publishing.

Andreatta, B. (2019). *Wired to grow: Harness the power of brain science to master any skill* (2nd ed.). Santa Barbara, CA: 7th Mind Publishing.

I. THE SCIENCE OF BECOMING

Blattner, T. (2018, July 24). *The neuroscience of your purpose and personal mission*. Medium. https://medium.com/@trevor.blattner/the-neuroscience-of-your-purpose-and-personal-mission-f903b2e4f6c1

Chapter 1

Fredrickson B., Grewen K., Coffrey K., Algoe S., Firestine A. (2013). A functional genomic perspective on human well-being. *Proceedings of the National Academy of Sciences*. 13684-13689.

Bosché, B. & Bosché, G. (2020). *The purpose factor: Extreme clarity for why you're here and what to do about it*. Brentwood, TN: Post Hill Press.

Maslow, A. (1943). A theory of human motivation. *Psychological Review, 50*(4), 370-396.

Ravilochan, T. (2021, April 4). *Could the Blackfoot wisdom that inspired Maslow guide us now?* Medium. https://gatherfor.medium.com/maslow-got-it-wrong-ae45d6217a8c#6f9a

Blackstock, C. (2019). Revisiting the Breath of Life Theory. *British Journal of Social Work, 49*, 854–849.

Kaufman, S. B. (2018, November 7). What does it mean to be self-actualized in the 21st century? *Scientific American*. https://blogs.scientificamerican.com/beautiful-minds/what-does-it-mean-to-be-self-actualized-in-the-21st-century/

Aristotle (1925/1998). *The Nicomachean ethics*. Ross, W.D., trans. Oxford: Oxford University Press.

Boyce, C. (2023, February 18). What actually makes a happier life. *Fast Company*. https://www.fastcompany.com/90851677/ive-spent-years-studying-happiness-heres-what-actually-makes-for-a-happier-life

Fredrickson, B. (2011). *Positivity: Groundbreaking research to release your inner optimist and thrive*. London: Oneworld.

Achor, S. (2018). *The happiness advantage: How a positive brain fuels success in work and life*. New York, NY: Currency.

Harris, R. (2022) *The happiness trap: How to stop struggling and start living*. Boulder, CO: Shambhala.

Lyubomirsky, S. (2008). *The how of happiness: A new approach to getting the life you want*. New York, NY: Penguin.

Price, C. (2021). *The power of fun: How to feel alive again*. New York, NY: Dial Press.

Brooks, A. (2022). *From strength to strength: Finding success, happiness, and deep purpose in the second half of life*. New York, NY: Penguin.

Seligman , M. P. (2013). *Authentic happiness: Using the new positive psychology to realize your potential for lasting fulfillment*. New York, NY: Free Press.

Waldinger, R. J., & Schulz, M. S. (2023). *The good life: Lessons from the world's longest scientific study of Happiness*. New York, NY: Simon & Schuster.

Madeson, M. (2023, March 27). The PERMA model: Your scientific theory of happiness. *Positive Psychology*. https://positivepsychology.com/perma-model/

Sato, W., Kochiyama, T., Uono, S., Kubota, Y., Sawada, R., Yoshimura, S., & Toichi, M. (2015). The structural neural substrate of subjective happiness. *Scientific Reports, 5*, 16891. https://doi.org/10.1038/srep16891

Wang, Y., Wu, R., Li, L., Ma, J., Yang, W., & Dai, Z. (2022). Common and distinct neural substrates of the compassionate and uncompassionate self-responding dimensions of self-compassion. *Brain Imaging and Behavior, 16*(6), 2667–2680. https://doi.org/10.1007/s11682-022-00723-9

Jung, H. Y., Pae, C., An, I., Bang, M., Choi, T. K., Cho, S. J., & Lee, S. H. (2022). A multimodal study regarding neural correlates of the subjective well-being in healthy individuals. *Scientific Reports, 12*(1), 13688. https://doi.org/10.1038/s41598-022-18013-1

Lewis, G. J., Kanai, R., Rees, G., & Bates, T. C. (2014). Neural correlates of the 'good life': eudaimonic well-being is associated with insular cortex volume. *Social Cognitive and Affective Neuroscience*, 9(5), 615–618. https://doi.org/10.1093/scan/nst032

Jamshidi, J., Park, H. R. P., Montalto, A., Fullerton, J. M., & Gatt, J. M. (2022). Wellbeing and brain structure: A comprehensive phenotypic and genetic study of image-derived phenotypes in the UK Biobank. *Human Brain Mapping*, 43(17), 5180–5193. https://doi.org/10.1002/hbm.25993

Remnick, D. (2022, May 10). Stephanie Hsu on "Everything everywhere all at once": *The New Yorker Radio Hour*. WNYC Studios.https://www.wnycstudios.org/podcasts/tnyradiohour/articles/stephanie-hsu-everything-everywhere-all-once-pod2

Martin, M. (2023, February 25). Mormon church leader uses his faith to spread anti-racist principles. *National Public Radio*. https://www.npr.org/2023/02/25/1159565361/mormon-church-leader-uses-his-faith-to-spread-anti-racist-principles\

Hurst, A. (2019). *The purpose economy: How your desire for impact, personal growth and community is changing the world* (3rd ed.). Boise, ID: Elevate.

Hillard, G. (2022, December 21). The 'Street Vet' provides free care to homeless people's beloved pets. *All Things Considered*. NPR. npr.org/2022/12/21/1144821737/the-street-vet-provides-free-care-to-homeless-peoples-beloved-pets

Chapter 2

Kim, E. S., Sun, J. K., Park, N., & Peterson, C. (2013). Purpose in life and reduced incidence of stroke in older adults: The health and retirement study. *Journal of Psychosomatic Research*, 74(5), 427–432. https://doi.org/10.1016/j.jpsychores.2013.01.013

Koizumi, M., Ito, H., Kaneko, Y., & Motohashi, Y. (2008). Effect of having a sense of purpose in life on the risk of death from cardiovascular diseases. *Journal of Epidemiology*, 18(5), 191–196. https://doi.org/10.2188/jea.je2007388

Boyle, P. A., Buchman, A. S., Barnes, L. L., & Bennett, D. A. (2010). Effect of a purpose in life on risk of incident Alzheimer disease and mild cognitive impairment in community-dwelling older persons. *Archives of General Psychiatry*, 67(3), 304–310. https://doi.org/10.1001/archgenpsychiatry.2009.208

Sutin, A. R., Luchetti, M., & Terracciano, A. (2021). Sense of purpose in life and healthier cognitive aging. *Trends in Cognitive Sciences*, 25(11), 917–919. https://doi.org/10.1016/j.tics.2021.08.009

Kim, G., Shin, S. H., Scicolone, M. A., & Parmelee, P. (2019). Purpose in life protects against cognitive decline among older adults. *The American Journal of Geriatric Psychiatry*, 27(6), 593–601. https://doi.org/10.1016/j.jagp.2019.01.010

Musich, S., Wang, S. S., Kraemer, S., Hawkins, K., & Wicker, E. (2018). Purpose in life and positive health outcomes among older adults. *Population Health Management*, 21(2), 139–147. https://doi.org/10.1089/pop.2017.006

Shin, S. H., Behrens, E. A., Parmelee, P. A., & Kim, G. (2022). The role of purpose in life in the relationship between widowhood and cognitive decline among older adults in the U.S. *The American Journal of Geriatric Psychiatry*, 30(3), 383–391. https://doi.org/10.1016/j.jagp.2021.07.010

Kim, E. S., Shiba, K., Boehm, J. K., & Kubzansky, L. D. (2020). Sense of purpose in life and five health behaviors in older adults. *Preventive Medicine*, 139, 106172. https://doi.org/10.1016/j.ypmed.2020.106172

Hedburg P, Gustafson Y, Alex L, Brulin C. (2010). Depression in relation to purpose in life among a very old population: A five-year follow-up study. *Aging and Mental Health*, 14(6), 757–763.

Telzer, E. H., Fuligni, A. J., Lieberman, M. D., & Galván, A. (2014). Neural sensitivity to eudaimonic and hedonic rewards differentially predict adolescent depressive symptoms over time. *Proceedings of the National Academy of Sciences*, 111(18), 6600–6605. https://doi.org/10.1073/pnas.1323014111

Office of the Surgeon General [OSG]. (2021). *Protecting youth mental health: The U.S. surgeon general's advisory*. U.S. Department of Health and Human Services.

Homan, K. J., & Kong, J. (2020). Longitudinal health consequences of childhood adversity: The mediating role of purpose in life. *Journal of Gerontological Social Work*, 63(8), 864–877. https://doi.org/10.1080/0163 4372.2020.1808140

Starecheski, L. (2015, March 2). Take the ace quiz and learn what it does and doesn't mean. NPR. npr.org/sections/health-shots/2015/03/02/387007941/take-the-ace-quiz-and-learn-what-it-does-and-doesnt-mean

Centers for Disease Control and Prevention. (2021, April 2). *Adverse childhood experiences (ACES)*. Centers for Disease Control and Prevention. https://www.cdc.gov/violenceprevention/aces/index.html

Harris, N. (2021). *The deepest well: Healing the long-term effects of childhood trauma and adversity*. New York, NY: Mariner Books.

Harris, N. (2014). *How childhood trauma affects health across a lifetime* [Video]. TED Conferences. https://www.ted.com/talks/nadine_burke_harris_how_childhood_trauma_affects_health_across_a_lifetime

Echeverria, I., Peraire, M., Haro, G., Mora, R., Camacho, I., Almodóvar, I., Mañes, V., Zaera, I., & Benito, A. (2021). "Healthcare Kamikazes" during the COVID-19 pandemic: Purpose in life and moral courage as mediators of psychopathology. *International Journal of Environmental Research and Public Health*, 18(14), 7235. https://doi.org/10.3390/ijerph18147235

Hill, P. L., Sin, N. L., Almeida, D. M., & Burrow, A. L. (2022). Sense of purpose predicts daily positive events and attenuates their influence on positive affect. *Emotion (Washington, D.C.)*, *22*(3), 597–602. https://doi.org/10.1037/emo0000776

Hill, P. L., Sin, N. L., Turiano, N. A., Burrow, A. L., & Almeida, D. M. (2018). Sense of purpose moderates the associations between daily stressors and daily well-being. *Annals of Behavioral Medicine: A Publication of the Society of Behavioral Medicine*, *52*(8), 724–729. https://doi.org/10.1093/abm/kax039

Koizumi, M., Ito, H., Kaneko, Y., & Motohashi, Y. (2008). Effect of having a sense of purpose in life on the risk of death from cardiovascular diseases. *Journal of Epidemiology*, 18(5), 191–196. https://doi.org/10.2188/jea.je2007388

Kim E, Sun J, Park N, Kubzansky L, Peterson C. (2013). Purpose in life and reduced risk of myocardial infarction among older US adults with coronary heart disease: A two year followup. *Behavioral Medicine*, *36*, 124–133.

Rohleder N. (2014). Stimulation of systemic low-grade inflammation by psychosocial stress. *Psychosomatic Medicine*, 181–189.

Friedman E., Hayney M., Love G., Singer B., Ryff C. (2007). Plasma interleukin-6 and soluble IL-6 receptors are associated with psychological well-being in aging women. *Health Psychology*, 305–313.

Hedburg P., Gustafson Y., Alex L., Brulin C. (2010). Depression in relation to purpose in life among a very old population: A five-year follow-up study. *Aging and Mental Health*, *14*(6):757–763.

Hill, P. & Turiano. N. (2014). Purpose in life as a predictor of mortality across adulthood. *Psychological Science*, *25*(7), 1482-1486.

Shiba, K., Kubzansky, L. D., Williams, D. R., VanderWeele, T. J., & Kim, E. S. (2021). Associations between purpose in life and mortality by SES. *American Journal of Preventive Medicine*, *61*(2), e53–e61. https://doi.org/10.1016/j.amepre.2021.02.011

Chapter 3

Burrow, A. L., Stanley, M., Sumner, R., & Hill, P. L. (2014). Purpose in life as a resource for increasing comfort with ethnic diversity. *Personality & Social Psychology Bulletin*, *40*(11), 1507–1516. https://doi.org/10.1177/0146167214549540

Burrow, A. L., Hill, P. L., & Sumner, R. (2016). Leveling mountains: Purpose attenuates links between perceptions of effort and steepness. *Personality & Social Psychology Bulletin*, *42*(1), 94–103. https://doi.org/10.1177/0146167215615404

Little, G. L., & Robinson, K. D. (1989). Effects of moral reconation therapy upon moral reasoning, life purpose, and recidivism among drug and alcohol offenders. *Psychological Reports*, *64*(1), 83–90. https://doi.org/10.2466/pr0.1989.64.1.83

Gandbhir, G. & Peltz, P. (2016). *Prison dogs* [Film]. Journeyman Pictures.

Prison Fellowship. *What is the Warden Exchange?* https://www.prisonfellowship.org/about/warden-exchange/warden-exchange-details/

Prison Policy Initiative. (n.d.). *United States profile*. https://www.prisonpolicy.org/profiles/US.html

Prison Policy Initiative. (n.d.). *Race and ethnicity*. https://www.prisonpolicy.org/research/race_and_ethnicity/

Cohen, G. L., Garcia, J., Purdie-Vaughns, V., Apfel, N., & Brzustoski, P. (2009). Recursive processes in self-affirmation: intervening to close the minority achievement gap. *Science*, *324*(5925), 400–403. https://doi.org/10.1126/science.1170769

Walton, G. M., & Cohen, G. L. (2011). A brief social-belonging intervention improves academic and health outcomes of minority students. *Science*, *331*(6023), 1447–1451. https://doi.org/10.1126/science.1198364

Cook, G. (2013, October 22). Why we are wired to connect. *Scientific American*. https://www.scientificamerican.com/article/why-we-are-wired-to-connect/

Steele, C. M., & Aronson, J. (1995). Stereotype threat and the intellectual test performance of African Americans. *Journal of Personality and Social Psychology*, *69*(5), 797–811. https://doi.org/10.1037//0022-3514.69.5.797

Andreatta, B. (2018). *Wired to connect: The brain science of teams and a new model for creating collaboration and inclusion.* Santa Barbara, CA: 7th Mind Publishing.

Good, C., Aronson, J., & Inzlicht, M. (2003). Improving adolescents' standardized test performance: An intervention to reduce the effects of stereotype threat. *Applied Developmental Psychology*, *24*, 645-662.

Yong E. (2013). Armor against prejudice. *Scientific American*, *308*(6), 76–80. https://doi.org/10.1038/scientificamerican0613-76

Cohen, G. L., & Sherman, D. K. (2005). Stereotype threat and the social and scientific contexts of the race achievement gap. *The American Psychologist*, *60*(3), 270–272. https://doi.org/10.1037/0003-066X.60.3.270

Milam, L. A., Cohen, G. L., Mueller, C., & Salles, A. (2018). Stereotype threat and working memory among surgical residents. *American Journal of Surgery*, *216*(4), 824–829. https://doi.org/10.1016/j.amjsurg.2018.07.064

Yoshino, K., & Smith, C. (2014, March). Fear of being different stifles talent. *Harvard Business Review*. https://hbr.org/2014/03/fear-of-being-different-stifles-talent

Sepulveda, J. A., Lincoln, B., Liang, B., Klein, T., White, A. E., Hill, N., & Perella, J. (2021). MPOWER: The impact of a purpose program on adolescents' intrinsic and extrinsic motivations. *Frontiers in Psychology, 12*, 761580. https://doi.org/10.3389/fpsyg.2021.761580

Sumner, R., Burrow, A. L., & Hill, P. L. (2018). The development of purpose in life among adolescents who experience marginalization: Potential opportunities and obstacles. *The American Psychologist, 73*(6), 740–752. https://doi.org/10.1037/amp0000249

Yeung, P., & Breheny, M. (2021). Quality of life among older people with a disability: the role of purpose in life and capabilities. *Disability and Rehabilitation, 43*(2), 181-191. https://doi.org/10.1080/09638288.2019.1620875

Staff. (2018, January 18). Remembering the victims of the Montecito mudslides. *The Santa Barbara Independent.* https://www.independent.com/2018/01/18/remembering-victims-montecito-mudslides/

Cowan, J., & Knoll, C. (2023, January 17). In Montecito, the million-dollar views still come with mudslide risks. *The New York Times.* https://www.nytimes.com/2023/01/17/us/montecito-mudslide-2018-california-storms.html

Wikipedia (2023, March 18). *2014 Isla Vista killings.* https://en.wikipedia.org/wiki/2014_Isla_Vista_killings

Wikipedia (2023, March 3). *Sinking of MV conception.* https://en.wikipedia.org/wiki/Sinking_of_MV_Conception

Dhingra, N., & Schaninger, B. (2021, June 3). *The search for purpose at work.* McKinsey & Company. https://www.mckinsey.com/business-functions/people-and-organizational-performance/our-insights/the-search-for-purpose-at-work

Albinus, P. (2022, March 2). The strong business case for giving employees a sense of purpose. *Human Resource Executive.* https://hrexecutive.com/the-strong-business-case-for-giving-employees-a-sense-of-purpose/

Schuyler, S. (2016, June). Putting purpose to work: A study of purpose in the workplace. *PricewaterhouseCoopers.* https://www.pwc.com/us/en/about-us/corporate-responsibility/assets/pwc-putting-purpose-to-work-purpose-survey-report.pdf

Mankins, M. (2017, March 1). Great companies obsess over productivity, not efficiency. *Harvard Business Review.* https://hbr.org/2017/03/great-companies-obsess-over-productivity-not-efficiency

Hurst, A. (2019). *The purpose economy: How your desire for impact, personal growth and community is changing the world* (3rd ed.). Boise, ID: Elevate.

Singhania, P. (Ed.). (2020). Global Human Capital Trends. *Deloitte Insights.* https://www2.deloitte.com/us/en/insights/focus/human-capital-trends/2020.html

Sperry, K., & Ferran, D. (2022, September 19). *Do company ethics and stakeholder focus equal greater long-run shareholder profits?* Torrey Project. https://www.torreyproject.org/post/ethics-stakeholder-focus-greater-long-run-shareholder-profits

Aziz, A. (2019, November 11). The power of purpose: Kantar Purpose 2020 study shows how purposeful brands grow twice as fast as their competition. *Forbes.* https://www.forbes.com/sites/afdhelaziz/2019/11/11/the-power-of-purpose-kantar-purpose-2020-study-shows-how-purposeful-brands-grow-twice-as-fast-as-their-competition

Aziz, A. (2020, March 7). The power purpose: The business case for purpose. *Forbes.* https://www.forbes.com/sites/afdhelaziz/2020/03/07/the-power-of-purpose-the-business-case-for-purpose-all-the-data-you-were-looking-for-pt-1/

WeSpire (2020, January 22). *15 critical insights into Gen Z, purpose, and the future of work.* https://cdn.sanity.io/files/umko2xz8/production/95463f27c4c356ea986c04013ce6cb0d82b4ed0f.pdf

Andreatta, B. (2022, February 24). *How to embrace purpose as the path to innovation, profitability.* HR Executive https://hrexecutive.com/how-to-embrace-purpose-as-the-path-to-innovation-profitability

Vranica, S. (2018, October 2). Consumers believe brands can help solve societal ills. *Wall Street Journal.* https://www.wsj.com/articles/consumers-believe-brands-can-help-solve-societal-ills-1538478000

Barton, R., Ishikawa, M., Quiring, K., Theofilou, B. (2018). *From me to we: The rise of the purpose-led brand.* Accenture. https://www.accenture.com/_acnmedia/thought-leadership-assets/pdf/accenture-competitiveagility-gcpr-pov.pdf

Cone Communications (2018). *Cone/Porter Novelli Purpose Study.* https://conecomm.com/2018-purpose-study

Chapter 4

Gulati, R., Nohria, N., & Wohlgezogen, F. (2014, October 6). Roaring out of recession. *Harvard Business Review.* https://hbr.org/2010/03/roaring-out-of-recession

Iger, B. (n.d.). *Bob Iger quotes.* BrainyQuote. https://www.brainyquote.com/quotes/bob_iger_177671

Kounios, J., & Beeman, M. (2014, January). The cognitive neuroscience of insight. *Annual Review of Psychology, 65,* 71-93.

Kounios, J., & Beeman, M. (2015). *The eureka factor: aha moments, creative insight, and the brain.* New York, NY: Random House.

Kaufman, S.B. (2017, December 6). The real neuroscience of creativity. *HuffPost.* https://www.huffpost.com/entry/the-real-neuroscience-of_b_3870582/

Kaufman, S.B., & Gregoire, C. (2015). *Wired to create: Unraveling the mysteries of the creative mind.* New York, NY: Penguin.

Vartanian, O., Bristol, A.S., & Kaufman, J.C. (Eds.). (2013). *Neuroscience of creativity.* Cambridge, MA: MIT Press.

Nichols, W. J., & Cousteau, C. (2015). *Blue mind: The surprising science that shows how being near, in, on, or under water can make you happier, healthier, more connected and better at what you do*. Boston, MA: Little Brown Spark.

Streep, A. (2014, July 22). How water makes us healthier, happier, and more successful. *Outside*. https://www.outsideonline.com/culture/books-media/how-water-makes-us-healthier-happier-and-more-successful/

Weir, K. (2020, April 1). Nurtured by nature. *American Psychological Association Monitor, 51*(3). https://www.apa.org/monitor/2020/04/nurtured-nature

Merrett, R. (2015, July 27). A neuroscience approach to innovative thinking and problem solving. *CIO*. https://www2.cio.com.au/article/580509/neuroscience-approach-innovative-thinking-problem-solving/

Andreatta, B. (2019). *Wired to grow: Harness the power of brain science to master any skill* (2nd ed.). Santa Barbara, CA: 7th Mind Publishing.

MacKenzie, G. (1998). *Orbiting the giant hairball: A corporate fool's guide to surviving with grace*. New York, NY: Penguin.

Gardner, H. (2006). *Multiple intelligences: New horizons in theory and practice*. New York, NY: Basic Books.

Gardner, H. (2011). *Frames of mind: The theory of multiple intelligences*. New York, NY: Basic Books.

Shearer, C.B., & Karanian, J.M. (2017). The neuroscience of intelligence: Empirical support for the theory of multiple intelligences? *Trends in Neuroscience and Education, 6*, 211-223.

Shearer, B. (2018). Multiple intelligences in teaching and education: Lessons learned from neuroscience. *Journal of Intelligence, 6*(3), 38.

Armstrong, T. (2017). *Multiple intelligences in the classroom* (4th ed). Alexandria, VA: Association for Supervision and Curriculum Development (ASCD).

Calaprice, A. (2010). *The ultimate quotable Einstein*. Princeton, NY: Princeton University Press.

Chapter 5

McKinsey & Company. (n.d.) *Growth & innovation: Strategy & corporate finance*. https://www.mckinsey.com/capabilities/strategy-and-corporate-finance/how-we-help-clients/growth-and-innovation

CB Insights. (2020, July 17). *7 innovation frameworks to navigate disruption: Apple, Netflix, Amazon, & more*. https://www.cbinsights.com/research/report/innovation-frameworks-navigate-disruption/

Jaruzelski, B., Chwalik, R., & Goehle, B. (2018, October 30). What the top innovators get right. *Strategy+business*. https://www.strategy-business.com/feature/What-the-Top-Innovators-Get-Right

Knapp, J. (2016). *Sprint: How to solve big problems and test new ideas in just five days*. New York, NY: Simon & Schuster.

Govindarajan, V., & Trimble, C. (September 2, 2010). *The other side of innovation: Solving the execution challenge*. Cambridge, MA: Harvard Business Review Press.

McChesney, C., Covey, S., & Huling, J. (2012). *The 4 disciplines of execution: Achieving your wildly important goals*. New York, NY: Simon & Schuster.

McChesney, C. (n.d.). *The 4 disciplines of execution*. Franklin Covey. https://resources.franklincovey.com/home/the-4-disciplines-of-execution

Duhigg, C. (2016, February 25). What Google learned from its quest to build the perfect team. *The New York Times*. https://www.nytimes.com/2016/02/28/magazine/what-google-learned-from-its-quest-to-build-the-perfect-team.html

Edmondson, A. (March 20, 2012) *Teaming: How organizations learn, innovate, and compete in the knowledge economy*. San Francisco, CA: Jossey-Bass.

Andreatta, B. (2018). *Wired to connect: The brain science of teams and a new model for creating collaboration and inclusion*. Santa Barbara, CA: 7th Mind Publishing.

Ban Breathnach, S. (n.d.). *Sarah Ban Breathnach quotes*. BrainyQuote. https://www.brainyquote.com/quotes/sarah_ban_breathnach_108282

II. OUR RISING HUNGER FOR PURPOSE

Oldster, K. *Dead toad scrolls*. Trenton, GA: Booklocker, Inc.

Chapter 6

Horovitz, B. (2022, May 13). Young people seek jobs with a higher purpose. *Time*. https://time.com/6176169/what-young-workers-want-in-jobs/

McFall, M. (2022, June 23). Council post: Employees want purpose at work: How to deliver on this priority. *Forbes*. https://www.forbes.com/sites/forbesbusinesscouncil/2022/06/22/employees-want-purpose-at-work-how-to-deliver-on-this-priority/

Dhingra, N., & Schaninger, B. (2021, June 3).*The search for purpose at work*. McKinsey & Company. https://www.mckinsey.com/business-functions/people-and-organizational-performance/our-insights/the-search-for-purpose-at-work

Teamstage (2022, January 12). *Millennials in the workplace statistics 2022: Latest trends*. https://teamstage.io/millennials-in-the-workplace-statistics/

Goleman, D. (2021, April 2). *Millennials: The purpose generation*. Korn Ferry. https://www.kornferry.com/insights/this-week-in-leadership/millennials-purpose-generation

Beresford Research. (2023, January 19). *Age range by generation.* https://www.beresfordresearch.com/age-range-by-generation/

Hecht, E. (2022, September 2). What years are Gen X? *USA Today.* https://www.usatoday.com/story/news/2022/09/02/what-years-gen-x-millennials-baby-boomers-gen-z/10303085002/

Kaplan, Z., & Pelta, R. (2022, November 2). *Generation Z workplace statistics.* Forage. https://www.theforage.com/blog/basics/generation-z-statistics

WeSpire (2020, January 22). *15 insights into gen Z, purpose, and the future of work.* https://www.wespire.com/15-insights-gen-z-purpose-and-future-of-work/

Wiles, J. (2022, January 13). *Employees increasingly seek value and purpose at work.* Gartner. https://www.gartner.com/en/articles/employees-seek-personal-value-and-purpose-at-work-be-prepared-to-deliver

Gallup. (2022, September 22). State of the American workplace. *Gallup.com.* https://www.gallup.com/workplace/238085/state-american-workplace-report-2017.aspx

Laloux, F. (2014). *Reinventing organizations: A guide to creating organizations inspired by the next stage of human consciousness.* Millis, MA: Nelson Parker.

Mackey, J., & Sisodia, R. (2013). *Conscious capitalism: Liberating the heroic spirit of business.* Cambridge, MA: Harvard Business Review Press.

Kofman, F. (2006). *Conscious business: How to build value through values.* Louisville, CO: Sounds True Publishing.

Sisodia, R., Wolfe, D., & Sheth, J. (2014). *Firms of endearment: How world class companies profit from passion and purpose* (2nd ed). London: Pearson.

Robertson, B. (2015). *Holacracy: The new management system for a rapidly changing world.* New York, NY: Henry Holt.

Andreatta, B. (2017, April 12). *Cracking the code: How organizational growth and consciousness shape talent development* [Presentation]. Society for Human Resource Management International Conference and Exposition. New Orleans, LA.

Zak, P. (2017, January). The neuroscience of trust. *Harvard Business Review.* https://hbr.org/2017/01/the-neuroscience-of-trust

Zak, P. & Miller, D. (2017). *Trust factor: The science of creating high-performance companies.* New York, NY: Amacom.

Andreatta, B. (2017). *Wired to resist: The brain science of why change fails and a new model for driving success.* Santa Barbara, CA: 7th Mind Publishing.

Hurst, A. (2019). *The purpose economy: How your desire for impact, personal growth, and community is changing the world* (3rd ed.). Boise, ID: Elevate Publishing.

Hurst, A., & Tavis, A. (2015). *Workforce purpose index.* Imperative. https://cdn.imperative.com/media/public/Purpose_Index_2015

Frankl, V.E. (2006). *Man's search for meaning.* Boston, MA: Beacon Press.

Warren, R. (2002). *The purpose driven life: What on earth am I here for?* Grand Rapids, MI: Zondervan Books.

Inglehart, R., Miller, J., Dennis, M., Jwo, S., & Rosta, G. (2021, February 26). *Religion's sudden decline revisited.* Center for Political Studies. https://cps.isr.umich.edu/news/religions-sudden-decline-revisited/

Mitchell, T. (2020, June 9). *In U.S., decline of Christianity continues at rapid pace.* Pew Research Center's Religion & Public Life Project. https://www.pewresearch.org/religion/2019/10/17/in-u-s-decline-of-christianity-continues-at-rapid-pace/

Levitt, M. (2022, September 17). *America's Christian majority is on track to end.* NPR. npr.org/2022/09/17/1123508069/religion-christianity-muslim-atheist-agnostic-church-lds-pew

Chapter 7

Andreatta, B. (2019). *Wired to grow: Harness the power of brain science to master any skill* (2nd ed.) Santa Barbara, CA: 7th Mind Publishing.

Maslow, A. (1943). A theory of human motivation. *Psychological Review, 50*(4), 370-396.

Berinato , S. (2020, March 23). That discomfort you're feeling is grief. *Harvard Business Review.* https://hbr.org/2020/03/that-discomfort-youre-feeling-is-grief

The COVID States Project (2022, April). *COVID-19 deaths and Depression: The covid states project.* https://www.covidstates.org/reports/covid-19-deaths-and-depression

Cara, E. (2021, September 15). 72% of Americans know someone killed or hospitalized by covid-19, Pew Poll finds. *Gizmodo.* https://gizmodo.com/72-of-americans-know-someone-killed-or-hospitalized-by-1847679026

World Health Organization (2023). WHO coronavirus (COVID-19) dashboard. *World Health Organization.* https://covid19.who.int/

Kubler-Ross, E. (1969). *On death and dying: What the dying have to teach doctors, nurses, clergy, and their own families.* New York, NY: Simon & Schuster.

Kessler, D. (2019). *Finding meaning: The sixth stage of grief.* New York, NY. Scribner.

Grief.com (n.d.). *Help for grief because love never dies.* https://grief.com/

Chapter 8

Oliver, M. (n.d.). Mary Oliver Quotes. *Goodreads.* https://www.goodreads.com/author/quotes/23988.Mary_Oliver

Saad, A. H. and L. (2022, November 29). Reviewing remote work in the U.S. under covid-19. *Gallup.* https://news.gallup.com/poll/311375/reviewing-remote-work-covid.aspx

Dowell, E. K. P. (2022, April 13). *Remote working, commuting time, life events all affect home buyers' decisions.* US Census. https://www.census.gov/library/stories/2021/10/zillow-and-census-bureau-data-show-pandemics-impact-on-housing-market.html

Taylor, P. L. (2021, December 10). Covid-19 has changed the housing market forever: Here's where Americans are moving (and why). *Forbes.* https://www.forbes.com/sites/petertaylor/2020/10/11/covid-19-has- changed-the-housing-market-forever-heres-where-americans-are-moving-and-why

Beck, R. H. (2022, September 7.). *Covid's impact on the housing market.* Bankrate. https://www.bankrate.com/real-estate/covid-impact-on-the-housing-market/

Luscombe, B. (2021, July 6). What we learned about relationships during the pandemic. *Time.* https://time.com/6076596/relationship-lessons-during-covid-19/

Lillie, H.M., Chernichky-Karcher, S. & Venetis, M.K. (2021). Dyadic coping and discrete emotions during COVID-19: Connecting the communication theory of resilience with relational uncertainty. *Journal of Social and Personal Relationships.* 38(6) 1844–1868.

Prasso, S. (2020, March 31). Divorce rate after coronavirus quarantine in China is warning. *Bloomberg.* https://www.bloomberg.com/news/articles/2020-03-31/divorces-spike-in-china-after-coronavirus-quarantines#xj4y7vzkg

Wolfe, J. (2022, January 21). Coronavirus briefing: love in the time of Covid. *The New York Times.* https://www.nytimes.com/2022/01/21/briefing/coronavirus-briefing-love-in-the-time-of-covid.html

Apollo Technical LLC. (2023, January 17). *19 important hybrid working statistics to know now.* https://www.apollotechnical.com/hybrid-working-statistics/

Kiersz, A. K., Kaplan , J., & Hoff, M. (2021, October 12). Another 4 million workers quit in the 5th month in a row of record exits, and it shows how the pandemic is still making people rethink what they want out of work and life. *Business Insider.* https://www.businessinsider.com/over-4-million-workers-quit-record-labor-shortage-great-resi gnation-2021-10

US Bureau of Labor Statistics. (2023, March 8). *Job openings and labor turnover summary: 2023 M01 results.* US Bureau of Labor Statistics. https://www.bls.gov/news.release/jolts.nr0.htm

Cook, I. (2021, September 15). Who is driving the Great Resignation? *Harvard Business Review.* https://hbr.org/2021/09 /who-is-driving-the-great-resignation

Henderson, T. (2022, May 3). As women return to jobs, remote work could lock in gains. *Pew Charitable Trust.* https://www.pewtrusts.org/en/research-and-analysis/blogs/stateline/2022/05/03/as-women-return-to-jobs-remote-work-could-lock-in-gains

Bhattarai, A., & Melgar, L. (2023, February 14). Women lost more jobs early in the pandemic. they're also returning faster. *The Washington Post.* https://www.washingtonpost.com/business/2023/02/12/women-workforce-jobs- flexibility-remote/

Kaplan, J. (2023, February 18). Welcome to generation quit. *Business Insider.* https://www.businessinsider.com/ gen-z-jobs-generation-quiet-quitting-great-resignation -recession-economy-2023-2

Liebman, W., & Kochan, T. (2022, September 5). America's seeing a historic surge in worker organizing. here's how to sustain it. *Cognoscenti.* https://www.wbur.org/cognoscenti/2022/09/05/worker-organizing-labor-day-thomas- kochan-wilma-liebman

Dawkins, J.O. (2022, January 12). The Great Resignation is spurring a new class of entrepreneurs: Full-time side hustlers, solopreneurs, and freelancers. *Business Insider.* https://www.businessinsider.com/the-great-resignation-created-more-solo-entrepreneurs-and-freelancers

Center for Education and the Workforce. (2020, January). *Tracking COVID-19 unemployment and job losses.* Georgetown University. https://cew.georgetown.edu/cew-reports/jobtracker/ #tool-3-tracking

Bowman, C. P. (2022, November 17). *Coronavirus moving study shows more than 15.9 million people moved during COVID-19.* My Move. https://www.mymove.com/moving/coronavirus-moving-trends/

Kupietzky, J. (2022, November 22). The great resignation hits healthcare: Actions to take. *Newsweek.* https://www.newsweek.com/great-resignation-hits-healthcare-actions-take-1761064

Nieuwsma, J. A., O'Brien, E. C., Xu, H., Smigelsky, M. A., & Meador, K. G. (2022, April 5). Patterns of potential moral injury in post-9/11 combat veterans and Covid-19 Healthcare Workers. *Journal of General Internal Medicine.* https://link.springer.com/article/10.1007/s11606-022-07487-4

O'Brien, E.C., Xu, H. *et al.* (2022). Patterns of potential moral injury in Post-9/11 combat veterans and COVID-19 healthcare workers. *Journal of General Internal Medicine.* Vol. 37, 2033–2040.

Gordon, D. (2022, October 12). Amid Healthcare's great resignation, burned out workers are pursuing flexibility and passion. *Forbes.* https://www.forbes.com/sites/debgordon/2022/05/17/amid-healthcares-great-resignation-burned-out-workers-are-pursuing-flexibility-and-passion/

Harmon, G.E. (2022, February 3). Threats, intimidation against doctors and health workers must end. *American Medical Association.* https://www.ama-assn.org/about/leadership/threats-intimidation-against-doctors-and -health-workers-must-end

Nguyen, B. (2021, November 15). How to know if your employees will get swept up in The Great Resignation. *Business Insider.* https://www.businessinsider.com/great-resignation-what-to-know-who-is-quitting-2021-9

Khalid, A. (2021, March 17). The 6 emerging tech trends you need to know about. *Inc.* https://www.inc.com/amrita-khalid/tech-trends-forecast-future-amy-webb.html.

Rothwell, J. & Saad, L. (2021, March 8). How have U.S. working women fared during the pandemic? *Gallup.* https://news.gallup.com/poll/330533/working-women-fared-during-pandemic.aspx

Barnum, B. (2023, March 6). More teachers quitting than usual. *USA Today.* https://www.usatoday.com/story/news/education/2023/03/06/more-teachers-quitting-than-usual-driven-stress-politics-data-shows/11390639002/

Tan, H. & Flake, Eb. (2022, July 5). Will your CEO be next? Leaders are feeling burned out and are joining the great resignation in record numbers. *Business Insider.* https://www.businessinsider.com/ceos-burning-out-joining-great- reshuffle -2021-11?

Commerce Institute. (2023, January 18). *How many new businesses are started each year? (2022 data).* https://www.commerceinstitute.com/new-businesses-started-every-year/

Chapter 9

Schwantes, M. (2021, November 12). Why are people really quitting their jobs? Burnout tops the list new research shows. *Inc.* https://www.inc.com/marcel-schwantes/why-are-people-really-quitting-their-jobs-burnout-tops-list-new-research-shows.html

Mayer, K. (2022, February 1). What's behind the great resignation? Blame burnout. *HR Executive.* https://hrexecutive.com/whats-behind-the-great-resignation-blame-burnout/

Angell, M. (2022, January 25). The real reasons workers are leaving in droves. *Inc.* https://www.inc.com/melissa-angell/great-resignation-burnout-workers-upskilling-career-development.html

Ito, A. (2021, October 14). Boomerang employees who quit during the pandemic are starting to ask for their old jobs back. *Business Insider.* https://www.businessinsider.com/job-market-hiring-trends-expect-boo-merang-employees -labor-shortage-great-resignation

Hires, K. [@drkimhires]. (2021, August 30) *This moment! #futurework #leadership #coaching* [video] Tik Tok. https://www.tiktok.com/@drkimhires/video/7002335637714013445

Garton, E. (2021, August 27). Employee burnout is a problem with the company, not the person. *Harvard Business Review.* https://hbr.org/2017/04/employee-burnout-is-a-problem-with-the-company-not-the-person

World Health Organization (WHO). (2019, May 28). Burn-out an "occupational phenomenon": International Classification of Diseases. *WHO.* https://www.who.int/news/item/28-05-2019-burn-out-an-oc-cupational -phenomenon-international-classification-of-diseases

Sheppard, G. (n.d.). *When vacations aren't enough: new visier survey finds 70% of burnt out employees would leave current job.* Visier. https://www.visier.com/blog/new-survey-70-percent-burnt-out-employees-would-leave-current-job/.

Haelle, T. (2020, September 10). *Your 'surge capacity' is depleted-it's why you feel awful.* Medium. https://elemental.medium.com/your-surge-capacity-is-depleted-it-s-why-you-feel-awful-de285d542f4c

Hohlbaum, C. (2021, October 4). Bouncing back from Burnout. *Psychology Today.* https://www.psychology-today.com/us/blog/the-power-slow/202110/bouncing-back-burnout

Degges-White, S. (2021, August 31). Pandemic burnout and compassion fatigue. *Psychology Today.* https://www.psychologytoday.com/us/blog/lifetime-connections/202108/pandemic-burnout-and-compassion-fatigue

Wang, V. (2021, June 28). Council post: Why potential new hires ghost you. *Forbes.* https://www.forbes.com/sites/forbestechcouncil/2021/06/28/why-potential-new-hires-ghost-you/

Zabkowicz, J. (2021, July 6). *Being 'ghosted' ... by a new hire.* Korn Ferry. https://www.kornferry.com/insights/this-week-in-leadership/being-ghosted-by-a-new-hire

Woodyard, C. (2021, December 10). As millions of jobs go unfilled, employers look to familiar faces in 'Boomerang Employees.' *USA Today.* https://www.usatoday.com/story/money/careers/2021/12/09/boomerang-employees- appeal-great-resignation/6435370001/

Carter, S. (2013, November 26). The tell tale signs of burnout ... Do you have them? *Psychology Today.* https://www.psychologytoday.com/us/blog/high-octane-women /201311/the-tell-tale-signs-of-burnout-do-you-have-them.

Beckwith, G. (2021). (rep.). *Incivility on the rise, another harmful symptom of the pandemic.* Massachusetts Municipal Association. https://www.mma.org/advocacy/incivility-on-the-rise-another-harmful-symptom-of-the-pandemic

Pearson, C., Porath, C., & Bennis, W. (2009). *The cost of bad behavior: How incivility is damaging your business and what to do about it.* London: Portfolio Hardcover.

Stropoli , R. (2021, August 18). Are we really more productive working from home? *The University of Chicago Booth School of Business.* https://review.chicagobooth.edu/economics/2021/article/are-we-really-more-productive-working-home

Maurer, R. (2021, July 6). Remote employees are working longer than before. *Society for Human Resource Management.* https://www.shrm.org/hr-today/news/hr-news/pages/remote-employees-are-working-longer-than-before

Davis, M. F. (2020, April 25). Three hours longer, the pandemic workday has obliterated work-life balance. *BQPrime.* https://www.bloombergquint.com/coronavirus-outbreak/working-from-home-in-covid-era-means-three-more-hours-on-the-job

Chen, G. (2022, December 20). *Office space timeline: Past, present, and future.* Hubble. https://hubblehq.com/blog/office -space-timeline-past-present-future-infographic.

Bernstein, E., & Waber, B. (2021, September 2). The truth about open offices. *Harvard Business Review.* https://hbr.org/2019/11/the-truth-about-open-offices

Goldberg, E. (2021, December 4). Public displays of resignation: Saying 'I quit' loud and proud. *The New York Times.* https://www.nytimes.com/2021/12/04/business/public-resignation-quitting.html

Carroll, G. (2023, Feb. 10). Women of color are leaving the workforce and vanishing from unemployment statistics. *Fast Company.* https://www.fastcompany.com/90848858/women-of-color-are-leaving-the-workforce -and-vanishing-from-unemployment-statistics

Comaford, C. (2016, September 20). 75% of workers are affected by bullying—here's what to do about it. *Forbes.* https://www.forbes.com/sites/christinecomaford/2016/08/27/the-enormous-toll-workplace-bullying-takes-on-your-bottom-line/?sh=44040bef5595

Andreatta, B. & Lanham, R. (2021). *Hybrid workplace report 2021.* Voodle. https://www.brittandreatta.com/-hybrid-workplace- report-2021/

Lankes, C. (2021, March 7). How George Floyd reignited a global movement. *DW.* https://www.dw.com/en/how-george-floyds-death-reignited-a-worldwide-movement/a-56781938

Bogel-Burroughs, N. (2021, March 30). Prosecutors say Derek Chauvin knelt on George Floyd for 9 minutes 29 seconds, longer than initially reported. *The New York Times.* https://www.nytimes.com/2021/03/30/us/derek-chauvin-george-floyd-kneel-9-minutes-29-seconds.html

Cohn, M. (n.d.). *Listening sessions.* CEO Action for Diversity & Inclusion. https://www.ceoaction.com/actions/ listening-sessions/

Guynn, J. (2021, May 20). One year after George Floyd's death, two-thirds of workers want their companies to speak out against racism. *USA Today.* https://www.usatoday.com/story/money/2021/05/20/george -floyd- racism -workers-corporate-america-black-lives-matter/5154145001/

Harris Insights & Analytics LLC, (2018). *ASA workforce monitor: Job seeking perspectives.* American Staffing Association. https://d2m21dzi54s7kp.cloudfront.net/wp-content/uploads/2020/05/ASA_Workforce_Monitor_Job_Seeking_Perspectives-2022.pdf

Nguyen, T. (2021, April 5). *After Georgia, companies are banding together to condemn restrictive voting laws.* Vox. https://www.vox.com/the-goods/2021/4/5/22368566/corporate-response-georgia-sb202

Witherspoon, A., Milman, O., Liu, R., & Chang, A. (2021, October 14). The climate disaster is here—this is what the future looks like. *The Guardian.* https://www.theguardian.com/environment/ng-interactive/2021/oct/14/ climate-change-happening-now-stats-graphs-maps-cop26

Gibbens, S. (2021, December 6.). 2021's weather disasters brought home the reality of climate change. *National Geographic.* https://www.nationalgeographic.com/environment/article/this-year-extreme-weather-brought-home-reality-of-climate-change

Barnes, A. (2021, June 7). Climate crisis will crush world's biggest nations twice as hard as covid-19, says New Study. *The Hill.* https://thehill.com/changing-america/sustainability/climate-change/557118-climate -crisis-will-crush-worlds-biggest/

Dibdin, E. (2023, February 23). 6 podcasts to help tackle your climate anxiety. *The New York Times.* https://www.nytimes.com/2023/02/23/arts/podcasts-climate-change.html

Stillman, J. (2021, September 8). The biggest truth most leaders misunderstand about 'the great resignation': Want your employees to stick around? Flexibility is just the minimum. *Inc.* https://www.inc.com/jessica-stillman/great-resignation-work-meaning-esther-perel.html

Chapter 10

Cich, J. (2022, July 8). *PTSD vs. PTSI: Considerations for professional wellness.* Concordia University. https://www.csp.edu/publication/ptsd-vs-ptsi-considerations-for-professional-wellness/

National Center for PTSD (n.d.). *How Common is PTSD in Adults?* US Department of Veterans Affairs. https://www.ptsd.va.gov/understand/common/common_adults.asp

National Center for PTSD (n.d.). *How Common is PTSD in Children and Teens?* US Department of Veterans Affairs. https://www.ptsd.va.gov/understand/common/common_children_teens.asp

National Institute for Children's Health Quality (n.d.). Childhood Trauma Affects Nearly Half of American Children. NICQH Insight. https://www.nichq.org/insight/bringing-trauma-forefront-early-childhood-systems

VinZant, N. (2022, January 6). Pandemic fuels rise in mental health prescriptions. *QuoteWizard.* https://quotewizard.com/news/mental-health-prescriptions

EmpiRx Health. (2022, October 6). Rise in mental health prescriptions does not equate to rise in costs. *PR Newswire.* https://www.prnewswire.com/news-releases/rise-in-mental-health- prescriptions-does-not-equate -to-rise-in-costs-according-to-a-new-report-by-empirx-health-301641604.html.

EMDR Institute Inc. (2020). *What is EMDR?* https://www.emdr.com/what-is-emdr/

Brainspotting (2017).*What is brainspotting?* https://brainspotting.com/

Pollan, M. (2018). *How to change your mind: What the new science of psychedelics teaches us about consciousness, dying, addiction, depression, and transcendence.* New York, NY: Penguin.

National Human Trafficking Training and Technical Assistance Center. (n.d.). *Trauma-related responses.* https://nhttac.acf.hhs.gov/soar/eguide/observe/trauma_related_responses

Ercolano, A. (2023, February 7). *Psychedelic and consciousness research.* Johns Hopkins Center for Psychedelic and Consciousness Research. https://www.hopkinsmedicine.org/psychiatry/research/psychedelics- research.html

World Health Organization (2022, March 2). *Covid-19 pandemic triggers 25% increase in prevalence of anxiety and depression worldwide.* https://www.who.int/news/item/02-03-2022-covid-19-pandemic-triggers-25-increase-in-prevalence-of-anxiety-and-depression-worldwide

Kaufman, S. B. (2020, April 20). Post-traumatic growth: Finding meaning and creativity in adversity. *Scientific American Blog Network.* https://blogs.scientificamerican.com/beautiful-minds/post-traumatic-growth-finding-meaning -and-creativity-in-adversity/

Gay Travel. (2020, December 8). *How many flights per day? Airline and flight statistics (2023).* https://www.gay-travel.com/gay-blog/airline-and-flight-statistics

Olson, K., Shanafelt, T., & Southwick, S. (2020, October 8). Pandemic-driven posttraumatic growth for organizations and individuals. *JAMA Network.* https://jamanetwork.com/journals/jama/fullarticle/2771807

Weir, K. (2020). (rep.). Life after COVID-19: Making space for growth. *American Psychological Association.* https://www.apa.org/monitor/2020/06/covid-life-after

Kaufman, S. B. (2020, April 20). Post-traumatic growth: Finding meaning and creativity in adversity. *Scientific American Blog Network.* https://blogs.scientificamerican.com/beautiful-minds/post-traumatic-growth-finding-meaning -and-creativity-in-adversity/

Tedeschi, R., & Calhoun, L. (2004). Posttraumatic growth: conceptual foundations and empirical evidence. *Semantic Scholar.* https://www.semanticscholar.org/paper/Posttraumatic-Growth%3A -Conceptual-Foundations-and-Tedeschi-Calhoun/9948d303099caa7915eb23da1df89602f70a0f1d?p2df

Tedeschi, R.G. (2020, July). Growth after trauma. *Harvard Business Review.* https://hbr.org/2020/07/growth-after-trauma

Olson K., Shanafelt T., Southwick S. (2020). Pandemic-Driven Posttraumatic Growth for Organizations and Individuals. *Journal of the American Medical Association.* 324(18):1829–1830. doi:10.1001/jama.2020.20275

III. YOUR JOURNEY TO FIND PURPOSE

Viscott, D. (1993). *Finding strength in difficult times: A book of meditations.* New York, NY: McGraw Hill.

Chapter 11

Wilcox, B. (2022, February 15). *The Joys of Journaling: How Putting Pen to Paper Improves Mental Health.* https://www.goodingwellness.com/post/the-joys-of-journaling-how-putting

Shackelford, S. & Denzel, B. (2021). *You on purpose: Discover your calling and create the life you were meant to live.* Grand Rapids, MI: Baker Books.

Hudson, F. (1999). *The adult years: Mastering the art of self-renewal.* San Francisco, CA: Jossey-Bass.

Slavid, L. (2019). [Personal communication with author].

Dinning, D., Nichols, T., Phillips, G., Toad, R. (1997). Throw it all away [Song]. On *Coil.* Columbia Records.

Chapter 12

WRVO Public Media (2013, July 21). *Neuroscience shows the brain is "Wired for story."* https://www.wrvo.org/health/2013-07-21/neuroscience-shows-the-brain-is-wired-for-story

Cron, L. (2012). *Wired for story: The writer's guide to using brain science to hook readers from the very first sentence.* Berkeley, CA: Ten Speed Press.

Nichols, O. [@Shoelover99]. (2022, December 12). *These are my thoughts* [Video]. TikTok. https://www.tiktok.com/@shoelover99/video/7176310834182769963

Chapter 13

Ewing, M. (2022). *My life in winters: The extraordinary tales of one man's journey through the rise of the ski industry.* Santa Barbara, CA: 7th Mind Publishing.

Bolles, R. (2022). *What color is your parachute? Your guide to a lifetime of meaningful work and career success.* Berkeley, CA: Ten Speed Press.

Gallup (2023, February 13). *Cliftonstrengths.* Gallup.com. https://www.gallup.com/cliftonstrengths

Gardner, H. (2006). *Multiple intelligences: New horizons in theory and practice.* New York, NY: Basic Books.

Bosché, B. & Bosché, G. (2020). *The purpose factor: Extreme clarity for why you're here and what to do about it.* Brentwood, TN: Post Hill Press.

Csikszentmihalyi, M. (2008). *Flow: The psychology of optimal experience.* New York, NY: Harper Collins.

IV. EXPLORING PURPOSE + MEANINGFUL WORK

Hawking, S. (2010, June 4). Interview with Diane Sawyer. *ABC World News.* https://www.bbc.com/worklife/article/20180314-stephen-hawkings-advice-for-a-fulfilling-career

Chapter 14

Lufkin, B. (2022, February 25). Stephen Hawking's advice for a fulfilling career. *BBC Worklife*. https://www.bbc.com/worklife/article/20180314-stephen-hawkings-advice-for-a-fulfilling-career

Shackelford, S. & Denzel, B. (2021). *You on purpose: Discover your calling and create the life you were meant to live.* Grand Rapids, MI: Baker Books.

Martela, F., & Pessi, A. B. (2018). Significant work is about self-realization and broader purpose: Defining the key dimensions of meaningful work. *Frontiers in Psychology, 9.* https://doi.org/10.3389/fpsyg.2018.00363

Lips-Wiersma M., Haar, J., & Wright, S. (2020). The effect of fairness, responsible leadership, and worthy work on multiple dimensions of meaningful work. *Journal of Business Ethics, 161,* 35-52.

Bailey, C., Yeoman, R., Madden, A., Thompson, M., & Kerridge, G. (2019). A review of the empirical literature on meaningful work: Progress and research agenda. *Human Resource Development Review, 18*(1) 83–113. https://journals.sagepub.com/doi/pdf/10.1177/1534484318804653

Fletcher, L., Bailey, C., & Gilman, M. (2018). Fluctuating levels of personal role engagement within the working day: A multilevel study. *Human Resource Management Journal, 28,* 128-147.

Johnson, M., & Jiang, L. (2017). Reaping the benefits of meaningful work: The mediating versus moderating role of work engagement. *Stress & Health, 33,* 288-297. doi:10.1002/smi.2710

Duffy, R., Allan, B., Autin, K., & Bott, E. (2013). Calling and life satisfaction: It's not about having it, it's about living it. *Journal of Counseling Psychology, 60,* 42-52.

Duffy, R., Blake, A., Autin, K., & Douglass, R. (2014). Living a calling and work well-being: A longitudinal study. *Journal of Counseling Psychology, 61,* 605-615.

Leiter, M., & Harvie, P. (1997). Correspondence of supervisor and subordinate during major organizational change. *Journal of Occupational Health Psychology, 2,* 343-352.

Montani, F., Boudrias, J., & Pigeon, M. (2017). Employee recognition, meaningfulness, and behavioral involvement: Test of a moderated mediation model. *The International Journal of Human Resource Management,* 1-29. doi:10.1080/09585192.2017.1288153

Johns, G., Xie, J. L., & Fang, Y. (1992). Mediating and moderating effects in job design. *Journal of Management, 18,* 657-676.

Fairlie, P. (2011). Meaningful work, employee engagement, and other key outcomes: Implications for human resource development. *Advances in Developing Human Resources, 13,* 508-525.

Soane, E., Shantz, A., Alfes, K., Truss, K., Rees, C., & Gatenby, M. (2013). The association of meaningfulness, well-being and engagement with absenteeism: A moderated mediation model. *Human Resource Management, 52,* 441-456.

HR Forms & Checklists. (2022, April 26). *Society for Human Resource Management.* https://www.shrm.org/ResourcesAndTools/tools-and-samples/hr-forms/Pages/default.aspx

HSD Metrics (2022, March 16). *Understand the cost of turnover-free calculator.* https://hsdmetrics.com/the-cost-of-employee-turnover-calculator/

Andre, L. (2023, February 15). *112 employee turnover statistics: 2023 causes, cost & prevention data.* Finances Online. https://financesonline.com/employee-turnover-statistics/

Centers for Disease Control and Prevention. (2015, January 28). *CDC Foundation's New Business Pulse focuses on a healthy workforce.* https://www.cdc.gov/media/releases/2015/a0128-healthy-workforce.html

Albuquerque, I., Cunha, R., Martins, L., & Sa, A. (2014). Primary health care services: Workplace spirituality and organizational performance. *Journal of Organizational Change Management, 27,* 59-82.

Duchon, D., & Plowman, D. (2005). Nurturing the spirit at work: Impact on work unit performance. *The Leadership Quarterly, 16,* 807-833.

Chen, Z., Zhang, X., & Vogel, D. (2011). Exploring the underlying processes between conflict and knowledge sharing: A work engagement perspective. *Journal of Applied Social Psychology, 41,* 1005-1033.

Cohen-Meitar, R., Carmeli, A., & Waldman, D. A. (2009). Linking meaningfulness in the workplace to employee creativity. The intervening role of organizational identification and positive psychological experiences. *Creativity Research Journal, 21,* 361-375.

Chen, C.-Y., & Li, C.-I. (2013). Assessing the spiritual leadership effectiveness: The contribution of follower's self-concept and preliminary tests for moderation of culture and managerial position. *The Leadership Quarterly, 24,* 240-255.

Andreatta, B. (2022). *Calculating the Return on Investment (ROI) for Leader Training.* Brain Aware Training: Santa Barbara, CA.

Allan B. A., Douglass R. P., Duffy R. D., McCarty R. J. (2016). Meaningful work as a moderator of the relations between work stress and meaning in life. *Journal of Career Assessment, 24,* 429-440.

Chalofsky N. (2010). *Meaningful workplaces.* San-Francisco, CA: Jossey-Bass.

Chalofsky N., Cavallero L. (2013). A good living versus a good life: Meaning, purpose and HRD. *Advances in Developing Human Resources, 15,* 331-340.

Chalofsky N., Krishna V. (2009). Meaningfulness, commitment, and engagement: The intersection of a deeper level of intrinsic motivation. *Advances in Developing Human Resources, 11,* 189-203.

Lips-Wiersma M., Wright S. (2012). Measuring the meaning of meaningful work: Development and validation of the Comprehensive Meaningful Work Scale (CMWS). *Group & Organization Management, 37,* 665-685.

Lips-Wiersma M., Wright S., Dik B. (2016). Meaningful work: Differences among blue, pink- and white collar occupations. *Career Development International, 21,* 534-551.

Pavlish C., Hunt R. (2012). An exploratory study about meaningful work in acute care nursing. *Nursing Forum, 47,* 113-122.

McCrae R., Boreham P., Ferguson M. (2011). Reducing work to life interference in the public service: The importance of participative management as mediated by other work attributes. *Journal of Sociology, 47,* 313-332.

Tummers L. G., Knies E. (2013). Leadership and meaningful work in the public sector. *Public Administration Review, 73,* 859-868.

Bailey, C., & Madden, A. (2017). Time reclaimed: temporality and the experience of meaningful work. *Work, Employment and Society, 31*(1), 3-18. https://doi.org/10.1177/0950017015604100

Littmann-Ovadia H., Steger M. (2010). Character strengths and well-being among volunteers and employees: Towards an integrative model. *The Journal of Positive Psychology, 5,* 419-430.

Pollet E., Schnell T. (2016). Brilliant: But what for? Meaning and subjective well-being in the lives of intellectually gifted and academically high achieving adults. *Journal of Happiness Studies,* 1-26.

Daniel J. L. (2015). Workplace spirituality and stress: Evidence from Mexico and US. *Management Research Review, 38,* 29-43.

Lips-Wiersma, M., Wright, S., & Dik, B. (2016). Meaningful work: Differences among blue-, pink-, and white-collar occupations. *The Career Development International, 21*(5), 534–551. https://doi.org/10.1108/CDI-04-2016-0052

Lips-Wiersma, M. (2000). *The map of meaning.* The Map of Meaning. https://www.themapofmeaning.org/resources/copy-of-map

Salvagno, D. (2020). *Finding purpose at work.* Rochester, MI: PurposePoint.

Lysova, E., Allan , B., Dik, B., Duffy , R., & Steger, M. (2018). Fostering meaningful work in organizations: A multi-level review and integration. *Journal of Vocational Behavior, 110* (Part B), 374–389.

Barrick, M. R., Mount, M. K., & Li, N. (2013). The theory of purposeful work behaviour: The role of personality, higher-order goals, and job characteristics. *Academy of Management Review, 38,* 132–153. https://doi.org/10.5465/amr.2010.0479.

Scroggins, W. (2008). The relationship between employee fit perceptions, job performance, and retention: Implications of perceived fit. *Employee Responsibilities and Rights Journal, 20*(1), 57–71. https://doi.org/10.1007/s10672-007-9060-0.

Tims, M., Derks, D., & Bakker, A. B. (2016). Job crafting and its relationships with person–job fit and meaningfulness: A three-wave study. *Journal of Vocational Behavior, 92,* 44–53. https://doi.org/10.1016/j.jvb.2015.11.007.

Vogel, R., Rodell, J., and Sabey, T. (2020). Meaningfulness Misfit: Consequences of Daily Meaningful Work Needs–Supplies Incongruence for Daily Engagement. *Journal of Applied Psychology, 105* (7), 760–770. http://dx.doi.org/10.1037/apl0000464

Van Zyl, L.E., Rothmann, S. & Nieman, C. (2020). Mental health, work engagement and meaningful work-role fit of Industrial Psychologists: A latent profile analysis. *Psychology Studies, 65,* 199–213. https://doi.org/10.1007/s12646-019-00544-9

Kupietzky, J. (2022, November 22). The great resignation hits healthcare: Actions to take. *Newsweek.* https://www.newsweek.com/great-resignation-hits-healthcare-actions-take-1761064

Oppland, M. (2023, March 9). 8 traits of flow according to Mihaly Csikszentmihalyi. *Positive Psychology.* https://positivepsychology.com/mihaly-csikszentmihalyi-father-of-flow/

Houghton, J., Neck, C., & Krishnakumar, S. (2016). The what, why, and how of spirituality in the workplace revisited: A 14-year update and Extension. *Journal of Management, Spirituality & Religion.* http://dx.doi.org/10.1080/14766086.2016.1185292

Joelle, M. & Coelho, A. (2019) The impact of spirituality at work on workers' attitudes and individual performance. *The International Journal of Human Resource Management, 30* (7), 1111-1135, DOI:10.1080/09585192.2017.1314312

Utami, N., Sapta, I., Verwati, Y., & Astakoni, I. (2021). Relationship between workplace spirituality, organizational commitment and organizational citizenship behavior. *The Journal of Asian Finance, Economics and Business, 8* (1), 507–517. https://doi.org/10.13106/JAFEB.2021.VOL8.NO1.507

Aboobaker, N., Edward, M. and Zakkariya, K. (2020). Workplace spirituality and employee loyalty: An empirical investigation among millennials in India. *Journal of Asia Business Studies, 14*(2), 211-225. https://doi.org/10.1108/JABS-03-2018-0089

Aboobaker, N., Edward, M. and Zakkariya, K. (2022). Workplace spirituality, well-being at work and employee loyalty in a gig economy: multi-group analysis across temporary vs permanent employment status. *Personnel Review, 51*(9), 2162-2180. https://doi.org/10.1108/PR-01-2021-0002

Hunsaker, W. and Ding, W. (2022). Workplace spirituality and innovative work behavior: The role of employee flourishing and workplace satisfaction. *Employee Relations, 44* (6), 1355-1371. https://doi.org/10.1108/ER-01-2021-0032

Conger, J. A. (1994). *Spirit at work: Discovering the spirituality in leadership.* San Francisco, CA: Jossey-Bass.

Warren, R. (2002). *The purpose driven life: What on earth am I here for?* Grand Rapids, MI: Zondervan Books.

Daniels, D. (2022). *Your purpose is calling: Your difference is your destiny.* Grand Rapids, MI: Zondervan Books.

Shackelford, S. & Denzel, B. (2021). *You on purpose: Discover your calling and create the life you were meant to live.* Grand Rapids, MI: Baker Books.

Moore, T. (2009). *A life at work: The joy of discovering what you were born to do.* New York, NY: Broadway Books.

Palmer, P. J. (2000). *Let your life speak: Listening for the voice of vocation.* San Francisco, CA: Jossey-Bass.

Millman, D. (2011). *The four purposes of life: Finding meaning and direction in a Changing World.* Novato, CA: HJ Kramer.

Ishida, R. (2011). Enormous earthquake in Japan: Coping with stress using purpose-in-life/ikigai. *Psychology, 2*(8), 773.

Ishida, R. (2012). Purpose in life (*Ikigai*), a frontal lobe function, is a natural. *Psychology, 3,* 272-276. doi: 10.4236/psych.2012.33038.

Kumano, M. (2018). On the concept of well-being in Japan: Feeling *shiawase* as hedonic well-being and feeling *ikigai* as eudaimonic well-being. *Applied Research Quality Life, 13,* 419–433. https://doi.org/10.1007/s11482-017- 9532-9

Wilkes, J., Garip, G., Kotera, Y. *et al.* (February 12, 2022). Can ikigai predict anxiety, depression, and well-being?. *International Journal of Mental Health Addiction.* https://doi.org/10.1007/s11469-022-00764-7

Eshak, E., Baba, S., Yatsuya, H., Iso, H., Hirakawa, Y., Mahfouz, E., Chifa, C., Sakaniwa, R., & El-khateeb, A. (2022, February 12). Work and family conflicts, depression, and "ikigai": A mediation analysis in a cross-cultural study between Japanese and Egyptian civil workers. *Journal of Epidemiology.* https://doi.org/10.2188/jea.JE20210338

Miyazaki, J., Shirai, K., Kimura, T., Ikehara, S., Tamakoshi, A., & Iso, H. (2022, October 10). Purpose in life (ikigai) and employment status in relation to cardiovascular mortality: The Japan collaborative cohort study. *BMJ open.* https://doi.org/10.1136/bmjopen-2021-059725

Yohko, M. (2021). Ikigai interventions for primary, secondary, and tertiary prevention of dementia. *Aging and Health Research, 1*(3). https://www.sciencedirect.com/science/article/pii/S266703212100024X?via%3Dihub.

Nakahara, S., & Ishikawa, M. (2012, October 20). Mortality in the 2011 tsunami in Japan. *Journal of Epidemiology.* https://pubmed.ncbi.nlm.nih.gov/23089585/

Ishida, R. (2011). Enormous earthquake in Japan: Coping with stress using purpose-in-life/Ikigai. *Psychology, 2*(8), 773-776.

Buettner, D. (2010). *The blue zones: Lessons for living longer from the people who've lived the longest.* Washington, DC: National Geographic Society.

Thomas, B. (2021). The art of resilience: The Japanese ikigai in sports. *SSRN Electronic Journal, 68*(1). https://doi.org/10.2139/ssrn.3952071

Kono, S., & Walker, G. (2019). Theorizing the temporal aspect of Ikigai or life worth living among Japanese university students: A mixed-methods approach. *Applied Research in Quality of Life, 16*(2), 845–873. https://doi.org/10.1007/s11482-019-09792-3

Chapter 15

Bailey, C. & Lips-Wiersma, M., Madden, A., Yeoman, R., Thompson, M., & Chalofsky, N. (2018). The five paradoxes of meaningful work: Introduction to the special issue 'Meaningful Work: Prospects for the 21st Century'. *Journal of Management Studies, 56,* 481-499. https://doi.org/10.1111/joms.12422

Ouwerkerk, J., & Bartels, J. (2022). Is anyone else feeling completely nonessential? Meaningful work, identification, job insecurity, and online organizational behavior during a lockdown in The Netherlands. *International Journal of Environmental Research and Public Health, 19*(3), 1514. https://doi.org/10.3390/ijerph19031514

Gui, W., Bai, Q., & Wang, L. (2022). Workplace incivility and employees' personal initiative: A moderated mediation model of emotional exhaustion and meaningful work. *SAGE Open, 12*(1). https://doi.org/10.1177/21582440221079899

Wells, S. (2022, December 8). *Violence against healthcare professionals: When will it stop?* American Association of Critical-Care Nurses (AACN). https://www.aacn.org/blog/violence-against-healthcare-professionals

Kavaklı, B. D., & Yildirim, N. (2022). The relationship between workplace incivility and turnover intention in nurses: A cross-sectional study. *Journal of Nursing Management, 30*(5), 1235–1242. https://doi.org/10.1111/jonm.13594

Weeks, K.P., Schaffert, C. (2019). Generational differences in definitions of meaningful work: A mixed methods study. *Journal of Business Ethics, 156,* 1045–1061. https://doi.org/10.1007/s10551-017-3621-4

Bunderson, J. and Thompson, J. (2009). The call of the wild: zookeepers, callings, and the double-edged sword of deeply meaningful work. *Administrative Science Quarterly, 54,* 32–57.

Hudson, F. (1999). *The adult years: Mastering the art of self-renewal.* San Francisco, CA: Jossey-Bass.

Oelberger, C. (2018). The dark side of deeply meaningful work: Work-relationship turmoil and the moderating role of occupational value homophily. *Journal of Management Studies, 56*(3), 558–588. https://doi.org/10.1111/joms.12411

Toraldo, M., Islam, G., & Mangia, G. (2018). Serving time: Volunteer work, liminality and the uses of meaningfulness at music festivals. *Journal of Management Studies, 56*(3), 617–654. https://doi.org/10.1111/joms.12414

Florian, M., Costas, J., & Kärreman, D. (2018). Struggling with meaningfulness when context shifts: Volunteer work in a refugee shelter. *Journal of Management Studies, 56*(3), 589–616. https://doi.org/10.1111/joms.12410

Symon, G., & Whiting, R. (2018). The sociomaterial negotiation of social entrepreneurs' meaningful work. *Journal of Management Studies, 56*(3), 655–684. https://doi.org/10.1111/joms.12421

Norman, S. B., & Maguen, S. (2020, April 20). *Moral injury.* US Department of Veteran Affairs. https://www.ptsd.va.gov/professional/treat/cooccurring/moral_injury.asp#

Schwartz, S. (2019, May 23). Teachers often experience 'moral injury' on the job, study finds. *EducationWeek.* https://www.edweek.org/teaching-learning/teachers-often-experience-moral-injury-on-the-job-study-finds/2019/05

Goldman, R. (2021, November. 10). Teachers are hurting and a new approach is needed. *Psychology Today.* https://www.psychologytoday.com/us/blog/building-resilient-minds/202111/teachers-are-hurting-and-new-approach-is-needed

Lewis, C. (2020). An exploratory analysis of the association between moral injury and mental health-care-seeking attitudes and behaviors in returning veterans of the Iraq and Afghanistan wars. *MedRxiv.* https://doi.org/10.1101/2020.08.25.20182147

Van Beusekom, M. (2022, April 6). COVID-19 health workers suffer combat-type moral trauma. *Center for Infectious Disease Research and Policy.* https://www.cidrap.umn.edu/covid-19-health-workers-suffer-combat-type-moral-trauma

Nieuwsma, J., O'Brien, E., Xu, H., Smigelsky, M., & Meador, K. (2022). Patterns of potential moral injury in post-9/11 combat veterans and covid-19 healthcare workers. *Journal of General Internal Medicine, 37*(8), 2033–2040. https://doi.org/10.1007/s11606-022-07487-4

Cartolovni, A., Stolt, M., Scott, P. A., & Suhonen, R. (2021). Moral injury in healthcare professionals: A scoping review and discussion. *Nursing Ethics, 28*(5), 590–602. https://doi.org/10.1177/0969733020966776

Williamson, V., Murphy, D., & Greenberg, N. (2020). Covid-19 and experiences of moral injury in front-line key workers. *Occupational Medicine, 70*(5), 317–319. https://doi.org/10.1093/occmed/kqaa052

Greenberg, N., Docherty, M., Gnanapragasam, S., & Wessely, S. (2020). Managing mental health challenges faced by healthcare workers during covid-19 pandemic. *BMJ (Clinical research ed.),* 368, m1211. https://doi.org/10.1136/bmj.m1211

Bartzak P. J. (2015). Moral injury is the wound: PTSD is the manifestation. *Medsurg nursing: Journal of the Academy of Medical-Surgical Nurses, 24*(3), 10–11.

Williamson, V., Murphy, D., & Greenberg, N. (2023). Veterinary professionals' experiences of moral injury: A qualitative study. *The Veterinary Record, 192*(2), e2181. https://doi.org/10.1002/vetr.2181

Chan, M. (2019, September 12). Here's why suicide among veterinarians is a growing problem. *Time.* https://time.com/5670965/veterinarian-suicide-help/

Luccesi, E.L. (2022, May 12). Researchers try to understand the high suicide rate among veterinarians. *Discover Magazine.* https://www.discovermagazine.com/mind/researchers-try-to-understand-high-suicide-rate-among-veterinarians

Bullis, A. (2023, February. 5). Our business is killing us. *Slate.* https://slate.com/human-interest/2023/02/veterinarians-euthanasia-mental-health-dogs-cats.html

Stoewen D. L. (2015). Suicide in veterinary medicine: Let's talk about it. *The Canadian Veterinary Journal / La Revue Veterinaire Canadienne, 56*(1), 89–92.

Nakatsuka, C. (2023, February 16). *Moral injury of a different kind.* Christian Medical & Dental Associations (CMDA). https://cmda.org/moral-injury-of-a-different-kind/

Smith, J. G., Urban, R. W., & Wilson, S. T. (2022). Association of stress, resilience, and nursing student incivility during COVID-19. *Nursing Forum, 57*(3), 374–381. https://doi.org/10.1111/nuf.12694

Park, E., & Kang, H. (2020). Nurse educators' experiences with student incivility: A meta-synthesis of qualitative studies. *Journal of Educational Evaluation for Health Professions, 17*, 23. https://doi.org/10.3352/jeehp.2020.17.23

Yanchus, N., Periard, D., & Osatuke, K. (2016). Further examination of predictors of turnover intention among mental health professionals. *Journal of Psychiatric and Mental Health Nursing, 24*(1), 41–56. https://doi.org/10.1111/jpm.12354

Hudson, F. (1999). *The adult years: Mastering the art of self-renewal.* San Francisco, CA: Jossey-Bass.

Chapter 16

Fraser-Thill, R. (2019, August 7). The 5 biggest myths about meaningful work. *Forbes.* https://www.forbes.com/sites/rebeccafraserthill/2019/08/07/the-5-biggest-myths-about-meaningful-work/

Chamberlain, M. (2016, September 11). The purpose-driven career: Myth or possibility? *HuffPost.* https://www.huffpost.com/entry/the-purposedriven-career_b_8118128

Hurst, A. (2019). *The purpose economy: How your desire for impact, personal growth, and community is changing the world* (3rd ed.). Boise, ID: Elevate Publishing.

Bosché, B. & Bosché, G. (2020). *The purpose factor: Extreme clarity for why you're here and what to do about it.* Brentwood, TN: Post Hill Press.

Anxiety and Depression Association of America (n.d.). *Anxiety disorders: Facts & statistics.* https://adaa.org/understanding-anxiety/facts-statistics

Campaign to End Loneliness (n.d.). *The facts on loneliness.* https://www.campaigntoendloneliness.org/the-facts-on-loneliness/

Statista Research Department. (2022, November 29). *Loneliness among adults worldwide by country 2021*. Statista. https://www.statista.com/statistics/1222815/loneliness-among-adults-by-country/

Strecher, V. (2016). *Life on purpose: How living for what matters most changes everything*. New York, NY: Harper Collins.

Winfrey, O. The Path Made Clear: Discovering Your Life's Direction and Purpose

Brooks, A. (2022). *From strength to strength: Finding success, happiness, and deep purpose in the second half of life*. New York, NY: Penguin.

Bolles, R. (2022). *What color is your parachute? Your guide to a lifetime of meaningful work and career success*. Berkeley, CA: Ten Speed Press.

Shetty, J. (2020). *Think like a monk: Train your mind for peace and purpose every day*. New York, NY: Simon & Schuster.

Sisodia, R. (2023). *Awaken: The path to purpose, inner peace, and healing*. Hoboken, NJ: Wiley.

V. CONTINUING YOUR JOURNEY TO FIND PURPOSE

Winfrey, O. (2018, June 8). *Ask Oprah: How did you discover your purpose?* National Museum of African American History and Culture. YouTube video. https://www.youtube.com/watch?v=fAz9qLTC4EY

Chapter 17

Goleman, D. (2006). *Emotional intelligence: Why it can matter more than IQ*. New York, NY: Bantam.

Kouzes, J. and Posner, B. (2023). *The leadership challenge: How to make extraordinary things happen in organizations* (7th ed). San Francisco, CA: Jossey-Bass.

Andreatta, B. (2020, October 9). Emotional intelligence: Why you need it and how to spot it at work. *Entrepreneur*. https://www.entrepreneur.com/growing-a-business/emotional-intelligence-why-you-need-it-and-how-to-spot-it/356292

Landry , L. (2019, April 3). Emotional intelligence in leadership: Why it's important. *Harvard Business School*. https://online.hbs.edu/blog/post/emotional-intelligence-in-leadership

Pontefract, D. (2022, November 14). Is emotional intelligence the number one indicator of a good leader? *Forbes*. https://www.forbes.com/sites/danpontefract/2022/11/12/is-emotional-intelligence-the-number-one- indi cator-of-a-good-leader/?sh=208f88464c02

Brown, B. (2021). *Atlas of the heart: Mapping meaningful connection and the language of the heart*. New York, NY: Random House.

Bosché, B. & Bosché, G. (2020). *The purpose factor: Extreme clarity for why you're here and what to do about it*. Brentwood, TN: Post Hill Press.

Pachter, R. (2020, July 20).Upskilling Employees in the Evolving Remote-Learning Environment. *Brandon Hall Group*. https://www.brandonhall.com/blogs/brandon-hall-group-research-highlights-july-13-17-2020/

Hurst, A. (2019). *The purpose economy: How your desire for impact, personal growth, and community is changing the world* (3rd ed.). Boise, ID: Elevate Publishing.

Van Sustern, L. and Colino, S. (2020). *Emotional inflammation: Discover your triggers and reclaim your equilibrium during anxious times*. Louisville, CO: Sounds True.

Chapter 18

Bosché, B. & Bosché, G. (2020). *The purpose factor: Extreme clarity for why you're here and what to do about it*. Brentwood, TN: Post Hill Press.

Moore, T. (2009). *A life at work: The joy of discovering what you were born to do*. New York, NY. Broadway Books.

Warren, R. (2002). *The purpose driven life: What on earth am I here for?* Grand Rapids, MI: Zondervan Books.

Brown, B. (2015). *Daring greatly: How the courage to be vulnerable transforms the way we live, love, parent, and lead*. New York, NY: Avery Publishing.

Brown, B. (2010, December). *The power of vulnerability* [Video]. TED Conferences. https://www.ted.com/talks/brene_brown_the_power_of_vulnerability/comments

Brown, B. (2012, March). *Listening to shame* [Video]. TED Conferences. https://www.ted.com/talks/brene_brown_listening_to_shame

Brown, B. (2019). *The call to courage* [Film]. Netflix. https://www.netflix.com/title/81010166

Brown, B. (2019). *Braving the wilderness: The quest for true belonging and the courage to stand alone*. New York, NY: Random House.

Brown, B. (2021). *Atlas of the heart: Mapping meaningful connection and the language of the heart*. New York, NY: Random House.

Brown, B. (2017). *Rising strong: How the ability to reset transforms the way we live, love, parent, and lead*. New York, NY: Random House.

Brown, B. (2018). *Dare to lead: Brave work, tough conversations, whole hearts*. New York, NY: Random House.

Van Der Kolk, B. (2015). *The body keeps the score: Brain, mind, and body in the healing of trauma*. New York, NY: Penguin.

Daniels, D. (2022). *Your purpose is calling: Your difference is your destiny*. Grand Rapids, MI: Zondervan Books.

Chapter 19

Psychology Today (n.d.). *EMDR.* https://www.psychologytoday.com/us/therapy-types/emdr

Cleveland Clinic. (n.d.). *EMDR therapy: What it is, Procedure & Effectiveness.* https://my.clevelandclinic.org/health/t reatments/22641-emdr-therapy

Brainspotting. (n.d.). *What is brainspotting?* https://brainspotting.com/

Psychology Today (n.d.). *Cognitive processing therapy.* https://www.psychologytoday.com/us/ therapy-types/cognitive-processing-therapy

Andreatta, B. (2014, July 22). *Human potential* [Video]. TED Conferences. https://www.youtube.com/watch?v=yXt_70Ak670

Carter-Scott, C. (2021, May 16). *Inner negotiation workshop.* MMS Worldwide Institute, LLC. https://www.mmsworldwideinstitute.com/inner-negotiation-workshop/

Van Der Kolk, B. (2015). *The body keeps the score: Brain, mind, and body in the healing of trauma.* New York, NY: Penguin.

Carter-Scott, C. (1998). *If life is a game, these are the rules: Ten rules for being human.* New York, NY: Harmony Books.

Carter-Scott, C. (2021, March 19). *Ten rules for being human.* Dr. Chérie Carter-Scott, MCC. https://www.drcherie .com/ten-rules-for-being-human/

Millman, D. (2011). *The four purposes of life: Finding meaning and direction in a changing world.* Novato, CA: New World Library.

Tolle, E. (2008). *A new earth: Awakening to your life's purpose.* New York, NY: Penguin.

Goleman, D. and Davidson, R. (2017). *Altered traits: Science reveals how meditation changes your mind, brain, and body.* New York, NY: Avery.

Chapter 20

Daniels, D. (2022). *Your purpose is calling: Your difference is your destiny.* Grand Rapids, MI: Zondervan Books.

Dalton-Smith, S. (2019). *The real reason why we are tired and what to do about it* [Video]. TED Conferences. https://www.youtube.com/watch?v=ZGNN4EPJzGk

Myers, E.[elysemeyers]. (December 2022) *Wherever you go, there you are, be good to yourself. #resolution #loveyourself* [Video]. Tik Tok. https://www.tiktok.com/t/ZTRnDFvMK/

Andreatta, B. (2018). *Wired to connect: The brain science of teams and a new model for creating collaboration and inclusion.* Santa Barbara, CA: 7th Mind Publishing.

West, L. (2021, June 8). Ask not for whom the bell trolls; it trolls for thee. *This American Life.* https://www.thisamericanlife.org/545/if-you-dont-have-anything-nice-to-say-say-it-in-all-caps/act-one-0

Brown, B. (2015). *Daring greatly: How the courage to be vulnerable transforms the way we live, love, parent, and lead.* New York, NY: Avery Publishing.

Glass, I., West, L., Menjivar, J., & Vogt, P. J. (2021, June 8). If you don't have anything nice to say, say it in all caps. *This American Life.* https://www.thisamericanlife.org/545/if-you-dont-have-anything-nice-to-say-say-it-in-all-caps

Brown, B. (2010, December). *The power of vulnerability* [Video]. TED Conferences. https://www.ted.com/talks/brene_brown _the_power_of_ vulnerability/comments

Brown, B. (2012, March). *Listening to shame* [Video]. TED Conferences. https://www.ted.com/talks/brene_brown_listening_to_shame

Winfrey, O. & Brown, B. (2013, March 17). *Super Soul Sunday,* Episode 413, Season 4. https://www.oprah.com/own-super-soul-sunday/dr-brene-brown-two-dangerous-words-in-your-vocabulary-video

Roosevelt, T. (1910, April 23). A quote by Theodore Roosevelt. *Goodreads.* https://www.goodreads.com/quotes/7-it-is-not-the-critic-who-counts-not-the-man

Wikipedia contributors. (2023, February 16). Citizenship in a Republic. *Wikipedia, The Free Encyclopedia.* https://en.wikipedia.org/w/index.php?title=Citizenship_in_a_Republic&oldid=1139685867

VI. BUILDING PURPOSE-DRIVEN ORGANIZATIONS

Mead, M. (1978, March 11). Meeting of the Planetary Initiative for the World We Choose. https://quoteinvestigator.com/2017/11/12/change-world/

Chapter 21

Johnson, S., Spehr, M., Rowan, R., Berghoff, J., Kelley, J., and Sisodia, R. (2019). Editor's desk: The potential and promise of purpose-driven organizations. *American Journal of Health Promotion,* 33(6), 958-973. doi:10.1177/0890117119855446

Laloux, F. (2014). *Reinventing organizations: A guide to creating organizations inspired by the next stage of human consciousness.* Shrewsbury, MA: Nelson Parker.

Reinventing Organizations (n.d.). *Reinventing organizations.* https://www.reinventingorganizations.com/

Mackey, J., & Sisodia, R. (2014). *Conscious capitalism: Liberating the heroic spirit of business.* Cambridge, MA: Harvard Business Review Press.

Sisodia, R. S., Wolfe, D. B., & Sheth, J. N. (2013). *Firms of endearment: How world-class companies profit from passion and purpose.* Upper Saddle River, NJ: Prentice Hall.

Gelb, R. S. M. J. (2019). *The Healing Organization: Awakening the conscience of business to help save the world*. Nashville, TN: HarperCollins Leadership.

Robertson, B. J. (2015). *Holacracy: The new management system for a rapidly changing world*. New York, NY: Henry Holt and Company.

Edwards, R. (2022, May 3). *The highest stages of human development: At the cutting edge*. The Great Updraft. https://thegreatupdraft.com/at-the-cutting-edge-the-highest-stages-of-human-development/

Edwards, R. (2023, March 14). *Ken Wilber fundamentals: Altitudes of development explained*. The Great Updraft. https://thegreatupdraft.com/ken-wilber-fundamentals-altitudes-of-development-explained/

Herway, J. (2023, March 30). *Just how purpose-driven is your organizational culture?* Gallup. https://www.gallup.com/workplace/356093/purpose-driven-organizational-culture.aspx

Dhingra, N., Samo, A., Schaninger, B., & Schrimper, M. (2021, April 5). *Help your employees find purpose-or watch them leave*. McKinsey & Company. https://www.mckinsey.com/capabilities/people-and-organizational-performance /our-insights/help-your-employees-find-purpose-or-watch-them-leave

O'Brien, D., Main, A., Kunkel, S., & Stephan, A. (n.d.). *Purpose is everything*. Deloitte Insights. https://www2.deloitte.com/us/en/insights/topics/marketing-and-sales-operations/global-markeing-trends/2020/purpose-driven-companies.html

Gast, A., Illanes, P., Probst, N., Schaninger, B., & Simpson, B. (2020, April 22). *Purpose: Shifting from why to how*. McKinsey & Company. https://www.mckinsey.com/capabilities/people-and-organizational-performance/our-insights/purpose-shifting-from-why-to-how

US Surgeon General (n.d.). *Workplace mental health & well-being: Current priorities of the U.S. Surgeon General*. https://www.hhs.gov/surgeongeneral/priorities/workplace-well-being/index.html

Miller, K. (2020, December 8). *The triple bottom line: What it is & why it's important*. Business Insights Blog. https://online.hbs.edu/blog/post/what-is-the-triple-bottom-line

Pfeffer, J. (2018). *Dying for a paycheck: How modern management harms employee health and company performance—and what we can do about it*. New York, NY: Harper Business.

Global Fashion Agenda (2023, March 30). Global Fashion Agenda. https://globalfashionagenda.org/

Ernst Young (2020, December 15). *Why business must harness the power of purpose*. EY Americas. https://www.ey.com/en_us/purpose/why-business-must-harness-the-power-of-purpose

Kolhatkar, S. (2019, February 26). The P.G. & E. Bankruptcy and the coming climate-related business failures. *The New Yorker*. https://www.newyorker.com/business/currency/the-pg-and-e-bankruptcy-and-the-coming-climate-related-business-failures

Bailey, R. (n.d.). *Climate change has claimed its biggest corporate victim*. Marsh McLennan. https://www.marshmclennan.com/insights/publications/2019/mar/climate-change-has-claimed-its-biggest-corporate-victim.html

Turner, J. (2020, January 27). *Mined into extinction: Is the world running out of critical minerals?* Mining Technology. https://www.mining-technology.com/features/featuremined-into-extinction-is-the-world-running-out-of-critical-minerals-5776166/

Nowatschin, J. (2023, February 28). *Top 10 extinct animals*. Animals Around the Globe. https://www.animalsaroundtheglobe.com/extinct-animals/

World Wildlife Fund. (n.d.). *Species list*. WWF. https://www.worldwildlife.org/species/directory?direction=-desc&sort=extinction_status

World Wildlife Fund (2022). *Living Planet Report 2022: Building a Nature Positive Society*. https://wwflpr.awsassets.panda.org/downloads/lpr_2022_full_report.pdf

Hasell, J., Roser, M., Ortiz-Ospina, E., & Arriagada, P. (2022, October 17). *Poverty*. Our World in Data. https://ourworldindata.org/poverty

Chapter 22

Glassdoor. (n.d.). *Glassdoor Job Search: You deserve a job that loves you back*. https://www.glassdoor.com/index.htm

Clifton, J. (2023, March 30). *The World's workplace is broken—here's how to fix it*. Gallup. https://www.gallup.com/workplace/393395/world-workplace-broken-fix.aspx

Rumi (n.d.). [Quote]. https://www.goodreads.com/quotes/936898-everyone-has-been-made-for-some-particular-work-and-the

Chapter 23

Suellentrop, A. S., & Bauman, E. B. (2022, November 11). *How influential is a good manager?* Gallup. https://www.gallup.com/cliftonstrengths/en/350423/influential-good-manager.aspx

Bloom, N., Van Reenen, J., & Brynjolfsson, E. (2021, August 31). Good management predicts a firm's success better than it, R&D, or even employee skills. *Harvard Business Review*. https://hbr.org/2017/04/good-management- predicts-a-firms -success-better-than-it-rd-or-even-employee-skills

Kaye, B. & Giulioni, J. *Help them grow or watch them go: Career conversations organizations need and employees want*. San Francisco, CA: Berrett-Koehler Publishers.

Kelly, M. (2207). *The dream manager*. New York, NY: Hyperion Press.

Andreatta, B. (2018). *Wired to connect: The brain science of teams and a new model for creating collaboration and inclusion.* Santa Barbara, CA: 7th Mind Publishing.

Edmondson, A. (2012). *Teaming: How organizations learn, innovate, and compete in the knowledge economy.* San Francisco, CA: Jossey-Bass.

Lencioni, P. (2007). *The three signs of a miserable job: A fable for managers.* San Francisco, CA: Jossey-Bass.

Chapter 24

Gulati, R. (2022). *Deep purpose: The heart and soul of high-performance companies.* New York, NY: HarperCollins.

Sisodia, R., Henry, T. & Eckschmidt, T. (2018). *Conscious capitalism field guide: Tools for transforming your organization.* Boston, MA: Harvard Business Review Press.

Sisodia, R. (2023). *Awaken: The path to purpose, inner peace, and healing.* Hoboken, NJ: Wiley.

Weetman, C. (2021, August 18). *Using Ikigai to clarify business purpose.* Rethink Global. https://www.rethink-global.info/ikigai-business-purpose/

Ikigai Coaching (2022). *Ikigai for business.* https://www.ikigaiprocoaching.com/ikigai-for-business

Andreatta, B. (2022, February 24). How to embrace purpose as the path to innovation, profitability. *HR Executive.* https://hrexecutive.com/how-to-embrace-purpose-as-the-path-to-innovation-profitability

Cone (2018). *2018 Purpose study: How to build deeper bonds, amplify your message and expand the consumer base.* https://conecomm.com/2018-purpose-study/

United Nations. (n.d.). *Sustainable development.* United Nations. https://sustainabledevelopment.un.org/

GRI (n.d.). *Global standards for sustainability impacts.* Global Reporting. https://www.globalreporting.org/standards/

Gibson, K. (2022, September 29). *What is a purpose-driven firm?* Business Insights Blog. https://online.hbs.edu/blog/post/purpose-driven-firms

Timberland (n.d.). *How we serve.* ttps://www.timberland.com/responsibility/stories/how-we-serve.html

Cone, C. (2022, August 5). *What does a purpose-driven company look like?* Salesforce. https://www.salesforce.org/blog/what-does-a-purpose-driven-company-look-like

Beck, R., & Harter, J. (n.d.). *Why great managers are so rare.* Gallup. https://www.gallup.com/workplace/231593/why-great-managers-rare.aspx

Bolden-Barrett, V. (2019, December 11). *Employees really do leave bad bosses, research shows.* HR Dive. https://www.hrdive.com/news/employees-really-do-leave-bad-bosses-research-shows/568774/

Veldsman, T. (2022, September 13). How toxic leaders destroy people as well as organizations. *The Conversation.* https://theconversation.com/how-toxic-leaders-destroy-people-as-well-as-organisations-51951

Kurter, H. L. (2022, November 9). Employees, here are 3 tell-tale signs your boss is toxic. *Forbes.* https://www.forbes.com/sites/heidilynnekurter/2021/04/28/employees-here-are-5-tell-tale-signs-your-boss-is-toxic/

SHRM. (2020, August 12). Survey: 84 percent of U.S. workers blame bad managers for creating unnecessary stress. *Society for Human Resource Management.* https://www.shrm.org/about-shrm/press-room/press-releases/pages/survey-84-percent- of -us -workers-blame-bad-managers-for-creating-unnecessary-stress-.aspx

SHRM. (2020, February 28). SHRM reports toxic workplace cultures cost billions. *Society for Human Resource Management.* https://www.shrm.org/about-shrm/press-room/press-releases/Pages/SHRM-Reports-Toxic-Workplace-Cultures-Cost-Billions.aspx

Dhingra, N., & Schaninger, B. (2021, June 3). *The search for purpose at work.* McKinsey & Company. https://www.mckinsey.com/business-functions/people-and-organizational-performance/our-insights/the-search-for-purpose-at-work

Gelles, D. (2022, Sept. 21). Billionaire no more: Patagonia founder gives away the company. *The New York Times.* https://www.nytimes.com/2022/09/14/climate/patagonia-climate-philanthropy-chouinard.html

Clinkenbeard, R. (2021, June 16). *Help your employees find purpose—or watch them leave.* The Radix Group. https://theradixgroupllc.com/help-your-employees-find-purpose-or-watch-them-leave/

Laloux, F. (2014). *Reinventing organizations: A guide to creating organizations inspired by the next stage of human consiousness.* Brussels: Nelson Parker.

Sisodia, R. & Gelb, M. (2019). *The healing organization: awakening the conscience of business to help save the world.* New York, NY: HarperCollins.

Sisodia, R., Wolfe, D., and Sheth, J. (2014). *Firms of endearment: How world-class companies profit from passion and purpose* (2nd ed). Upper Saddle River, NJ: Pearson Education.

Clifton, J. & Harter, J. (2021). *Wellbeing at work: How to build resilient and thriving teams.* New York, NY: Gallup Press.

Chapter 25

Lovich, D. (2023, March 22). How exactly will ChatGPT change work? *Forbes.* https://www.forbes.com/sites/deborahlovich/2023/03/22/how-exactly-will-chatgpt-change-work/

Saviom (2021, March 22). *12 jobs that robots (AI) will replace in the future.* https://www.saviom.com/blog/12-jobs-that-robots-ai-will-replace-in-the-future-and-12-that-wont/

Melfi, T. (Director). (2017). *Hidden Figures* [Film]. 20th Century Studios.

ChatGPT (2023, January 20). *How ChatGPT will change the world. According to ChatGPT.* Medium. https://becoming-human.ai/how-chatgpt-will-change-the-world-according-to-chatgpt-the-answer-will-surprise-you-2dacfddc6ad9

Butler, O. (1998). *Parable of the talents.* New York, NY: Seven Stories Press. 5.18.23

ACKNOWLEDGMENTS: PRACTICING GRATITUDE

This book has been a joy to research and write. The topic resonated with me personally and I was further motivated by seeing the issues play out in real time. I am comforted by all I have learned and I'm more hopeful for the future than ever. We are living through an amazing transformation on our way to a more connected and caring world.

I could not have written this book without the help of many others and I'm grateful for every single person who played a part. I'll start by thanking the teams of neuroscientists and researchers who shared their work with me. Jenefer Angell (PassionfruitProjects.com) brought her amazing editing skills and polished my words while traveling in an RV with her husband!

Claudia Arnett (BeTheMarkets.com) did a great job coordinating the Purpose Stories, cover design poll, press releases, and posts. Claudia continues to amplify my voice through her marketing and social media expertise. Nicole Lazar, my executive assistant, did a fabulous job with the hundreds of citations, as well as managing my calendar so I could finish the book. The book is better for the input from my team of incredible learning professionals at Brain Aware Training: Heloisa Vila, Justin Reinert, Lisa Slavid, Steve Caputo, and Angeli Mancuso.

I'd also like to thank the rest of my team at Brain Aware Training because, without their talent I wouldn't be able to step away to focus on the research and writing. I'm grateful for Kyle Nickel and Brandon Blake (Customer Partnerships), Richard Hilton (Webdev and Video Production), Al Dea (Competitor Analysis), and Chris Sneathen (Operations). I'm grateful for my partnerships and friendships with Iñigo Sanchez-Cabezudo, Margarita Lozano-Job, Alejandra Langarica, Flora Alves, Tatiany Melecchi, Jessica Schweizer, Koko Nakahara, and Satomi Uno. You have all expanded the reach of this important research around the world.

I'm grateful for my wonderful husband Chris and my teen Kiana who support and love me all of the time, even when I am deep in my research and writing. My kitties, Ellie and Rosie, also lent their support by sitting on my lap and shedding on the drafts. And of course, my family and friends who keep me sane on a daily basis.

Finally, to my tribe of leadership and learning professionals who work hard to bring out the best in their people and organizations through the power of learning: I am honored to share this important work with you and hope that it helps you help others in return.

I wish all of you a meaningful life filled with a deep sense of purpose. Here's to following your North Star!

ABOUT THE AUTHOR

Dr. Britt Andreatta is an internationally recognized thought leader who creates science–based solutions for today's challenges. As CEO of Brain Aware Training, Britt Andreatta draws on her unique background in leadership, neuroscience, psychology, and learning to unlock the best in people and organizations.

In 2022, she was named a Top 10 Influencer in Learning. In 2021, she was a Top 20 Learning Influencer and a Top 20 HR Influencer for Leadership Development. Britt's industry accolades include the Global Training & Development Leadership Award from the World Training & Development Congress, and the Gold Medal for *Chief Learning Officer* magazine's Trailblazer Award. *Talent Development* magazine featured her as an "outstanding thought leader and pioneer."

Britt's other titles include *Wired to Connect: The Brain Science of Teams and a New Model for Creating Collaboration and Inclusion, Wired to Grow: Harness the Power of Brain Science to Master Any Skill* and *Wired to Resist: The Brain Science of Why Change Fails and a New Model for Driving Success.*

  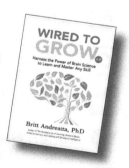

She is a regular contributor to *Entrepreneur, Training Industry, Chief Learning Officer,* and *Talent Management* magazines.

The former Chief Learning Officer for Lynda.com (now LinkedIn Learning), Britt is a seasoned professional with more than 25 years' experience. She regularly consults with businesses, universities, and nonprofit organizations on leadership development and learning strategy. Corporate clients include Fortune 100 companies like Comcast and Apple, and also Ernst & Young, John Deere, Microsoft, LinkedIn, Domino's, Franklin Covey, Evergreen-Health, Splunk, DPR Construction, Rust-Oleum, Zillow, Pacific Life, SHI, and Dell.

Dr. Andreatta has worked with major educational institutions like the University of California, Dartmouth University, and the University of New Mexico, and nonprofit organizations like the YMCA and Prison Fellowship's Warden Exchange Program. She has served as professor and dean at the University of California, Antioch University, and several graduate schools.

Her courses on LinkedIn Learning, Skillsoft, and Cornerstone On Demand have received over 10 million views worldwide. Titles include Leading with Emotional Intelligence, Advice for Leaders During a Crisis, Increasing Collaboration on Your Team, Creating Winning Teams, Organizational L&D, and 20 Questions to Improve Learning at Your Organization.

A highly sought-after and engaging speaker, Britt delivered a TEDx talk called "How Your Past Hijacks Your Future." She regularly speaks at corporate events and international conferences, receiving rave reviews and awards for "best session of conference."

Due to popular demand, Dr. Andreatta now offers certifications in her brain-based training programs. These award-winning programs drive sustained behavior change at organizations across a wide range of industries like technology, healthcare, finance, food, media, and manufacturing. Learn more at BrainAwareTraining.com.

Dr. Andreatta regularly consults with executives and organizations on how to maximize their full potential. To learn more, visit her website and social channels:

www Website: BrittAndreatta.com

Instagram: Instagram.com/brittandreatta/

LinkedIn: Linkedin.com/in/brittandreatta/

Twitter: @BrittAndreatta

Youtube: Youtube.com/c/BrittAndreattaTraining

LEARN MORE ABOUT TRAINING

Dr. Andreatta's robust, science-based training solutions feature her ground-breaking research, trademarked models, and uniquely effective learning design that drives real behavior change. Signature products include:

Brain Aware® Leader

This award-winning program gives leaders the critical skills they need to drive success. Discover the neuroscience of what brings out the best in others. In every engaging session, leaders actively apply content and concepts to their current teams and projects. There are six interconnected sessions as well as industry-specific versions for Sales, Healthcare, and Technology/Engineering.

| Managing People | Coaching For Impact | Increasing Emotional Intelligence | Creating Peak Performing Teams | Leading Effective Change | Driving Execution + Accountability |

Brain Aware® Executive

This program gives executives the sophisticated skills they need to drive successful strategy, vision, and innovation in their organizations for years to come.

Change Quest®

Why do 50 to 70 percent of change initiatives fail? Typical approaches don't take into account human biology and that we are wired to resist change. But once you understand the brain structures activated by change, you can mitigate their effects, increasing adaptability and resilience. With content for senior leaders, managers, and the recipients of change (i.e., employees, customers, etc.), participants gain new strategies they can use immediately.

Four Gates to Peak Team Performance®

Teams power more and more of today's work. Recent discoveries in neuroscience illuminate what differentiates high-performing teams from the rest. Learn how safety, inclusion, purpose, and belonging create the necessary conditions for true collaboration and team excellence. With sessions specifically for team leaders, team members, and senior executives, participants will gain effective strategies to consistently create peak-performing teams.

To get certified, contact us at:

Info@BA-Train.com

(805) 883-6616

BrainAwareTraining.com

SCAN ME

PRAISE

Speaking

"You were not only the best keynote we have had for this annual conference, you were the best keynote I have seen, EVER."

Mark Walker, Board Member at Technology Affinity Group

"The top two sessions were Britt Andreatta and President Barack Obama" + "Your research/presentations are THE BEST! Thank you for pouring your passion and curiosity into your work and sharing it with us."

Attendees, Association for Talent Development's (ATD)
International Conference and Expo 2023

"Britt, sending a ton of thanks for your support of the Leader meeting last week—a TERRIFIC experience. The talk you gave spirited people in such a positive way AND your delivery was flawless. Thank you for helping us to get our leaders into the "think differently" space. Loved it!"

Martha Soehren, Chief Talent Officer at Comcast

Training

"When a company has a major culture shift, you can rarely look to one person. Britt was an exception to this. What looked like company-wide management training became the foundation for the conversations, relationships, and plans to positively impact the culture. She was the rock star in the organization making sure the culture was solid."

Hilary Miller Headlee, EVP of Global Sales & Customer Success,
Insight Partners (formerly Altryx and Zoom)

"You have powerful influence in our field and a whole generation of Learning & Development professionals is hungry for your message. People are better because of what you do."

Cory Kreeck, Executive Director for Training and
Development, Beachbody

Executive Coaching

"I absolutely credit Britt's executive training and coaching for helping us to change our culture. As a result of working with her, we were able to have critical conversations, build better trust, and become a peak-performing team."

Tim Tully, Chief Technology Officer at Splunk

"I have partnered with Britt on several major initiatives. She rapidly assesses a business situation and is able to apply the perfect concepts and craft a learning journey that enhances participants' capability to achieve their goals. I can't imagine taking a company through rapid growth or major change without her."

Dr. Kelly McGill, Chief People Officer at Lighthouse
(formerly Amazon, Avvo, and LinkedIn)

CPSIA information can be obtained
at www.ICGtesting.com
Printed in the USA
BVHW050118060723
666779BV00016B/647